KURDISH
ETHNONATIONALISM

KURDISH ETHNONATIONALISM

NADER ENTESSAR

LYNNE RIENNER PUBLISHERS ▪ BOULDER & LONDON

Published in the United States of America in 1992 by
Lynne Rienner Publishers, Inc.
1800 30th Street, Boulder, Colorado 80301

and in the United Kingdom by
Lynne Rienner Publishers, Inc.
3 Henrietta Street, Covent Garden, London WC2E 8LU

Library of Congress Cataloging-in-Publication Data
Entessar, Nader.
   Kurdish ethnonationalism / by Nader Entessar
      p.   cm.
   Includes bibliographical references (p.   ) and index.
   ISBN 1-55587-250-6
   1. Kurds—Ethnic identity. 2. Kurds—Politics and government.
3. Middle East—Politics and government.   I. Title.
DS59.K86E58   1992
950'.049159—dc20   92–3655
                                                              CIP

British Cataloguing in Publication Data
A Cataloguing in Publication record for this book
is available from the British Library.

Printed and bound in the United States of America

The paper used in this publication meets the requirements
of the American National Standard for Permanence of
Paper for Printed Library Materials Z39.48–1984.

CONTENTS

PREFACE

The purpose of this book is to analyze the political and social dimensions of Kurdish integration into the mainstream of sociopolitical life in Iran, Iraq, and Turkey. The central thesis of the book is that ethnic conflict constitutes a major challenge to the contemporary nation-state system in the Middle East. In other words, the book challenges the long-held view that assimilation is an inevitable result of modernization and the emergence of the relatively strong and centralized nation-state system in the Middle East. Perhaps no single phenomenon illustrates this thesis more vividly than the historical Kurdish demands for self-determination.

In addition to Western literature, I have relied on Middle Eastern sources and publications of various Kurdish organizations, such as the Kurdish Democratic Party and Komala. Notwithstanding the importance of the Kurds for nation building and regime maintenance in Iran, Iraq, and Turkey, there are few comprehensive scholarly books on this subject. Many of the recent books on the Kurds are either anecdotal or written to support the ideological position of a particular group or political movement. Of the few other books that have been written by scholars, most are either out of date or have a narrower focus than this one. I hope that it will provide a balanced treatment of the Kurdish dilemma in the late twentieth century that will be useful to both scholars and informed readers.

In transliterating Arabic and Persian names and other words into English, I have relied on the most commonly used spellings. For simplicity, I have avoided using diacritical marks. Since modern Turkish, unlike Arabic and Persian, uses the Latin alphabet, I have tried to maintain the spellings of Turkish names as they are used in Turkish publications. For this reason, some names may be spelled differently in Turkish than they are spelled in Arabic or Persian.

A number of sources have aided in the research for this book. Spring Hill College awarded me several faculty research grants for data collection. The National Endowment for the Humanities provided me with two summer grants for college teachers to participate in seminars on ethnic minorities and cultural pluralism at Harvard University and the University of Wisconsin-Madison. The staff of the interlibrary loan service at the Thomas Byrne

Memorial Library at Spring Hill College was especially helpful in obtaining various books and documents for me in a timely and efficient manner. Anonymous reviewers provided useful insight and critical comments on earlier drafts of this manuscript. I also want to thank Martha Peacock for her cooperation and support of this project, and Gia Hamilton and Steve Arney for their astute editorial work. Last but not least, my wife, Marie, provided expert word-processing skills and help in revising the various drafts of this manuscript. I am indebted to all of them. Any errors of fact and interpretation are, of course, my sole responsibility.

—*Nader Entessar*

1
KURDISH ETHNICITY:
INTRODUCTION AND OVERVIEW

The end of the Cold War has augured a new vision of the global order and conflict management. In a controversial article, policy analyst Francis Fukuyama even suggests that with the apparent triumph of Western liberalism over Soviet communism, all underlying causes of conflict in the world have been eliminated.

> What we may be witnessing is not just the end of the Cold War or the passing of a particular period of history, but the end of history as such: that is, the end point of mankind's ideological evolution and the universalization of Western liberal democracy as the final form of human government.[1]

Although Fukuyama in his neo-Hegelian theory acknowledges the importance of religious fundamentalism and ethnonationalism in global politics, he nevertheless asserts that Western liberalism will eventually prevail over possible challenges presented by these and similar phenomena.[2]

Though it is beyond the scope of this book to examine the validity of Fukuyama's theory, one could reasonably assert that the phenomenon of ethnonationalism will continue to pose a major challenge to the nation-state system and will continue to be a serious source of conflict in multiethnic societies irrespective of the predicted triumph of Western liberalism on a global scale. The revival of ethnonationalism in the Middle East, the former Soviet Union, Europe, and the Americas in the late twentieth century is a clear manifestation of the existence of sources of conflict that cannot be dealt with satisfactorily through the application of the macro theories of world order.

The rise of ethnic consciousness and the political demands of many minority or ethnic groups for self-determination has run against the perceived interests of the state as the dominant actor in global politics. As the history of Kurdish ethnonationalism clearly demonstrates, politicization of Kurdish ethnicity coincided with the formation of the modern nation-state system in the Middle East.[3] In other words, competing claims of ethnic groups and the state have transformed ethnicity from a purely "personal quest for meaning and belonging into a group demand for respect and power."[4]

STATE AND ETHNICITY

One of the most salient features of Third World societies has been the expansion of the role of the state as an independent variable in shaping the balance of societal forces, including managing competing socioeconomic and political claims of ethnic groups. As David Brown noted, Third World multiethnic societies that "formerly attained only spasmodic and limited control outside their core regions and capital cities have sought increasingly systematic control over peripheral regions through the expansion of their administrative bureaucracies, armies and educational systems. At the same time, the range of governmental interference has expanded beyond the concern with raising revenues and maintaining order, as the need to direct, train and motivate labour has increased."[5]

The pervasive role of the state has allowed it to develop into an institution that is autonomous from all other actors in the society while maintaining monopoly control over coercive forces that enable the state to shape, inter alia, class formations and ethnic relations.[6] The relative independence of the state vis-à-vis other social forces has allowed the state to shape and alter ethnic identities in multiethnic societies. In many Third World settings, the state has been instrumental in fostering and/or altering ethnic identities to suit its own policy objectives, legitimize its authority, promote national unity, and generate interethnic rivalries and has devised a "divide-and-rule" strategy to enhance its hegemonic position over individuals and groups in society.

The Soviet Union, for example, traditionally promoted ethnic rivalries and even fostered primordial identities among the country's diverse ethnic groups to advance Moscow's domestic and foreign policy objectives. By the same token, governments in the modern Middle East have succeeded at times in maintaining their political control by exploiting ethnic enmities in their societies. The statist paradigm, however, does not necessarily negate the role played by dominant classes or other groups in shaping state policies. It simply affirms the supremacy of the state as the manager and controller of competing ethnic claims in society.

KURDISH IDENTITY

Kurdish demands for autonomy or independence for Kurdistan (the land of the Kurds) have been one of the most enduring sources of ethnic conflict in the modern Middle East. Today, the Kurds are primarily concentrated in Turkey,

Iraq, and Iran, but Kurdish communities are also found in Syria and the former Soviet Union. There are no reliable figures available on the total number of Kurds in the Middle East. Kurdish sources have, at times, claimed that the Kurds number thirty-five million people. This is probably an exaggerated estimate and is generally given by Kurdish leaders to accentuate the importance of this neglected minority. Governments of the region, also for political reasons, have tended to undercount their Kurdish populations.

The origin of the Kurds has been a source of controversy and uncertainty. Modern-day Kurds trace their origin to the Medes, an Indo-European tribe that descended from Central Asia into the Iranian plateau around 614 B.C. They ruled the area until 550 B.C. as one of the principal pre-Islamic Iranian dynasties.[7] The Medes fought with a host of other tribes, including the Persians, who later defeated them and became the rulers of Iran. The Kurds, along with the Persians, the Baluchis, the Tadjiks, and the Afghans then constituted the Iranian people. After the Arab defeat of Iranian forces and conquest of the area in the seventh century, outsiders increasingly used the name "Kurd" to refer to all people inhabiting the Zagros mountain ranges of northwestern Iran.[8] These people included not only those who claimed to be original descendants of the Medes, but also a host of other ethnic and tribal groups, who had intermingled with each other over the years and had created new communities and groups through miscegenation.

For over four centuries after the Arab conquest, the Kurds played a crucial political role in western Asia. For example, they provided important leaders in the Islamic world, the most notable of whom was the legendary Salah-ed-din Ayyubi (Saladin), who led Islamic forces against Richard Lion-Heart and the Crusaders. It is important to note, however, that Salah-ed-din did not rule over or control the major part of what is today Kurdistan, nor did he claim to be a warrior for the Kurds. He was first and foremost an Islamic leader and not a Kurdish nationalist.

From 1258 to 1509, the Kurds were not involved in any major exploits in the region. But the advent of the Safavid dynasty in Iran at the turn of the sixteenth century and the ensuing rivalry between the Iranians and the Ottoman Turks brought the Kurds once again to the fore as important players in regional politics. Both the Persians and the Ottoman Empire began to view the Kurdish-inhabited regions as buffer zones between their rival empires. This allowed the Kurds to become more assertive politically as they became more aware of their strategic importance in southwest Asia. As a result, a number of semi-independent Kurdish principalities flourished, and many of them survived into the first half of the nineteenth century. Examples of such principalities included Botan, Hakkari, Badinan, Soran, and Baban in the Ottoman-ruled areas, and Ardalan and Mukriyan in Iran.[9] After the defeat and eventual disintegration of the Ottoman Empire after World War I, the Kurds intensified their struggle for self-determination. However, as will be discussed, a number of internal and external factors inhibited the emergence of an independent Kurdish homeland.

KURDISH LANGUAGE AND RELIGION

The degree of shared experience, especially in language and religion, has long been recognized as a principal contributor to the development of ethnic consciousness and ethnonationalism. Kurdish belongs to the family of Iranian languages and, like other Iranian languages, has an Indo-European origin; Kurdish is therefore more akin to Persian than to Arabic. Nevertheless, Kurdish dialects are distinct from other Iranian languages or dialects and are generally unintelligible to speakers of Persian. Unlike many other minority groups in the Middle East, the Kurds have failed to adopt a lingua franca. This has not only hindered inter-Kurdish communication, it has also reduced the importance of language as a symbol of ethnic identity for the Kurds. As I have argued elsewhere, the reasons for the heterogeneity of Kurdish languages are threefold:

> First, the rugged, mountainous terrain of Kurdistan has historically impeded communication between Kurdish tribes and clans. Second, the absence of a strong, centralized administrative structure to unify the many rival Kurdish groups encouraged the development of diverse languages among the Kurds. Finally, the emergence in the twentieth century of a sovereign nation-state system in the Middle East further fragmented the Kurds and placed them under the jurisdiction of countries which themselves displayed linguistic diversity.[10]

There are three major Kurdish languages and several dialects. Although Kurdish nationalists have contended that the three Kurdish languages are different dialects of a single Kurdish language, variations among them are "far too great by any standard linguistic criteria to warrant the classification of these tongues as simply dialects of the same language. To the discomfort of any lay Kurdish patriot, and the gratitude of prudence, one should speak of Kurdish languages."[11] In brief, the three Kurdish languages are:

1. *Kurdi*, which includes the Gurani and Sulaymani dialects. Gurani is spoken mostly by the Kurds in Kermanshah (Bakhtaran) in Iran and is very similar to *Lori*, an Iranian language spoken by the Lors, who along with the Kurds constitute the two major ethnic groups in Kermanshah. *Kurdi* is also spoken by some Iraqi Kurds.

2. *Kurmanji*, which is used by the largest number of Kurds, especially those in Turkey. It is, for all practical purposes, the literary language of the Kurds and as such is considered the most prestigious of all Kurdish

vernaculars. *Kurmanji* is divided into North and South *Kurmanji*. The former dialect is spoken by most western Kurds and those Kurds living in the Caucasus region of the former Soviet Union, while the latter is used by the people of central Kurdistan.

   3. *Zaza*, which predominates in the north and northwest sectors of Kurdistan. It is also used by some Kurds in the Iranian province of Western Azerbaijan and central Turkey.[12] Zaza is the least developed Kurdish literary language. In addition, because of the absence of radio broadcasts and printed media in *Zaza,* this Kurdish language has remained in a "stagnant state of development and usage" and has not been used as a means for inter- and intra-Kurdish communication.[13]

As was mentioned, these Kurdish languages are mutually exclusive and, in the case of *Zaza*, inaccessible to the speakers of the other two languages. Nevertheless, the perception of a common language as an integral part of the Kurdish nation remains very strong among Kurdish nationalists. However, as George Harris noted, the very existence of linguistic differences has had an inhibiting impact on the development of a common Kurdish identity.[14]

   With the exception of some fifty thousand Yazidis (known to outsiders as devil-worshippers but in reality practitioners of an offshoot of the Ismailia branch of Shi'a Islam), a few thousand Christians and Zoroastrians, and some two hundred Jewish families in the Iranian city of Sanandaj,[15] the overwhelming majority of Kurds are Muslim.[16] Overall, at least two-thirds of the Kurds are followers of the Shafai school of Sunni jurisprudence. The overwhelming majority of the Kurds residing in the Kermanshah region of Iran are followers of Shi'a Islam, which is also the predominant religion of other Iranians and the official state religion of the country. There are also pockets of various Sufi orders of Nagshbandi and some Ali-Allahis (those who deify Ali, the first Shi'a Imam).

   Sunni and Shi'a Kurds have not exhibited major religious hostility toward each other. Sunni-Shi'a tensions, however, have erupted into clashes between Sunni Kurds and Shi'a Azeri-speaking inhabitants of Western Azerbaijan. Also, conflicts have arisen in postrevolutionary Iran between Shaikh Ezzedin Husseini, the spiritual leader of the Sunni Kurds in Iran, and Ahmad Moftizadeh, a supporter of the Islamic Republic and a leader of the Shi'a Kurds of Kermanshah. However, these and similar conflicts have not occurred over religious disputes and doctrinal differences between Sunni and Shi'a Islam; they have occurred over differences in loyalty to the Iranian government. While Moftizadeh remained loyal to the Iranian theocracy, Shaikh Husseini became an ardent critic of the Islamic Republic and an active supporter of the Kurdish demand for autonomy.[17]

KURDISH SOCIOECONOMIC MARGINALIZATION

Cultural and sociopolitical discrimination against an ethnic group by the larger society is what Joan Nagel has called "unequal center-periphery relations."[18] This discrimination has contributed to the enduring quality of Kurdish ethnic consciousness. The relatively greater development of the center vis-à-vis the periphery, Kurdish regions, and the subsequent sociopolitical and economic inequality experienced by the Kurds have given rise to a condition akin to internal colonialism and to what Frank Young has termed "reactive subsystems."[19] Reactive movements are those organized by the periphery or marginalized groups in reaction to their exclusion from the state machinery dominated by the center or the dominant groups in society. Of course, the existence of center-periphery inequality is not, in and of itself, sufficient to give rise to ethnic conflict. A catalyst is necessary, such as the one provided when the center seeks to "take over, influence, or control some portion of the periphery."[20] The response of the ethnic group in the periphery is normally volatile in cases where the political center is heavily controlled by the dominant cultural entity in the larger society.[21]

Unequal center-periphery relations have long characterized the Kurdish condition in Iran, Iraq, and Turkey, although specific causes for the Kurdish predicament have differed in each country. In Iran, for example, ethnic inequality is partly due to uneven modernization during the Pahlavi monarchy and partly the result of the integration of the Iranian economy into the world capitalist system. A by-product of the modernization programs of the two Pahlavi monarchs was the creation of a strong central government capable of exercising near total political and economic hegemony over nonstate actors, such as ethnic groups. That is, the central government was able to transform the country's provincial areas, inhabited by ethnic and/or linguistic minorities, into economic zones controlled by the machinery of the political center in Tehran.

The use of force and repressive measures certainly played a major role in perpetuating unequal center-periphery relations, but other techniques were also employed. The tribal khans, or chiefs, were integrated into a growing state-centered socioeconomic system, and the expansion of state bureaucracy brought much of the tribal sociopolitical system under the central government's control, allowing the government to spread its financial apparatus into those areas. The introduction of a nationwide military draft further transformed the socioeconomic structure of tribal areas as the army began to function as an integrative and centripetal force in Iran. As a growing number of Kurdish tribes became sedentary, the agricultural village became the principal unit of taxation and a primary source of rural labor for both Kurdish and non-Kurdish absentee landholders.[22]

The modernization of Iran generated demand for manual labor in such booming enterprises as housing construction and road building. Peripheral tribal areas provided a substantial number of unskilled or semiskilled manual laborers for these projects; they provided the cheap labor for the purpose of modernizing the center. Although modernization did not destroy traditional patterns of tribal leadership, it did give rise to a new pattern of class structure and dependency relations in the periphery:

> The existence of a statewide economy linked the propertied classes in the periphery to those in the center. However, Persians controlled the state and imposed a program of cultural uniformity throughout the country that denied the minorities rights of cultural expression. The initial manifestation of national awareness among the minorities occurred, therefore, as reactions to Persian cultural domination and reflected the interests of the minority elites. Thus, they were limited to demands for cultural autonomy and did not challenge class domination, either in the minority region or in the country as a whole.[23]

Other dimensions of ethnic inequality in Iran have been reflected in education, public health and public utilities, and the overall level of poverty in ethnic communities. While the literacy rate for Kurds residing in the province of Kurdistan rose from 14.3 percent in 1960 to 30 percent in 1976, this was well below the 66.1 percent literacy rate observed in the central, Persian-speaking province.[24]

With respect to public health and public utilities, 80.7 percent of household units in the central province had electricity in 1976, while only 19.5 percent of households in Kurdistan had electricity. At the same time, only 12 percent of households in Kurdistan had indoor plumbing, as opposed to 74.9 percent in the central province.[25] Although there are no reliable statistics on the number of medical doctors in Kurdistan, there is an acute shortage of medical staff and hospital beds and clinics in ethnic regions of the country. This situation has been exacerbated since the Iranian Revolution of 1978–1979 and the subsequent flight of doctors from the country. Out of the estimated fifteen thousand medical doctors in Iran, about eight thousand reside in Tehran, and most of the rest are in a few other major cities, such as Isfahan and Shiraz.

With regard to the overall degree of poverty, ethnic inequality has been quite evident throughout Iran. Taking Akbar Aghajanian's criterion of poverty as households with a yearly consumption expenditure of less than $875, the percentage of Kurdish families below the poverty line in the mid-1970s was 30.8, while the corresponding figure for the central province was 21 percent.[26]

In Iraq, the paucity of reliable statistics with respect to the socioeconomic conditions of the Kurds has hindered objective comparative studies of Kurdish-Arab inequalities. Nevertheless, certain general observations can be made. The Kurdish areas have experienced less modernization and industrialization than the rest of the country. When major industrial projects have been introduced, usually in the petroleum sectors of the economy, they have been located in Kurdish cities such as Kirkuk and Mosul, which are not a part of the officially designated "Autonomous Kurdish Region."

Despite the Kurdish region's abundance of natural resources, such as oil, iron ore, and fertile land, the budget allocation for this area has traditionally been very low, ranging from 7 to 12 percent of the total Iraqi budget. Until the US-led Gulf War in 1991, Kurdish areas had provided much of the raw material for the iron and steel industries in Iraq, but these industries have been located elsewhere in the country. Tobacco, traditionally a major cash crop in Kurdish regions, has not benefited the Kurds because the government has used its monopoly over the tobacco industry to exert economic pressure on the Kurds.[27] All in all, internal colonialism and unequal center-periphery relations have permeated the economic dimensions of Kurdish-Arab relations in recent decades.

In the area of infrastructural development, road-building projects were most common in Kurdish areas until destruction of Iraq's economic infrastructures during the Gulf War paralyzed reconstruction activities in the country. The Kurds, however, have contended that the main purpose for these projects was to facilitate the "quick movement and dispatch of large Iraqi land forces into and within the region in case of unrest."[28] Government-subsidized public housing also received some attention before the war. The Iraqi government undertook a program of constructing "cluster villages" in which compact houses were built in such a fashion as to allow easy monitoring of activities. Again, the Kurds have charged that the purpose of cluster villages was to seal off their inhabitants and prevent contact with Kurdish guerrillas, or *peshmergas* (those who confront death).[29]

In 1958, with the overthrow of the Iraqi monarchy, a major attempt was made by the new government to remedy some of the socioeconomic imbalances in the Kurdish areas of the country. Educational reforms were to receive top priority, and education was to become an integrative vehicle for building a new republican Iraq. In recognition of the Kurdish component of Iraqi society, the government inaugurated in 1960 a new Directorate-General office for Kurdish studies.[30] With the government's twelve-point program in 1966, the Kurds were given nominal control over educational affairs in their areas. Furthermore, the study of Kurdish was encouraged for all Iraqis.

Nevertheless, conflict developed when the Iraqi government began to emphasize increasingly the role of education in developing and advancing a "feeling of national identity and awareness of Arab cultural heritage" and Arab nationalism.[31] In response, the Kurds continued to demand recognition of Kurdish as a medium of instruction in Kurdish schools and as a tool to promote Kurdish nationalism. Eventually, in an agreement signed on March 11, 1970, between the Iraqi government and the Kurdish Democratic Party, the government acceded to the Kurdish demand. In addition, it agreed to re-establish the defunct Kurdish Academy for the promotion of the Kurdish language and culture.[32]

The Kurds extracted further concessions from the Iraqi government in the area of Kurdish linguistic and cultural autonomy when the so-called Law of Autonomy of March 1974 became effective. It is important to note that all the concessions were extracted when the Iraqi regime was trapped in a debilitating war with the Kurdish *peshmergas*. However, as will be discussed, the Iraqi government re-imposed its hegemony over Kurdish affairs as a result of the 1975 Algiers Agreement between Iraq and Iran, which, among other things, terminated Iranian support for the Kurdish guerrillas.

Thereafter, attempts at Arabization increased. Many Kurdish towns and villages were renamed, albeit unsuccessfully. For example, Kirkuk became Ta'mim, and Haj Umran was renamed Al-Nasr, or victory. Many Kurdish cultural organizations were abolished, and school textbooks were reprinted to omit references to Kurdistan, replacing it with the term "Autonomous Area." Kurdish staff members at Sulaymanieh University were transferred to non-Kurdish areas of the country. Through a centrally administered registration policy, the Baghdad government allowed increasing numbers of non-Kurdish students to enter Sulaymanieh University, limiting educational opportunities for the Kurds at an institution designed to serve the Kurdish community in Iraq.[33] The weakening of the Ba'thi government in Iraq today may once again lead to a modus vivendi between the government and Kurdish leaders and a lessening of discrimination against the ethnic Kurds in Iraq.

Unlike Iran and Iraq, where ethnic minorities have received official recognition, the twelve million Kurds in Turkey for a long time have been the subject of officially sanctioned discrimination and neglect. As will be discussed in Chapter 4, the modern state of Turkey has been preoccupied with forging a single Turkish identity and, as such, has reacted violently to manifestations of any other ethnic nationalistic impulse within its borders. Consequently, Kurdish demands for self-determination have been viewed as tantamount to treason.

The Kurds, or the "mountain Turks" as they have been euphemistically called in Turkey, have had virtually no guarantee of cultural freedom in Turkey. Until recently even the use of Kurdish dialects was forbidden by law. Because of the severe official discrimination against them, the Kurds in Turkey have developed a more uncompromising posture vis-à-vis the Turkish state than Kurds in Iran and Iraq. Unlike the major Kurdish parties in Iran and Iraq, the dominant Kurdish political party in Turkey—the Workers' Party of Kurdistan (PKK)—openly advocates the establishment of a separate Kurdish state, as opposed to an autonomous region within Turkey. The over-whelming power of the Turkish state, however, will make it almost impossible for the Kurds to achieve their goals in Turkey.[34]

To a large extent, this is true in the case of Iran, and even a weakened Iraq. In the final analysis, the Kurdish struggle for independence will have to compete with the territorial integrity and national security imperatives of these three nation-states. Given the primacy of the nation-state system in international affairs and the desire for maintaining stability and security in the region on the part of major outside powers, the irredentist claims of the nonstate Kurdish "nation" will not likely receive the outside support they need for the Kurds to succeed.

Despite oft-repeated support for the principle of self-determination, governments tend to "resist separatist claims and support the territorial status quo even in the face of public support for a particular 'captive nation,' because states fear the potential mischief in international affairs if every stateless nation demanded and obtained political independence."[35] However, recognition of the legitimate rights of the Kurds that do not threaten the territorial integrity and political viability of Iran, Iraq, and Turkey must be promoted by these states and by other regional states and the international community.[36] This is not just morally right, but a sound policy essential for maintaining long-term stability in the region.

2

THE KURDS IN IRAN

A BRIEF HISTORICAL REVIEW

The modern Kurdish movement for autonomy in Iran is a new historical phenomenon and can be traced to the late nineteenth century. However, as was mentioned in Chapter 1, the Kurds became an important pawn in the Persian-Ottoman rivalry beginning in the early sixteenth century, with the coming to power of the Safavid dynasty in Iran. Taking advantage of their religious (Sunni) affinity with the Kurds, the Ottoman sultans sought to attract the allegiance of the Kurds against the Shi'a Safavid Iran.[1] With the assistance of the Ottoman sultan, Selim, a number of Kurdish tribal leaders revolted against Safavid Shah Ismail's reign. Recognizing the potential danger to his kingdom, Shah Ismail reacted swiftly against the Kurdish upheavals. Most prominent Kurdish tribal leaders were rounded up, and their domain was placed under the court-appointed leaders of the Qizilbash Turks, who were the backbone of the Safavid army.

Shah Ismail's initial success in containing the Kurdish uprisings was reversed in August 1514 when Sultan Selim's forces, with the help of the Kurds, defeated Shah Ismail's army at the Battle of Chaldiran in northwest Uromiyah. This marked the first time that a part of the Kurdish region was separated from Iran and controlled by the Ottomans.[2] Throughout the sixteenth century, both Ottoman and Safavid administrations embarked upon sustained programs of creating strong centralized states, a policy that ran counter to the relative freedom of Kurdish principalities and led to Kurdish revolts. Although the rebellions were crushed by Ottoman or Iranian armies, the state leaders found it necessary to reach an agreement to control the Kurds. In 1639, an Ottoman-Iranian treaty was signed by Sultan Murad and Shah Abbas, effectively designating the Kurdish regions to the Ottoman Empire and Iran. With this agreement, the central government in Iran was able to subdue the Kurdish khans and eliminate the de facto semisovereign status of the Kurdish principalities. To contain the Kurdish rebellions, Iranian monarchs took advantage of tribal hostilities among the Kurds, pursuing a carrot-and-stick policy and a selective system of rewards and punishment.[3] Almost all of the Kurdish principalities had come under the direct control of the central government of Iran by the mid-nineteenth century, with Ardalan being the last to succumb, in 1865. The last, and perhaps the most significant Kurdish revolt in the nineteenth century occurred in 1880 under the leadership of Shaikh Obeydollah. For a brief period, Obeydollah succeeded in unifying the region between Lake Uromiyah and Lake Van, thus bringing together the two parts of Kurdistan. This revolt, however, was crushed through a two-pronged attack by the Persian and Ottoman armies.[4]

The end of World War I and the disintegration of the Ottoman Empire created a power vacuum in the region, allowing Kurdish tribes to once again challenge Iranian and Turkish control of Kurdistan. Sometimes these rebellions "assumed more the character of inter-tribal wars of plundering expeditions, involving only one tribe at a time, and not directed against the structure of the State,"[5] but at other times, they were more complicated, and involved inter-Kurdish tribal fighting and conflicts between the Kurds and other religious or linguistic minorities. The revolt of Ismail Agha Simko was a prime example of this type of rebellion. Simko was the chief of the Shakkak tribe, which exercised control over the region west of Lake Uromiyah and called for the independence of Kurdistan under Simko's leadership. After overcoming neighboring tribes, Ismail Agha Simko exercised tenuous authority over much of Iranian Kurdistan from 1920 to 1924.

One major problem with Simko's vision of an independent Kurdistan was that to the west of Lake Uromiyah resided not only Kurds, but also Azeri-speaking Shi'as and Christian Assyrians, both of whom had had long-standing conflicts with the Kurds and had fought them bitterly. In fact, the cities of Uromiyah (Rezaiyeh), Salmas, and Khoi were overwhelmingly Azeri in composition and did not wish to become part of Simko's Kurdistan. Consequently, battles between the Azeris and the Kurds became incessant.

Ismail Agha Simko had also to contend with the forces of Reza Khan, who had come to power in a military coup in February 1921 as the minister of war and commander in chief of the Iranian army. Reza Khan, who reorganized the Iranian army into a well-integrated, centralized force, had begun a sustained and organized campaign against Simko and other rebellious tribal leaders. Reza Khan contended that the previous practice of confronting tribal rebellions with small detachments of the armed forces was counterproductive and played into the hands of the rebel forces. Instead, he ordered organized brigades to overwhelm rebels with superior firepower and manpower, and the Iranian army gradually recaptured major towns from the Kurdish rebels. By 1924, Simko's ten-thousand-man army had been reduced to one thousand men from his Shakkak tribe. After the surrender of his forces in 1924, Simko was pardoned by the Iranian government.

In 1925, when Reza Khan had become Reza Shah, the first monarch of the Pahlavi dynasty, Simko pledged eternal loyalty to him and to the Iranian state. Nonetheless, Simko participated in another Kurdish rebellion in 1926, aligning himself with the two Kurdish chiefs, Haji Agha of the Herki tribe and Begzadeh of Mergever and Tergever. After entering Salmas and encircling Shahpur, the Kurdish forces were attacked by Iranian forces dispatched from Uromiyah, Sharafkhaneh, and Khoi in Azerbaijan and were forced to retreat to the Turkish frontier where Simko was captured and jailed. After his release from Turkish internment, Simko returned to Iran, where, in a brief skirmish with Iranian forces near the city of Oshnu (Oshnoviyeh), in June 1930, he was killed.[6] (Some Kurdish and Western sources have stated that Simko was not killed in battle against the Iranian forces but was assassinated on June 21, 1930, by the Iranian military, after he accepted their invitation to meet with them to negotiate a settlement of the Kurdish revolt.[7])

Simko's revolt was the first major attempt by the Kurds to establish an independent Kurdistan in Iran. Despite some initial military success, Simko's ultimate failure to establish a genuine Kurdish nation-state has been attributed to his inability to overcome his parochialism and his inability to create "a state in the modern sense of the word, with an administrative organization. He was chiefly interested in plunder, and as he could not loot his own tribe or the associated tribes, he raided and tried to dominate non-Kurdish regions, like Salmas, Rezaiyeh [Uromiyah], and eventually Khoi, reducing the population of these districts to utter ruin and despair."[8]

Reza Shah's military victory over Simko and other tribal leaders throughout Iran initiated a new repressive era to many ethnic groups in the country. Reza Shah's attempt to create a centrally controlled state based on the national unity of all Iranian peoples, an artificially imposed Persian consciousness, was spearheaded by the so-called Society for Public Guidance. This organization controlled all means of communication, suppressed all non-Persian ethnic identities and cultural characteristics, including radio broadcasts, textbooks, and other publications, and Reza Shah's obsession with instilling a Persian national consciousness led to the establishment of an Iranian academy to purge foreign (i.e., Arabic and Turkish) words from the Persian language[9]—which proved to be impossible, given the centuries-long intermingling of Persian, Arabic, and Turkish cultures. The use of Kurdish dialects in education, publication, and public speech was forbidden. Many Kurdish schools were forced to close down as their education was disrupted and their funding frozen. A European-style dress code was imposed on Kurds and on other Iranians.[10] Following Attaturk's example in Turkey, Reza Shah even stressed the use of the term "mountain Iranians" to refer to the Kurdish population of the country, although public use of the term "Kurd" was never banned, as was the case in Turkey.

Reza Shah staffed government bureaucracies in the Kurdish region with Persian and Azeri officials. Considering the history of Azeri-Kurdish hostility and Kurdish-Persian tensions in the twentieth century, this policy was tantamount to Kurdish political disenfranchisement and marginalization. Furthermore, at the urging of the Society for Public Guidance, some traditionally Kurdish-inhabited areas were declared to be part of the new province of West Azerbaijan, hence further exacerbating Kurdish-Azeri tensions.[11]

The Kurdish economy, which relied heavily on the production of tobacco as a cash crop, was severely disrupted by the introduction of a state monopoly on tobacco as Reza Shah injected heavy government subsidies into his own estates at the expense of Kurdish estates,[12] but otherwise, Reza Shah's economic modernization policies generally did not extend to Iranian Kurdistan. No new roads or factories were built in Kurdistan, and health care remained highly primitive, the worst in the country. The pattern of land ownership remained largely intact. That is, large landowners, including absentee landowners, were allowed to keep their estates. Even the *waqf* estates, or religious endowments, remained basically intact despite the fact that *waqf* lands in other parts of the country were removed from the control of the clergy and placed under the jurisdiction of the ministry of education or another governmental agency. This meant that the traditional powerholders in Kurdistan—the tribal khans and religious shaikhs—were able to continue to exploit their own people.[13] Kurdistan remained "provincial, extremely undeveloped, and unintegrated with the national economy. The Kurdish petty bourgeoisie resented state monopolies as well as the government's neglect of the province."[14]

World War II transformed Iran's politics and weakened the authority of the central government over outlying provinces and tribal areas. With the Anglo-Soviet invasion of Iran on August 25, 1941, the forced abdication and departure from Iran of Reza Shah, and the lack of authority of Mohammad Reza, his son and successor, the tribal sociopolitical order began to reassert itself. The British and the Soviets were the de facto rulers in areas under their military occupation. One manifestation of the loss of authority of the Iranian government in the provinces, especially in Azerbaijan and Kurdistan, where the Soviet army was in control, was the flight of thousands of Iranian army officers and conscripts to Tehran.[15] It was within this context that Kurdish nationalism reasserted itself.

THE KURDISH REPUBLIC OF MAHABAD

The most serious twentieth-century Kurdish challenge to Iranian authority occurred in 1945, when the autonomous Kurdish Republic of Mahabad was established. The rise and fall of the Mahabad republic must be analyzed within the context of Soviet expansionist policies in Iranian Azerbaijan, where the Soviets hoped sponsorship of a communist-oriented secessionist movement would pressure the Iranian government into granting them economic concessions, especially long-sought access to the Gulf. To advance their policies, the Soviets attempted to establish a united Kurdish-

Azeri front. Well aware of the historical animosity between the Kurds and the Azeris, the Soviets invited various Kurdish tribal chiefs to visit Soviet Azerbaijan in 1944 and early 1945. Ja'far Baghirov, prime minister of the Azerbaijan Soviet Socialist Republic, sought to convince the chiefs of the necessity of forging a Kurdish-Azeri front in order to attain Kurdish autonomy.[16] There was little indication, however, that the Soviets understood the tribal and communal structures of Kurdish society.

Indeed, many orthodox Iranian Marxists—including the pro-Soviet Tudeh (Masses) Party, which was formed in 1941 and reflected the views of the Persian and/or Persianized intelligentsia[17]—did not understand how linguistic and regional variables affected the political behavior of tribal and non-Persian ethnic groups. In contrast, many non-Persian Iranian Marxists understood the importance of cultural and regional variables to their constituency. This crucial difference between Persians and non-Persians led to a schism between the Tudeh leadership and its counterpart in Azerbaijan. This schism led Ja'far Pishevari, a prominent Azeri leftist, to lay the foundation for the establishment of *Firqah-e Demokrat-e Azerbaijan* as the Marxist party representing the interests of the Azeris. Officially formed on September 3, 1945, the *Firqah* was immediately accused by the Iranian government of being an extension of the Tudeh, and by implication the Soviet Union, in Iranian Azerbaijan. In fact, the Tudeh and *Firqah* "were not simply two sides of the same coin. On the contrary, they were separated from each other by contrasting social bases, conflicting interests, and, at times, clashing policies."[18]

Whereas the Tudeh emphasized the familiar Marxist principles of class conflict and democratic centralism, the *Firqah* promoted autonomy for minorities and use of the Azeri language as the principal vehicle for the realization of Azeri rights. Responding to the Tudeh's criticism of his party's policies of sectarianism, Pishevari declared that it was time for the Persian intellectuals to recognize their own chauvinism and to recognize linguistic differences between themselves and other Iranians. Speaking on Tabriz Radio, Pishevari announced that his party considered the right to use the mother tongue in Azerbaijan as a nonnegotiable principle.[19]

The issue of linguistic autonomy bedeviled Tudeh and Soviet policies in Kurdistan, and, as Ervand Abrahamian noted, the Tudeh's policies toward linguistic minorities remained ambiguous. It was not until after the second Tudeh Party Congress in April 1948 (after the defeat of the Kurdish and Azeri autonomous republics) that the party formulated a coherent statement on ethnic issues.[20] In a pamphlet published in September 1949 entitled *Mellat va Melliyat* (Nation and Nationality), the Tudeh applied Leninist and Stalinist nationality principles to Iran. The pamphlet concluded that Iran was composed of different nationalities, each with its own language and customs. However, their participation in the creation of a rich (Iranian) culture and "their joint struggles against feudalism, despotism, and imperialism" created an enduring bond among them. This cohesive bond of friendship could best be maintained if linguistic minorities were protected and their rights of self-determination respected.[21]

Although Soviet influence in shaping events in Kurdistan was significant, there were important differences between the autonomy-seeking movements in Iranian Azerbaijan and Kurdistan. In Azerbaijan, the Soviet Union had a built-in advantage of relying on the vast reservoir of Azeri Marxists in the Azerbaijan Soviet Socialist Republic. Many of the founders and theoreticians of the *Firqah* spent years in the Soviet Union and established strong ties to their Soviet counterparts in Baku. Furthermore, Stalin's southern policy envisaged the secession of Iranian Azerbaijan and its unification with northern (Soviet) Azerbaijan under Moscow's suzerainty.

There is no convincing evidence to suggest that the Soviet Union's Kurdish policy mirrored its Azerbaijan policy. The Soviet government did help create a Kurdish state in Iran and probably would have favored the establishment of an independent Kurdish state in Iran, Iraq, and Turkey had it been able to ascertain the Kurdish state's loyalty to the Soviet Union. However, Stalin did not pursue a policy supporting the creation of a greater Kurdistan lest this new state show "a spirit of independence which would not coincide with Soviet policies and perhaps even ultimately fall under Western influence, since political power in all the Kurdish regions was concentrated in the hands of big landowners, chiefs, and religious leaders, who were all conservative and even reactionary-minded people, and likely to be suspicious of Soviet intentions and hostile to the spreading of Communist ideas."[22] Indeed, the rise and fall of the Kurdish Republic of Mahabad reflected the Soviet Union's conflicting and tentative views on the issue of Kurdish autonomy.

THE FORMATION OF THE KOMALA

The city of Mahabad was a principal center of Kurdish nationalist ferment even before the Soviet occupation of northern Iran during World War II. Mahabad had a vibrant middle-class community, and its leading citizens were familiar with the intellectual ferments of the time. After the establishment of the Soviet zone of occupation in Iran, which included the city of Mahabad, government employees were systematically replaced by local Kurds with Soviet approval. Many of these local Kurds did not enjoy the necessary stature within the Kurdish community to govern effectively. For example, Amir As'ad, the nominal chief of the Dehbokri tribe, was appointed governor of the Mahabad region. As'ad was an old man, visually impaired, and did not command the respect of many clans within his own tribe, let alone the respect of other tribes in the region. For this reason, a group of Mahabad Kurds began to organize their own political party to control their destiny in a more independent and effective fashion.

On September 16, 1942, several Mahabad Kurds gathered to form a committee (*komala* in Kurdish) to plan actions to further the cause of Kurdish self-determination. This committee called itself *Komala-e Zhian-e Kurdistan* (Committee for the Resurrection of Kurdistan), or *Komala*. Within a few weeks of its formation, the *Komala* had increased its membership to about one hundred Kurds from Mahabad. In order to avoid detection by hostile authorities, the *Komala* functioned on a secretive basis, with self-contained cells as its basic organizational unit. Members of the *Komala* were aware only of the identities of members of their own cells. Membership remained highly restrictive and was limited to those whose parents were Kurdish. Azeris who had lived within the Kurdish communities and spoke Kurdish were expressly excluded from membership in the *Komala*, as were Kurds who were the product of miscegenation.[23] Because of its selectivity and narrow base of support outside Mahabad, the *Komala* was unable to extend its appeal to all Kurds in greater Kurdistan.

Notwithstanding its objective of establishing an autonomous region in all of Iranian Kurdistan, with the eventual aim of linking this autonomous region with Kurdish lands outside Iran, the *Komala* was unsuccessful in extending its activities to important Kurdish cities such as Sanandaj and to the province of Kermanshah. Not only were these areas controlled by the Iranian army, they were also the stronghold of prominent Kurdish Shi'a families, who for generations had established close links with the Persians and the Iranian government. Because these families viewed themselves as an inseparable part of the Iranian nation, the *Komala's* secessionist calls fell on deaf ears in most major Kurdish-inhabited areas outside Mahabad. Thus, the *Komala* decided to rely on the Soviet Union in a marriage of convenience to further its cause of Kurdish autonomy.[24] Ironically, no known Marxist or Communist members joined the *Komala* during its first two years of existence.

Marxist and leftist rhetoric began to enter the *Komala's* pronouncements not so much through the Soviet Union's proselytizing activities as through the *Komala's* intensified contacts with Iraqi Kurdish groups. In particular, after the *Komala* increased its collaboration with *Razgar-e Kurd* (Kurdish Deliverance), an Iraqi Kurdish nationalist association dominated by Marxists and other leftists, its pronouncements were peppered with denunciations of Western imperialism and its surrogates.[25] At the same time, the *Komala* embarked upon a policy of formalizing its relations with other non-Iranian Kurdish movements. In August 1944, representatives of the *Komala* met with delegates from Iraqi and Turkish Kurdish regions at Mount Dalanpar, where the Iranian, Iraqi, and Kurdish frontiers intersect, and signed a pact entitled *Peman e Se Senur* (Pact of the Three Borders). Although this pact was more of a "symbolic affirmation of greater Kurdish unity" than a concrete plan for action, it did outline the geographic contours of what some

Kurdish nationalists consider to be a Kurdish homeland.[26]

The Kurdish region as outlined by these Kurdish leaders contained inaccuracies that have remained highly controversial. For example, the leaders extended the Kurdish region in Iran beyond Kermanshah and into areas inhabited by the Lors and Bakhtiari tribes, who are not Kurdish. Similarly, extending the Kurdish region into Iranian Azerbaijan has been a source of conflict between the Kurdish and Azeri nationalists for decades. Another controversial area involved the city of Kirkuk in Iraq. As William Eagleton noted, the population of this oil-rich city was equally divided between Kurds and Turkomans, and the outlying areas of the city have become home to Arab, Kurdish, and Turkoman villagers.[27] Despite the controversial nature of the proposed Kurdish homeland, it has symbolized the essence of Kurdish nationhood and has galvanized Kurdish ethnonationalist movements in the twentieth century.

The structure of the *Komala* reflected the party's initial desire to establish a nonhierarchical organization without a dominant clique or individual. During the first two years of its existence, the question of membership, especially membership in the party's central committee, was hotly debated. Some members of the central committee favored the admission of Qazi Mohammad, Mahabad's leading citizen, while others feared that his authoritarian personality would undermine the *Komala's* democratic decisionmaking structure. Furthermore, it was not clear whether and under what condition Qazi Mohammad would agree to join the *Komala's* central committee if invited to do so.

Qazi Mohammad was a Sunni religious leader and son of Qazi Ali, who collaborated with Ismail Agha Simko when Simko's forces briefly occupied Mahabad in the early 1920s. Through his brother Sadr Qazi, who was a member of the Iranian Parliament, Qazi Mohammad had met with a number of Iranian government officials to convey Kurdish grievances. As a religious leader with conservative sociopolitical inclinations, however, Qazi Mohammad remained suspect in the minds of radical nationalists and leftists in the *Komala*. Nevertheless, both the *Komala* nationalists and the Soviet Union knew that without the participation of a well-respected and authoritative figure like Qazi Mohammad the *Komala* probably could not overcome tribal rivalries. Consequently, in October 1944, Qazi Mohammad was invited to join the *Komala* as its spiritual leader, its guiding light, and its voice, but he was never formally elected to the central committee.

By early 1945, it became evident that for the *Komala* to succeed in implementing its broad objectives it needed outside military aid. Given the Soviet Union's occupation of northern Iran and its involvement with the *Komala*, it was natural that outside help would come from the Soviet Union. However, the Soviet authorities were not comfortable with the *Komala's* nationalist orientation and its unwillingness to establish closer ties with the Soviet-supported *Firqah* in Iranian Azerbaijan. By influencing the *Komala*, the Soviet Union hoped to facilitate the merger of the Kurdish and Azeri secessionist movements and to bring both movements in line with Stalin's policy objectives in Iran.[28] In order to create a Kurdish-Azeri union, the Soviet government once again invited a high-level Kurdish delegation to visit Baku and meet with the prime minister of Soviet Azerbaijan, Ja'far Baghirov. The Kurdish delegation, which arrived in Baku in September 1945, was headed by Qazi Mohammad and included other prominent members of the *Komala,* such as Ali Rayhani and Qazi Mohammad's cousin, Saif Qazi.

Baghirov promised the Kurds financial and military support in pursuit of their objectives. However, he outlined the Soviet nationalities policy and how the Kurdish desire for independence would fit into this policy:

> People with separate languages and cultures . . . should have separate governments. Iran contained four such "nations." These were Farsi-speaking Persians, the Gilaki-speaking peoples of the southern Caspian littoral, the Turki-speaking [sic] peoples of Azerbaijan, and the Kurdish-speaking peoples of Kurdistan. Each of these would eventually enjoy local autonomy and the first to be favored would be the Turks of Azerbaijan. There was no need . . . for the Kurds to hurry the formation of their own state. Kurdish freedom must be based on the triumph of popular forces not in Iran alone but also in Iraq and Turkey. A separate Kurdish state was a desirable thing to be considered in the future when the entire "nation" could be united. In the meantime Kurdish aspirations should be achieved within Azerbaijani autonomy.[29]

Qazi Mohammad replied that the Kurds needed their own state now and that they did not want their destiny united with Azerbaijan's. If anything, Kurdish unity should be achieved with their brethren in Iraq and Turkey. Baghirov responded that the *Komala* needed to transform itself into a more disciplined political party with its own army in order to realize the goal of establishing an independent Kurdistan and that the *Komala* needed to transcend its parochialism so the Soviet Union would support it. Thus, a new political party, the Kurdish Democratic Party, was established in September 1945. Qazi Mohammad urged all Kurds, including the *Komala* members, to join this new party as the umbrella group for achieving Kurdish independence.

It soon became evident that the Soviet-engineered Kurdish Democratic Party was at odds with the *Komala's* democratic decisionmaking structure. While the *Komala* modeled itself after liberal democracies, the Kurdish Democratic Party became identified with the one-man authoritarian rule of Qazi Mohammad.[30] Kurdish supporters, however, dismissed charges of authoritarianism levied against Qazi Mohammad. Abdul Rahman Ghassemlou, who later headed the Kurdish Democratic Party of Iran, praised Qazi Mohammad for his exemplary conduct and his indefatigable endeavor to further the Kurdish cause at the expense of his own life.[31]

The Kurdish Democratic Party's program was outlined in a manifesto drafted under the supervision of the Soviet consul in Uromiyah and signed by

Qazi Mohammad and 105 members of this new party. In brief, it included the following demands:

1. The Kurdish people in Iran should have freedom and self-government in the administration of their local affairs, and obtain autonomy within the limits of the Iranian state.
2. The Kurdish language should be used in education and be the official language in administrative affairs.
3. The provincial council of Kurdistan should be immediately elected according to constitutional law and should supervise and inspect all state and social matters.
4. All state officials must be of local [Kurdish] origin.
5. A single law for both peasants and notables should be adopted and the future of both secured.
6. The Kurdish Democratic Party will make a special effort to establish unity and complete fraternity with the Azerbaijani people and the other peoples living in Azerbaijan (Assyrians, Armenians, etc.) in their struggle.
7. The Kurdish Democratic Party will strive for the improvement of the moral and economic state of the Kurdish people through the exploration of Kurdistan's many natural resources, the progress of agriculture and commerce, and the development of hygiene and education.
8. We desire that peoples living in Iran be able to strive freely for the happiness and progress of their country.[32]

Another provision called for all government revenues collected in Kurdistan to be spent exclusively in the Kurdish region.

The Iranian government considered the manifesto a challenge to its authority in Kurdistan, a first attempt by the Kurdish Democratic Party to promote irredentism, and despite references in the manifesto to Iranian constitutional law, it became clear that the fears of the Iranian authorities were justified as the Kurdish Democratic Party established an independent republic in Mahabad. The formation of the Kurdish Republic of Mahabad was formally proclaimed on January 22, 1946, at a meeting attended by the leadership of the Kurdish Democratic Party, several tribal chiefs, Mullah Mostafa Barzani (a prominent Iraqi Kurdish leader whose forces had crossed into Iran to provide military support to the Kurdish uprising when the *Komala* was formed), and three Soviet Red Army officers. At this meeting, Qazi Mohammad was elected president of the new republic, and a new cabinet was formed, consisting primarily of the leadership of the Kurdish Democratic Party from Mahabad. Mullah Mostafa's fighters joined the local tribal contingents to form the backbone of the new republic's army. It is interesting to note that both Qazi Mohammad and Saif Qazi, the minister of war in the new republic's cabinet, donned Soviet general's uniforms. Qazi Mohammad, however, at the urging of his colleagues, wore his white turban to accentuate his religious standing.

By the time the Kurdish Republic of Mahabad had been formed, the Soviets had succeeded in helping their allies in the *Firqah* establish their own autonomous republic in Azerbaijan, the Democratic Republic of Azerbaijan.[33] In a brief speech given after the formation of the Mahabad republic, Qazi Mohammad, much to the satisfaction of his Soviet patrons, congratulated his "Azerbaijani brothers" for achieving independence and expressed hope that they would help the Kurds solidify the foundation of their own republic, leading to a lasting friendship between the two independent Soviet-supported republics. As William Eagleton noted, no one at the ceremony wanted to "spoil the joyous occasion by questioning the sincerity of Qazi's declaration of Kurdish-Azerbaijani brotherhood."[34] The Soviets, cognizant of significant differences between Kurdish and Azeri objectives, were keenly aware of the necessity of reaching a practical compromise between the Azerbaijan and Kurdish republics in order to maintain sufficient influence in northern Iran to allow them to extract maximum concessions from the Iranian government.

It was within this framework that a delegation headed by Qazi Mohammad, including Soviet representatives, traveled to Tabriz in Azerbaijan and met with representatives of the Azerbaijan republic to negotiate the formation of a united front against the central government in Tehran. Through Soviet prodding, Qazi Mohammad and his counterpart in the Azerbaijan republic, Ja'far Pishevari, signed a friendship and cooperation treaty on April 23, 1946. The treaty contained numerous references to "Kurdish-Azerbaijani brotherhood" and delineated areas of cooperation between the two newly established republics. The language of the treaty left no doubt in Tehran that, in spite of claims to the contrary, the two republics were moving toward total independence from Iran. For example, the treaty called for the exchange of representatives (akin to the exchange of diplomatic officials between two sovereign nation-states), joint military planning, and economic, trade, and cultural agreements between the two republics. The treaty further stipulated that future negotiations with the Iranian government would be conducted only with the joint interests of the Kurdish and Azerbaijan republics in mind.

The Kurdish-Azerbaijani treaty of 1946 addressed the thorny problem of the conflicting ethnic demands of the Kurds and the Azeris. Article 2 of the treaty stated: "In those areas of Azerbaijan where there are Kurdish minorities, Kurds will be appointed to government departments, and in those parts of Kurdistan where there are Azerbaijani minorities, Azerbaijanis will be appointed to government departments."[35] In a similar vein, Article 6 of the treaty said: "The Azerbaijan National Government will take the necessary steps to promote the use of the Kurdish language and the development of

Kurdish culture among the Kurds of Azerbaijan, and the Kurdish National Government will take similar steps with regard to the Azerbaijanis living in Kurdistan."[36]

Neither the Kurdish Republic of Mahabad nor the Democratic Republic of Azerbaijan took meaningful steps to implement the provisions of their treaty. In the end, ethnic nationalism and provincial exigencies proved to be problematic, the marriage of convenience between the republics, at the behest and for the benefit of a foreign power, faltered. Furthermore, the Kurdish and Azerbaijani republics were counting on long-term Soviet support to deter the Iranian military, but the Soviet Union and Iran had embarked upon a diplomatic course of action to improve their relationship.

In discussions with Iranian prime minister Ahmad Qavam, the Soviets promised to remove their troops from Iran in return for an oil concession in the northern oil fields. Prime Minister Qavam reminded the Soviets that the Iranian Parliament had to approve an oil concession and that since the term of the Parliament had expired elections were needed to convene a new Parliament. However, parliamentary elections were not permissible under Iranian law so long as foreign troops were occupying part of the country. In an April 1946 agreement, the Soviet Union promised to remove its troops from Iranian territory and to treat the Azerbaijan upheaval as a purely internal Iranian matter. The agreement also called for the establishment of a joint Iranian-Soviet oil company.[37] By May 9, 1946, the Soviets had withdrawn from Iran, but neither the oil concession nor the establishment of a joint oil company was approved by the Iranian Parliament.

Anticipating the withdrawal of the Red Army from Iran and the implications of a withdrawal on their survival, the Azerbaijanis began negotiations with Prime Minister Qavam that led them to accept Azerbaijan as an inseparable part of Iran. In return, Qavam offered a number of political and economic concessions. They included: recognizing the executive and legislative bodies of the Azerbaijan republic as the legal provincial government; promising to increase the size of Azerbaijan's representative delegation to the Iranian Parliament; allowing the Azerbaijan republic to maintain internal security through its own security forces; and permitting two-thirds of revenues generated in Azerbaijan to be used exclusively for internal economic development projects. Not wanting to betray the spirit of their treaty with the Kurdish Republic of Mahabad, the Azerbaijani delegation also compelled Qavam to reform the educational system and allow Azeri and Kurdish children to be taught exclusively in their native vernaculars in all primary schools.[38]

Even though the Kurdish Republic of Mahabad was represented occasionally by Sadr Qazi in the Azeri-Iranian negotiations, the Kurds concluded that the agreement achieved very little for the Kurdish cause. Therefore, a Kurdish delegation was dispatched from Mahabad to meet with Qavam. Unlike their Azeri counterparts, the Kurdish representatives were unable to obtain any concessions from the Iranian prime minister. Much to the chagrin of the Kurds, Qavam told them that Kurdistan was part of Azerbaijan. If the Kurds wanted their own province in Iran, they would have to negotiate with the Azerbaijan republic and obtain its acquiescence, because the Mahabad republic had no legal standing as far as Qavam was concerned. The Kurds were now placed in double jeopardy, as an ethnic minority in the Iranian state and as a minority in an Azeri state.

These negotiations exacerbated Azeri-Kurdish relations, leading to fighting that intensified as the Red Army began to remove its troops from Iran. As the Soviet pullout from Azerbaijan and Kurdistan continued, the Iranian army gradually moved in to disarm the Azeri and Kurdish forces and re-establish the central government's authority. With Soviet protection removed, the Azerbaijan republic's separate existence came to an abrupt end in early December 1946.

The same fate awaited the Mahabad republic as the Iranian Fourth Division under the command of General Homayuni, who had recently led a successful campaign to neutralize tribal uprisings in the southern province of Khuzistan, surrounded Mahabad. The Iranian army entered Mahabad on December 17, 1946, and less than a year after its formation, the Mahabad republic had crumbled. A military court found Qazi Mohammad, Sadr Qazi, and Saif Qazi guilty of treason, and they were publicly hanged in Mahabad's main square on March 31, 1947. The republic's infrastructures were destroyed, and overt manifestations of Kurdish nationalism, such as the teaching of Kurdish, were prohibited.

In spite of the fact that the Mahabad republic exercised authority over less than one-third of Iranian Kurds and lasted less than a year, it has remained the point of reference for Kurdish movements throughout the Middle East. During the republic's existence, many of the Kurds' aspirations came to fruition. Kurdish became the official language, and Kurdish-language periodicals and literary publications flourished. Kurdish *peshmergas* replaced Iranian police units, and a Kurdish governmental bureaucracy was set up. Attempts were made to encourage the creation of other autonomous regions in the country and to turn Kurdistan into a base for "all the democratic forces in Iran."[39] No Kurdish movement has succeeded in duplicating the modest achievements of the Mahabad republic.

AFTER MAHABAD: KURDISH
NATIONALISM AND THE PAHLAVI DICTATORSHIP

The demise of the Kurdish Republic of Mahabad accelerated Reza Shah's disarming of Iranian tribes and the reintegration of non-Persian ethnic groups into the emerging centralized power structure in Tehran. Many of the Kurdish tribes that had joined forces with the Mahabad republic returned to their tribal areas, and in the words of General Hassan Arfa, chief of staff of the Iranian Army in 1944–1946, the Kurds returned to their tribal homelands "not with the bitter and humiliated feelings of a vanquished nation which had lost its dearly-won but short-lived independence, but only with the knowledge that this venture, like many others before, had not come off and that for the time being they had better sit quietly and show themselves good citizens."[40] The sentiments expressed by General Arfa illuminated the Shah's policies toward ethnic nationalism throughout much of the Pahlavi dynasty.

With the autonomy-seeking movements in Azerbaijan and Kurdistan neutralized, the Shah began to consolidate his power. Prime Minister Qavam's friendly agreements with the Azerbaijan and Kurdish republics and the support given him by the Tudeh Party and the Soviet Union had shielded him from the Shah's political whims. With the downfall of these two republics and the withdrawal of the Soviet forces from northern Iran, however, Qavam's position weakened. The parliamentary elections of 1946 and 1947 in particular weakened Qavam's power base as many of his erstwhile allies lost their parliamentary seats, thus paving the way for the Shah's dismissal of Qavam as prime minister in late 1947.

Qavam's removal from the political center did not eliminate other potential rivals in the Shah's quest for absolute power. One potential rival was General Ali Razmara, chief of staff of the Iranian Army, who through restructuring of the command structures and the placing of sympathetic officers in key positions in the military, sought to place himself in a favorable position for a possible power struggle with the Shah. Razmara's prospects received an unexpected and indirect boost when the Truman administration informed the Shah that future US aid to his government would be contingent upon internal reforms to stamp out corruption and inefficiency. Eager to ingratiate himself with the United States, the Shah decided to enlist the aid of Razmara in effecting reforms. Without consulting Parliament, the Shah appointed General Razmara as prime minister on June 26, 1950.

As promised by the Shah, Razmara initiated a purge of top-level Iranian politicians, including Qavam's political associates, undertook steps to decentralize political power by introducing a bill to establish provincial assemblies, and called for the implementation of a massive land reform program. Having come to power through US support and US Embassy machinations,[41] Razmara next wanted to obtain the support of the British, a traditional outside power broker in Iranian politics, to solidify his position. To this end, he campaigned to obtain the Iranian Parliament's ratification of a supplemental oil agreement with the British-controlled Anglo-Iranian Oil Company (AIOC). Although this was an improvement over prior agreements with the British and its ratification would have doubled the Iranian government's financial returns, Razmara was confronted with strong opposition in Parliament from growing nationalist sentiment that favored nationalization of the Iranian oil industry. Razmara's insistence on ratification of the supplemental agreement, and his bellicose confrontation with nationalist forces in Parliament, resulted in a loss of prestige and his being labeled a British puppet.

In order to reassert his authority and deflect charges of antinationalism, Razmara began to tilt toward the Soviet Union. He signed a trade agreement with the Soviet Union and settled Soviet-Iranian territorial disputes. He also withstood US pressure to include Iran in a pro-Western military pact, removed US advisers overseeing his economic reform programs, and restricted the movement of American military advisers.[42] Perhaps the major motive for Razmara's policy toward the Soviet Union was to establish an equilibrium between the East and the West and to portray himself as a legitimate Iranian nationalist. However, the end result was that he lost US-British support while failing to establish his nationalistic credentials on the domestic front.

While Razmara's pro-British agreement with the AIOC and his concessional trade agreement with the Soviet Union eroded his base of support among Iran's secular nationalists, his courting of pro-Tudeh figures, whom the clergy considered to be atheistic Communists, and his confrontational style of politics vis-à-vis the leading religious figures alienated the clerical hierarchy. The Shah was more than delighted to see his chief rival besieged on all fronts. Razmara's political career came to an abrupt end when he was assassinated on March 7, 1951, by a member of a Muslim fundamentalist group called *Fadaiyan-e Islam*.

After the assassination of Prime Minister Razmara, nationalist deputies in the Iranian Parliament reiterated their insistence on nationalizing the country's oil industry. To the nationalists, British control of Iran's major source of revenue was tantamount to economic colonialism and robbed the country of its independence and freedom of action. The nationalist sentiments were echoed by the Iranian National Front under the leadership of Dr. Mohammad Mossadegh. The National Front, which was formed in the summer of 1949 to oppose ratification of the supplemental oil agreement with the AIOC, royal authoritarianism, and the emerging dictatorship of the Shah, was an umbrella group representing a broad spectrum of Iranian politics. It opposed granting political and economic concessions to either the capitalist or Communist bloc and favored equidistance from both superpowers (negative equilibrium). It called for the establishment of a strong central government that guaranteed basic freedoms to all Iranians, irrespective of their ethnic or linguistic background.[43]

The National Front opposed the establishment of quasi-autonomous provincial legislative bodies, as had been proposed by Razmara, as a means to guarantee the basic rights of all Iranians. Dr. Mossadegh and his colleagues argued that in a democratically controlled government, where free elections are conducted without royal intervention, the rights of every Iranian voter, Persian or non-Persian, could best be guaranteed when the government was strong enough to prevent the country's disintegration. Members of the

National Front, and other Iranian nationalists, feared that without a strong central government foreign powers would once again exploit regional and provincial sentiments and create disintegrative movements like the ones in Azerbaijan and Kurdistan. Given the increasing popularity of the National Front and the growing prestige of Dr. Mossadegh among the Iranian intelligentsia, the National Front's call for a strong central government did not engender strong opposition from the outlying provinces. In fact, the leadership of the National Front was well represented by non-Persians or those who had established records of supporting the rights of non-Persian Iranians. For example, Dr. Karim Sanjabi, a respected Kurdish intellectual, became a prominent member of the National Front and a member of Mosaddegh's cabinet.

The Shah viewed the emergence of the National Front and Mossadegh as an obstacle to developing the monarchy into an absolute center of power. Consequently, the Shah appointed Hussein Ala, a staunch royalist supporter and a pro-British politician, as the new prime minister. Ala proved to be no match for Dr. Mossadegh, however, and Ala's cabinet proved ineffective in stopping the momentum for oil nationalization that engulfed the Parliament. On April 26, 1951, the Parliament unanimously approved a National Front bill nationalizing the Iranian oil industry. The significance of the passage of this bill stems from the fact that the Iranian Parliament was composed primarily of deputies who represented the old pro-British, pro-monarchical power structure. However, they too recognized the overwhelming public support for terminating British neocolonial hegemony in Iran.[44]

The passage of the oil nationalization bill led to Prime Minister Ala's resignation. Ala's resignation and the Parliament's overwhelming vote of confidence for the National Front's leadership compelled the Shah to appoint Dr. Mossadegh as prime minister in April 1951. Mossadegh's nationalistic platform, liberal democratic ideals, and desire to govern the country through free elections generated enthusiasm among Kurdish intellectuals. The Kurdish Democratic Party, which was outlawed by the Shah's government after the demise of the Mahabad republic, began once again to engage in political activity, albeit clandestinely.

The first provincial election since the downfall of the Mahabad republic in which candidates from the Kurdish Democratic Party participated was held in early 1952. Its candidates won handily, but the election was nullified when the Shah's army entered Mahabad and the government appointed political officials who were royalist supporters. Prime Minister Mossadegh opposed the military's high-handed disregard of free election results, but he could not oppose the Shah because under the Iranian Constitution the Pahlavi monarch was the supreme commander in chief of the armed forces. In the same year, major uprisings occurred in other parts of Kurdistan. Most of these revolts were antifeudal and directed as much against Kurdish feudal landlords as they were against the Shah's military. Thus, an alliance of convenience was formed between the Shah and the major Kurdish khans and landlords to suppress peasant rebellions throughout Kurdistan.

Kurdish rank-and-file support for Dr. Mossadegh's government alienated the Shah and convinced him that the Kurds had to be contained at all costs. For example, in a massive display of support for Mossadegh's crusade to force the Shah to reign and not rule, as stipulated in the Iranian Constitution, Iranian Kurds on August 13, 1953, overwhelmingly voted to limit the Shah's power and make him into a constitutional monarch. According to Abdul Rahman Ghassemlou, in the city of Mahabad, where five thousand voters participated in the referendum, the Shah received only two votes.[45] This period of liberalism ended when the democratically elected government of Dr. Mossadegh was overthrown on August 19, 1953, in a British-US-sponsored coup with the code name Operation Ajax.[46] The Kurds, who hoped to attain their rights under Mossadegh's leadership, found themselves once again at the mercy of the Shah's regime, and the remnants of Kurdish resistance to the Shah's forces were easily overcome.

Nevertheless, sporadic rebellions continued to occur throughout Kurdistan. The most significant of these post-1953 revolts occurred in 1956 among the Javanioudi tribe near Kermanshah. The harsh mountainous terrain and the relative isolation of the Javanioudi Kurds had enabled them to withstand incursions by the Shah's armed forces in the past. However, they were no longer able to resist the vastly superior Iranian army and succumbed. No other significant Kurdish revolt occurred in Iran until the onset of the Islamic Republic in 1978.

In addition to reliance on military force, the Shah attempted to pacify Kurdistan by co-opting tribal leaders into the monarchical system through a policy of financial and political rewards. For example, the Shah's government identified traditional power holders in the Jaf tribe and gave them high-level positions in the local government and in the central government in Tehran. When he implemented his land reform program as a centerpiece of his White Revolution in 1960–1963, the Shah left the large landholdings of the Jaf tribal leaders essentially untouched. Salar Jaf was given a high-level position in the Shah's palace, while his brother, Sardar Jaf, became an influential tribal member in the Iranian Parliament.[47] The predominantly Shi'a Ardalan tribe provided a large number of prominent individuals during the Shah's reign; the Shah's last minister of the court was a Kurd from the Ardalan tribe. The Kurds also provided soldiers who rose to the highest ranks in the Shah's military. For example, one of the most loyal supporters of the Shah, even after the overthrow of the Pahlavi monarchy, was General Palizban, the Kurdish governor general of Kermanshah. Using his knowledge of the topography and demography of Kurdistan and his connections in the region, General Palizban haunted the Islamic Republic from his base in Iraq for several years.[48] Even though the Shah's carrot-and-stick policy rewarded some Kurds, life for the majority of Kurds remained unchanged during the

Shah's reign. The Kurdish economy, in particular, deteriorated as increased taxation of Kurdistan's main cash crop, tobacco, depleted needed funds from the region.

The Shah sought to stifle overt manifestations of Kurdish ethnicity by not only requiring Persian as the exclusive language in governmental matters, but also requiring it in all printed media and books. Although limited radio and television broadcasts in Kurdish were allowed, all primary and secondary teaching was to be in Persian. To ensure adherence to linguistic policies, the government sent nonnative speakers to staff educational institutions in Kurdish regions. Political activity and freedom were restricted in Kurdistan, but this was in line with the Shah's authoritarian policies as practiced in the rest of the country.[49]

Before the Iranian Revolution, the Shah initiated a final policy to weaken the Kurds. Precipitated by Kurdish revolts against the Iraqi government during the 1960s, it was disastrous for the Kurds. The Shah viewed the rise to power of the "radical" Ba'th Party in neighboring Iraq as a threat to his ambition to become the uncontested regional power in the Gulf and a threat to regional stability. Consequently, he decided to use the Kurdish revolts in Iraq to destabilize the Ba'thi regime in Baghdad. As will be discussed in Chapter 3, the primary Kurdish revolt was led by the veteran Kurdish fighter Mullah Mostafa Barzani.

Until 1966, the only significant outside aid for Mullah Mostofa's *peshmergas* came from the Kurdish Democratic Party of Iran. However, the Shah came to recognize the potential for using direct aid to Mullah Mostafa as a means to "secure some direct influence within the Kurdish national movement. The idea was to make Barzani's movement dependent upon the aid and to increase that aid as the movement grew so that eventually the Kurdish movement's very survival would depend upon it."[50] The Shah correctly calculated that by helping Mullah Mostafa he could compel him to cease aiding the Iranian Kurds and even use him to restrain Kurdish activities inside Iran.

As the Iranian government's aid to Mullah Mostafa increased, so did the Shah's influence. This resulted in the 1966 issuance of a major policy statement by Mullah Mostafa regarding the direction of the Kurdish movement in Iran. The statement directed Kurdish nationalists to cease hostilities against the Shah's regime. To do otherwise would result in the cutoff of Iranian support for the Kurdish *peshmergas* inside Iraq and lead to certain defeat of the Kurdish revolt against the Ba'thi regime. Every Kurdish fighter who continued fighting against the Shah's regime would be considered an enemy of the "Kurdish revolution." Mullah Mostafa concluded that his *peshmergas* had a greater chance of success against the Iraqi government than the Kurds in Iran had against the Shah's regime, and that Kurds would have to sacrifice their own objectives for the more immediate goal of a victory in Iraq.

Mullah Mostafa's policy of collaborating with the Shah's regime was an abject failure and a detriment to Kurdish autonomy. It resulted in a major schism between Iraqi Kurds and their Iranian counterparts in the Kurdish Democratic Party. Several Iranian rebels who had joined Mullah Mostafa's forces returned to Iran and began a new revolt against the Pahlavi regime. The Kurdish region bounded by Mahabad, Baneh, and Sardasht was selected as the center of this new revolt, and a committee was set up to guide and sustain it. However, the rebels soon found themselves surrounded by the Iranian army and their escape route blocked by Mullah Mostafa's *peshmergas*. Some key leaders of this revolt, such as Abdullah Moini and Sharif Zadeh, were killed fighting the Iranian army. Others, such as Sulayman Moini, the elder brother of Adbullah, were arrested by Mullah Mostafa and executed. By one estimate, forty Iranian Kurdish rebels were killed by Mullah Mostafa's forces or arrested and handed over to Iranian authorities to face certain death.[51] The Shah's policy of divide-and-rule had worked, and the Kurds, once again, became the victims of their own misguided and opportunistic leadership.

THE IRANIAN REVOLUTION, THE ISLAMIC REPUBLIC, AND THE KURDS

After years of suppression by the Shah's regime, it was natural that the Kurds would enthusiastically support the Iranian Revolution of 1978–1979. In fact, a broad spectrum of the Kurdish population participated in the revolutionary process from the outset. What the Kurds viewed as the Shah's betrayal of them without, as one observer called it, "the least bit of compunction,"[52] provided added incentive for the Kurds to join the revolutionary forces against the monarchical regime. As I have discussed elsewhere, the only Kurds who refrained from participating in anti-Shah activities were tribal leaders, such as the Jafs, who had become the beneficiaries of the Shah's policies of political and financial co-optation.[53] Initial Kurdish euphoria over the demise of the Pahlavi monarchy gave way to the bitter realization that Kurdish autonomy demands would go unheeded by the new Islamic Republic. It became evident that Ayatollah Khomeini's objective of establishing a strong centralized Islamic republic would clash with the goals of the autonomy-seeking Kurds. As Khomeini saw it, the demands of ethnic nationalities for autonomy would be superfluous in an Islamic state:

> Sometimes the word minorities is used to refer to people such as the Kurds, Lurs, Turks, Persians, Baluchis, and such. These people should not be called minorities, because this term assumes that there is a difference between these brothers. In Islam, such a difference has no place at all. There is no difference between Muslims who speak different languages, for instance, the Arabs or the Persians. It is very probable that such problems have been created by those who do not wish the

> Muslim countries to be united. . . . They create the issues of
> nationalism, of pan-Arabism, pan-Turkism, and such isms, which are
> contrary to Islamic doctrines. Their plan is to destroy Islam and the
> Islamic philosophy.[54]

Notwithstanding Ayatollah Khomeini's rejection of the importance of
ethnic and cultural pluralism, the constitution of the Islamic Republic
recognizes the existence of linguistic diversity among the Iranian people. In
article fifteen of the constitution, Persian is recognized as the official
language of Iran—official communication and instructional and educational
materials must be in Persian—however, the use of local vernaculars in the
media and in the classroom is permitted so long as they are used in
conjunction with Persian.[55] The only recognition given to minorities in the
constitution is for religious minorities (Christian, Jewish, and Zoroastrian)
and not for Islamic minorities such as the Kurds. The Kurds were viewed as
an integral part of the Islamic *umma*, or community, and hence were not to
be treated differently from other Muslim groups in the country.

The Kurds, however, considered the downfall of the Shah's regime as
having presented them with "an unrivaled opportunity for Kurdish demands
for autonomy, far greater than that offered to the men of Mahabad [the
Mahabad Republic], since Soviet or other Great Power interest or physical
presence was not involved."[56] To this end, the Kurdish leadership strove to
affect the shape of the emerging state structure in post-Pahlavi Iran. Dr.
Abdul Rahman Ghassemlou, who became secretary general of the Kurdish
Democratic Party of Iran (KDPI) in 1973, returned on the eve of the Iranian
Revolution after several years of exile in Europe and sought to transform the
essentially dormant KDPI into the principal Kurdish political organization in
the country.

Like other parties and interest groups in the country, the KDPI
recognized the importance the new constitution would have in guaranteeing
Kurdish rights. On March 30–31, 1979, the Iranian government conducted a
referendum, asking voters to vote on a single proposal: to maintain the
monarchical system or replace it with an Islamic republic. The KDPI and
other secular groups in the country boycotted the referendum because it only
offered two choices. Given the antipathy toward the Shah's regime, it was
evident that the majority of voters would opt for an Islamic republic.
Khomeini's exhortations for a massive turnout resulted in an overwhelming
victory for the clerics as 98.2 percent voted to replace the monarchy with an
Islamic republic.[57] The Kurds had lost their first political battle with the
revolutionary regime in Tehran.

The Kurds, as well as other nonclerical parties, shifted the focus of their
struggle to the new constitution, which the provisional government of
Mehdi Bazargan was given the task of drafting. The outlines of the
constitution had been formulated in Paris by moderate and nonclerical
supporters of Khomeini. It was heavily influenced by the Iranian

Constitution of 1906 and the constitution of France's Fifth Republic. Unveiled by Bazargan's government on June 18, 1979, the draft constitution called for the establishment of a strong presidency and a unitary system of government. Although it payed lip service to the individual and communal rights of Iranians, it fell far short of what the Kurds had hoped for in terms of their autonomy demands. However, much to the satisfaction of the secular parties, including the KDPI, the draft constitution did not give special privileges to the clergy, nor did it call for a political system dominated by Shi'a clerics. Surprisingly, Ayatollah Khomeini approved the draft constitution, with minor modifications, and asked Bazargan to submit it for public approval. Bazargan, and the opposition, objected, arguing for the election of a constituent assembly to debate the draft constitution and make any necessary modifications before a public referendum. They argued that a constitution should not be hastily drafted without debate by representatives of the people.

The KDPI joined the other opposition parties and demanded that a constituent assembly, consisting of no more than five hundred members, be elected to debate and revise the draft constitution. The position of the oppositionists was bolstered when Ayatollah Kazem Shariatmadari, a major clerical figure and spiritual leader of Azerbaijan, supported the idea of an elected constituent assembly. Eventually, a compromise was reached in which an elected assembly would review the draft. However, this new body, the Assembly of Experts, was to be composed of seventy-three members, not five hundred as requested by the opposition.

In formal and informal gatherings, Iranians expressed a multitude of views on the draft constitution. Among the ethnic groups, some were adamant that the final constitution include provisions guaranteeing autonomy for their provinces, while others were more conciliatory. On one hand, Shaikh Mohammad Taher Shubayr al-Khaqani, the spiritual leader of the Arabs of Khuzistan, cautioned his people about pressing too hard for autonomy lest they be seen as disloyal. On the other hand, Shaikh Ezzedin Husseini, the Sunni spiritual leader of the Mahabad Kurds, argued that as Iran was a multinational state, its constitution had to recognize the cultural, economic, and sociopolitical rights of all ethnic groups. He also took the view that securing Kurdish rights would require redrawing Iran's provincial borders, which would transfer territories from provinces such as Azerbaijan, Ilam, and Kermanshah into Kurdistan.[58] Once again, this highlighted the difficulty of granting autonomy to the Iranian Kurds without trampling on the rights of others, such as the Azeris. Nevertheless, a group calling itself the United Muslims of Kurdistan threatened an armed uprising if Kurdish autonomy demands were not satisfied in the revised constitution.[59]

Acrimonious debate about the draft constitution and Kurdish autonomy demands conjured up memories of the 1940s and the rise of secessionist movements in Azerbaijan and Kurdistan, whose objectives had also been couched in terms of gaining local autonomy. Furthermore, Ayatollah Khomeini and his clerical supporters feared that the foundation of their preferred system of government (an Islamic state) would be weakened if what were essentially secular ethnic demands were accommodated in the revised constitution. To counter the increasing demands of ethnonationalists, Ayatollah Khomeini delivered a major speech to a delegation of clerics from Mahabad. In the speech, Khomeini insisted that debates about the draft constitution be conducted only within an Islamic framework, and that the clergy had the right and obligation to prevent others from interjecting "non-Islamic principles" into the document. As Khomeini put it, the constitution of the Islamic Republic "means the constitution of Islam. Don't sit back while foreignized intellectuals, who have no faith in Islam, give their views and write the things they write. Pick up your pens and in the mosques, from the altars, in the streets and bazaars, speak of the things that in your view should be included in the constitution."[60] The gap between the emerging Islamic Republic of Iran and Kurdish aspirations seemed to have widened. The final draft of the Iranian Constitution, as approved by the clergy-dominated Assembly of Experts, established a state system as centralized as the Pahlavi state system had been, albeit within an Islamic framework.

Even before debates about the constitution soured relations between Islamic authorities and the Kurdish leadership, tensions had increased after units of the Iranian army and the newly created *pasdaran-e enghelab* (Revolutionary Guards) engaged in sporadic military clashes with the KDPI *peshmergas* and their supporters. Then, in March 1979, a Kurdish delegation met with Ayatollah Khomeini in the holy city of Qom to present him with autonomy demands. While acknowledging past discrimination against the Kurds by the Pahlavi regime, Khomeini told the delegates that their autonomy demands were unacceptable in Islamic Iran.[61] After this meeting, the Kurdish leadership became convinced that they would be unable to convince Khomeini that autonomy for Kurdistan in a federally structured Iran would not endanger Iran's territorial integrity.[62] Nevertheless, they continued to maintain a dialogue with central government authorities while reiterating their support for the Iranian Revolution.

In addition to political considerations, religion played a role in exacerbating tensions between the mostly Sunni Kurds and the Shi'a leadership in Tehran and Qom. While during the Shah's reign, "religion was not generally considered a crucial criterion of Kurdish ethnic identity, . . . [after the Revolution there emerged] several indications of increased consciousness among Kurds as among Persians of the religious factor."[63] The Kurdish concern was that the Islamic state, as envisioned by Ayatollah Khomeini, would result in a Shi'a dictatorship at the expense of the power and prestige of the Sunni religious leaders in Kurdistan. Furthermore, the Kurdish leaders were concerned that the clerical leadership in Tehran would replace Kurdish leaders, both secular and religious, with Shi'a leaders loyal to the Islamic Republic.[64] The Kurdish fears in this regard were not without foundation. As the *komitehs* (revolutionary committees) were set up throughout the country to act as the eyes and ears of the Revolution, and to ensure compliance with the new Islamic standards, their leaders became closely identified with the Shi'a clergy in Qom and Tehran.

Furthermore, as a result of Shaikh Ezzedin Husseini's increasing influence among the Kurds, the Qom clerics promoted Ahmad Moftizadeh, a conservative Kurdish Shi'a cleric from Kermanshah, as the authentic voice of the Kurdish nation and as the true religious representative of the Kurds. Shaikh Husseini continued to issue edicts opposing Ayatollah Khomeini's concept of Islamic government and his emphasis on the institution of *velayat-e faqih* (government of a just jurisconsult), which promoted absolutism by concentrating all power in the hands of an infallible *faqih*.[65] In an interview given in October 1982, Shaikh Ezzedin Husseini summarized his objections to the concept of *velayat-e faqih:*

> Many governments in the past have claimed to act in the name of Islam, but in reality they were not Islamic. The Safavid and Ottoman governments were cases in point; more recently we have the case of Khomeini in Iran. They are *qeshri*—backward and vulgar—and have ruined Islam and its spirit. What we have is not religious government, but a dictatorship under the name of Islam. They are using the name of religion to oppress the people, and the people know this. In Sunni Islam there is no imam as political leader or *na'ib* (deputy) imam. The role of the clergy is to be a *morshed*, or guide, in knowing God. You will also find some shi'i [sic] clergy who reject Khomeini's concept of the *faqih*. It is not an Islamic regime.[66]

In the same interview, Shaikh Husseini recalled his April 1979 meeting with Ayatollah Khomeini, during which he asked Khomeini to support autonomy for Kurdistan and to draft an Islamic constitution, as opposed to a Shi'a or Sunni one. According to Husseini, Khomeini said that everyone in Iran was oppressed, but that things were going to be better for everyone. Upon leaving, Khomeini told Husseini, "What I am asking from you is the security of Kurdistan." Husseini responded, "What I ask from you is autonomy for Kurdistan."[67] The two religious leaders never met again. However, their feud over the political direction of the Islamic Republic, and the role of minorities in it, continued unabated.

Even though Islamic authorities in Tehran expressed serious reservations about the nature and effects of Kurdish autonomy demands, the Kurds proceeded to hold elections in several cities for city councillors. Many of the newly elected councillors were members, or sympathizers, of the KDPI and were endorsed by the Marxist-Leninist guerrilla organization *Fadaiyan-e Khalq* (People's Sacrificers) and the Islamic leftist organization *Mujahidin-e Khalq* (People's Combatants). After brief honeymoons with the Islamic Republic, these organizations initiated sustained campaigns of armed struggle against the clerical authorities in Iran. In Kurdistan, they found fertile ground for recruitment of new members and a suitable base for operations against the new Iranian regime.[68] Due in part to the close cooperation between the anti-Khomeini Iranian "left," Kurdish fighters, and prominent leaders such as Dr. Ghassemlou and Shaikh Ezzedin Husseini, Ayatollah Khomeini declared the spring 1979 city councillor elections null and void. In addition, because of Ghassemlou's neo-Marxist orientation and Shaikh Husseini's socialist views couched in religious terms, Khomeini concluded that Kurdish autonomy demands were a Marxist-inspired conspiracy against the Islamic Republic of Iran. By the end of the summer of 1979, the KDPI was banned as a political party and both Ghassemlou and Shaikh Husseini were declared by Ayatollah Khomeini to be *mofsid-e fil arz* (corrupters of the earth), a charge that carried an automatic death penalty.

As I have alluded earlier, from the outset the Kurds denied that their aim was to weaken Iran or establish a separate sovereign nation-state of Kurdistan. As Ghassemlou stated emphatically, "Let me make one thing clear: no political force in Iranian Kurdistan wants to secede from Iran. Our demands are framed within the context of the Iranian state."[69] He helped coin the term "democracy for Iran, autonomy for Kurdistan" as a popular motto for the KDPI. In response, the Iranian authorities insisted that the KDPI prove its loyalty to Iran and the principles of the Islamic Revolution. Dr. Mostafa Chamran, the first defense minister of the Islamic Republic, said that if the KDPI and other Kurds really believed in the Islamic Revolution, "we would give them not just autonomy in Kurdistan but also the control of all of Iran so that they could show us how to give autonomy and freedom to every group in the country. However, if they simply use fancy and misleading slogans to hide their intention to harm Islam and the Revolution and to serve the interests of the foreign powers whose interests are diametrically opposed to those of the Iranian people, including the Kurds, we will fight them to the end."[70] Chamran further chastised the KDPI by saying: "If you are truly fighting for the liberation of the Kurdish people, then why do you need to threaten them constantly? Why do you have to terrorize or hang those Kurds who sympathize and cooperate with the Islamic government? Let the Kurdish masses freely choose which side they want to support—the Islamic Republic or a foreign-supported political party."[71] Dr. Chamran's efforts in 1979 were instrumental in defeating Kurdish uprisings in Iran and in damaging the military capabilities of the guerrilla units of the fadaiyan and mujahidin in Kurdistan. Furthermore, the question of what the KDPI meant by autonomy, and the implications of such an autonomy for the rest of the country, was never answered.

Shortly after coming to power, the provisional Islamic government of Prime Minister Bazargan sought to reassure non-Persian ethnic minorities of the government's commitment to remedy past injustices inflicted upon them by the Pahlavi monarchy. Bazargan, a member of the Azeri minority, traveled to Tabriz and delivered a major address on this topic to the people of Azerbaijan and Kurdistan. Bazargan's first postrevolutionary cabinet included two prominent Kurds in its ranks: Dr. Karim Sanjabi, the veteran leader of the National Front, and Dariush Foruhar. Sanjabi was appointed foreign minister while Foruhar was given the labor portfolio. Both of these men were respected nationalists with anti-Shah credentials.

After appointing the members of his cabinet, Prime Minister Bazargan sent a goodwill delegation headed by Dariush Foruhar to Kurdistan on February 14, 1979, to discuss autonomy demands with Kurdish leaders. Despite Bazargan's de jure authority as head of the government, de facto political power was in the Revolutionary Council, whose membership was dominated by anti-secularists. Because of Bazargan's weakness vis-à-vis the Revolutionary Council and the existence of multiple centers of power in Tehran, the Foruhar delegation was unable to make firm commitments to the Kurdish leaders. To compound the problem, the Kurds could not specify the powers they wanted in a local Kurdish government should autonomy be granted. Also, as described previously, the Kurdish leadership's demand to redraw the boundaries of the Kurdistan province at the expense of the provinces of West Azerbaijan, Ilam, and Kermanshah was unacceptable to Iranian authorities as well as to the residents of those provinces.[72]

The failure of the Foruhar mission to Kurdistan exacerbated tensions between the Kurds and the Islamic Republic, leading to an intensification of armed clashes between the Islamic *pasdarans* and the Kurdish *peshmergas*. Simultaneously, fighting in Kurdistan spilled over into adjacent areas in the form of skirmishes between Kurds and Azeris and Turkomans.[73] Moreover, fighting between conservative Kurdish landlords and Kurdish peasants, who had seized land from the owners as a result of the power vacuum created after the Shah's downfall, reflected deep divisions within Kurdish society. Needless to say, these conflicts undercut the Kurdish position in talks with government authorities and cast doubt on the prospects for peaceful coexistence among the various groups in the region.

After the inconclusive talks with the Foruhar delegation, the Kurds felt that future negotiations with the government would be fruitless as long as the Iranian army and *pasdarans* were attacking Kurdish forces. The major Kurdish cities of Mahabad and Sanandaj became battlegrounds between the government forces and the KDPI *peshmergas*. Of course, fighting in Kurdistan was not limited to these two cities. Paveh, Marivan, and other Kurdish cities were also the daily scenes of battles between the KDPI *peshmergas,* aided by the guerrilla forces of the Iranian fadaiyan and mujahidin, and government forces under the leadership of Defense Minister Chamran.[74] Without the decisive intervention of Chamran's forces, the KDPI forces and their leftist allies would have established a durable stronghold and the course of the Iranian Revolution might have changed dramatically.

Although intense battles were waged in all parts of Kurdistan, the cities of Mahabad and Sanandaj assumed symbolic importance as the soul of the Kurdish struggle for autonomy. As the capital of the Kurdish province and the site of the only independent Kurdish republic in history, Mahabad always carried a special status for Iranian Kurds. Sanandaj was the heart of the Kurdish region, a major center of socioeconomic activity, and a city from which SAVAK, the Shah's secret police, directed its anti-Kurdish activities. One of the activities that most incensed the Kurds occurred when the Iranian government dispatched Shaikh Sadeq Khalkhali to Kurdistan to hold impromptu trials for Kurdish fighters and those suspected of collaborating with the KDPI and its leftist allies. Khalkhali established his reputation as a merciless judge when he ordered the execution of officials of the Shah's regime after holding secret trials for them, and hundreds of Kurds were tried and summarily executed in public on his order. After his whirlwind trials in Kurdistan, Khalkhali was given the sobriquet "the hanging judge" by his opponents.

The intensity of fighting and the extent of the bloodshed in Kurdistan caused Ayatollah Taleghani to offer his services as a peacemaker between the government and the Kurds. Taleghani was a highly respected religious figure throughout the country, with a long history of struggle for the civil and political rights of all Iranians, and he was accepted by all parties as an impartial intermediary. Ayatollah Taleghani agreed to head a government delegation to mediate between the Kurds and the authorities in Tehran, and on March 24, 1979, an agreement was reached between the two sides by which the Kurds were to be given limited autonomy.

The agreement included three main parts: (1) Kurdish and Persian would be taught in schools in Kurdistan, (2) administration of the local government and economy would be conducted by elected Kurdish representatives, and (3) Kurds would participate in drafting a new national constitution in Iran. The logistics for implementing the provisions of this agreement were to be worked out between the central government and Kurdish representatives. In return for limited autonomy, the Kurds promised to support the abolition of the monarchy and the establishment of an Islamic state in the country and actively participate in the upcoming referendum on the constitution. However, the agreement brokered by Ayatollah Taleghani fell apart when the Kurds began to doubt the government's sincerity and as the more radical elements on the Kurdish side began to pressure the KDPI not to participate in the referendum without first obtaining autonomy for Kurdistan. Hence, they coined the slogan "no referendum, self-determination first." As a result, the fragile truce between the Kurds and the government broke down, and major clashes ensued. A Kurdish boycott of the March 1979 referendum was followed by a similar boycott in December 1979 of the vote on the new Iranian Constitution.

In early August 1979, the KDPI sent a letter to Ayatollah Khomeini, the text of which was published in the popular secularist Tehran daily

Ayandegan. The letter sought to clarify once again the goals of Kurdish autonomy and reassure Khomeini that the Kurds were loyal citizens and that the KDPI did not wish to dismember Iran.[75] The letter requested a face-to-face meeting between KDPI representatives and Ayatollah Khomeini to clear up any misrepresentation of Kurdish goals that the media may have conveyed. By that time, the Iranian army and *pasdarans* were well on their way to recapturing Kurdish areas from the insurgents. By the last week of August 1979, the strategically important cities of Paveh, Sanandaj, and Saqqez were under the control of the Iranian army, and by early September, all major cities in Kurdistan, including Mahabad and Sardasht, had been recaptured from the Kurdish *peshmergas*. The fall of these cities "was a sharp reminder that the Iranian army was not in disarray, and that its defeat in conventional warfare was not a Kurdish option."[76] Despite military defeat and loss of control of Kurdish cities, the *peshmergas* did maintain some freedom of action in the countryside and in areas close to the Iraqi border where Saddam Hussein's forces resupplied the KDPI *peshmergas*.

The government's failure to neutralize Kurdish guerrillas in the countryside and the KDPI's loss of control of the cities created a stalemate that led to another attempt at a negotiated settlement of the Kurdish problem in Iran. On August 26, 1979, a five-man Kurdish delegation arrived in Tehran to offer a new peace plan. The delegation, which was headed by Mullah Rahim Abbasi, the head of the Provincial Council of Mahabad, met with leading religious and political authorities, including Ayatollah Taleghani, Defense Minister Mostafa Chamran, and Deputy Prime Minister Sadeq Tabatabai. The Kurds offered a five-point plan that included: the immediate removal of Shaikh Sadeq Khalkhali from Kurdish areas, an end to the execution of Kurdish militants and activists, the withdrawal of non-Kurdish *pasdarans* from Kurdistan and their replacement with Kurds, an immediate cease-fire, and the convening of a comprehensive conference to discuss Kurdish autonomy within the framework of the Iranian state. Ayatollah Khomeini rejected these demands as long as the Kurds were armed and challenging his authority. Thereafter, Khomeini dispatched Hojjatoleslam Hussein Kermani as his personal representative to Kurdistan to oversee the crushing of the Kurdish insurgency.[77]

Although these newest Kurdish demands were rejected by Ayatollah Khomeini, Prime Minister Bazargan continued to search for a peaceful settlement of the Kurdish problem. On September 3, 1979, Bazargan went to Mahabad to personally offer concessions to the Kurds, including a promise of massive economic aid to bolster the sagging Kurdish economy, an amnesty for KDPI *peshmergas*, and the establishment of a university in Mahabad. The Bazargan mission was derailed as fighting between Kurdish and government forces intensified. This was a clear indication of the Bazargan administration's weakness vis-à-vis other multiple centers of power in the country.

A final attempt by the Bazargan government to negotiate an overall settlement was made in November 1979 when Labor Minister Dariush Foruhar headed another government delegation to Mahabad to negotiate with Kurdish leaders. Foruhar's delegation was presented with an eight-point plan containing the most detailed list of Kurdish autonomy demands since the victory of the Iranian Revolution. It called for legal recognition of Kurdish autonomy in the Iranian Constitution; recognition of West Azerbaijan, Ilam, Kermanshah, and Kurdistan provinces as a single integrated autonomous region; establishment of a freely elected Kurdish parliament with jurisdiction over all local matters (including internal security and police functions); inclusion of Kurdish representatives at all levels of central government; use of Kurdish (alongside Persian) in all official communications and in schools; and allocation of a specified amount of the national budget for the development of the Kurdish economy and infrastructures. The Kurdish plan reiterated the supremacy of the central government in the areas of international trade and defense and foreign policy.[78] These demands were accepted in principle by the Foruhar delegation, but as before, they were rejected by Ayatollah Khomeini.

As previously mentioned, the final draft of the Islamic Republic's constitution did not recognize Kurdish minority rights aside from the rights guaranteed to all Iranians. However, in an attempt to persuade the Kurds to participate in the Islamic Republic's first presidential election in 1980, Khomeini announced that he would consider asking the authorities to add an amendment to the constitution guaranteeing specific rights for Sunni minorities. Specifically, this amendment would have allowed Sunnis to have their own religious courts in areas where they constituted the majority of the population. Kurdish leadership rejected this idea as insufficient. They wanted recognition as a distinct ethnic, not religious, group because the Kurdish population contained both Sunni and Shi'a Muslims.

As the presidential election of 1980 approached, hopes for a negotiated settlement of the Kurdish issue had all but vanished. In the election, the KDPI supported the candidacy of Massoud Rajavi, the leader of the mujahidin, against Abol Hassan Bani-Sadr, who received the endorsement of Ayatollah Khomeini. Bani-Sadr's landslide victory was expected, and the KDPI's support for Rajavi did not deter Ghassemlou from approaching President Bani-Sadr in February 1980 to present him with a new plan for Kurdish autonomy.

The major difference in this latest plan was that the KDPI dropped its insistence on including the provinces of West Azerbaijan, Ilam, and Kermanshah as part of Kurdistan. Dr. Ghassemlou agreed to allow a majority popular vote to define the autonomous area of Kurdistan. Because Kurds were in the minority in West Azerbaijan and Ilam and the Shi'a Kurds in Kermanshah were more supportive of the Islamic Republic than the KDPI, Ghassemlou's concession, in effect, narrowed the contours of the Kurdish region to a substantially smaller area than previously had been demanded.

Bani-Sadr was positively inclined toward the Kurdish demands, but he insisted that there could be no progress toward settlement of the Kurdish issue until the Kurds laid down their arms and ended their military confrontation with government forces. Ghassemlou insisted that they would not disarm until their autonomy goals were achieved. Both sides parted company and new rounds of fighting broke out throughout Kurdistan.

The KDPI held its Fourth Congress in Mahabad in February 1980. In a resolution passed at this meeting, the KDPI reaffirmed its support for the Iranian Revolution and the country's territorial integrity while issuing autonomy demands that had already been rejected by the government. The resolution endorsed President Bani-Sadr's "liberal" views, particularly on internal freedom for the country's ethnic minorities.[79] Bani-Sadr, in turn, issued a conciliatory message expressing hope that peace would return to all of Iran.

One of the most vexing problems regarding the realization of Kurdish self-determination involved the meaning of the term "autonomy," which in Persian is referred to as *khodmokhtari*. The Persian term has a negative connotation; it equates autonomy with secession and total independence. Ayatollah Alame Nouri, a leading cleric with a reputation for having "progressive" views, suggested in late March 1980 that the Kurds cease using *khodmokhtari* in their publications and devise a new, less threatening term. The Kurds were amenable to using any term, including "Islamic autonomy" as suggested by Ayatollah Nouri, as long as the government "recognized the concept of decentralization for itself and home rule for the Kurds and other ethnic minorities."[80] However, developments in Iran—including Bani-Sadr's emerging power struggle with the clerical establishment, the increasing challenge to the government posed by the activities of opposition forces, and the need for unity in the face off with the United States over the holding of US hostages in Tehran—relegated the issue of Kurdish autonomy to a secondary concern of the government.

On September 22, 1980, Iraq launched a major invasion of Iran and occupied the Khuzistan province. Faced with the prospect of total war against an invading enemy, the loyalty of all Iranians was expected in defense of the motherland. The KDPI made the cardinal error of seeking military and logistical support from the invading forces of Saddam Hussein's Iraq. Ghassemlou's declarations in support of Iran's territorial integrity now rang hollow, and many supporters of the KDPI turned away from its leadership.

On October 12, Ayatollah Khomeini appointed President Bani-Sadr chairman of the Supreme Defense Council. The president's authority, however, was undermined by the clerical authorities associated with the Islamic Republican Party (IRP). Bani-Sadr began writing a regular column, "The President's Diary," in his daily newspaper, *Engelab-e Islami* (Islamic Revolution), in which he accused the IRP of practicing Stalinism and undermining his war efforts. The IRP retaliated by sponsoring a parliamentary motion to impeach the president for violating "Islamic principles." The powerful IRP clerics managed to shut down Bani-Sadr's newspaper in 1980. The embattled president found some unexpected allies, including members of the KDPI and the mujahidin. This provided ammunition to Bani-Sadr's enemies in the Parliament for forcing his dismissal from office. Bani-Sadr's alliance of convenience with the KDPI and the mujahidin left Khomeini no choice but to withdraw support from the president, and on June 20 and 21, 1981, in a highly charged atmosphere, the IRP-led deputies in the Parliament orchestrated the passage of a motion to impeach Bani-Sadr and remove him from office. Bani-Sadr's defiant speeches did little to alleviate tension and caused Khomeini to suspect that Bani-Sadr was being used as a tool of the opposition groups to undermine the foundation of the Islamic Republic.

After Bani-Sadr's overthrow in June 1981, the mujahidin organized their last major demonstration in the country, hoping to generate popular sentiment for their cause and for Bani-Sadr. The demonstration proved to be a failure, causing Bani-Sadr and Massoud Rajavi to plan their escape from the country. On July 29, 1981, Bani-Sadr and Rajavi were secretly flown to Paris on an air force jet piloted by a mujahidin supporter. After France granted political asylum, the two exiled leaders announced the formation of the National Council of Resistance (NCR) to fight the Iranian government. The KDPI joined the NCR as a principal partner.[81]

Initially, the mujahidin succeeded in expanding the NCR into a broad coalition encompassing many secular nationalists and leftist groups, but the NCR began to show signs of internal decay only a few months after its formation. As far as the KDPI was concerned, Rajavi's "personality cult" damaged the democratic image that the NCR wished to project. In his capacity as chairman of the NCR, Rajavi, leader of the mujahidin structured the voting system to ensure that the mujahidin and its front organizations "retained full control over all important decisions. [They] determined who could join the National Council; who was worthy of being given full voting rights as a 'prominent national figure'; and who could represent the National Council in international meetings."[82] Dr. Ghassemlou became increasingly agitated with the internal functioning of the NCR and the KDPI's inability to chart an independent course of action in Kurdistan.

Over time, Rajavi's open courting of the Ba'thi regime in Iraq at the height of Iraq's war against Iran alienated many supporters of the mujahidin and groups within the NCR. Former President Bani-Sadr offered his resignation from the NCR in 1984 in a blistering attack on Rajavi's leadership style, charging that the mujahidin had become a tool of the Iraqi regime. In March 1985, conflict between the KDPI and Rajavi intensified. Rajavi accused Ghassemlou of "betraying" the NCR's covenant by negotiating with Islamic authorities in Tehran without the NCR's approval. Ghassemlou retorted that the KDPI, as a guerrilla organization, reserved the right to negotiate with its adversaries at any time and that the mujahidin could not act as the sole decisionmaking body within the NCR.[83] At the end of March, the NCR lost an important component when the KDPI withdrew from the organization. The KDPI's withdrawal weakened the NCR, while in return, the KDPI was deprived of the support of an important ally at a time when factionalism had already reduced its organizational strength.

Shortly after the beginning of the Islamic Republic in Iran, three factions developed within the KDPI. The dominant faction, led by Ghassemlou, favored armed struggle against the Iranian government. The other two factions were associated with Karim Hessami and Ghani Bloorian, both of whom had developed close relations with the pro-Soviet Tudeh Party. Given the Tudeh Party's conciliatory posture vis-à-vis the Islamic Republic until 1982, the Hessami and Bloorian factions of the KDPI favored negotiations with the Islamic government. However, after the suppression of the Tudeh Party in 1982 and the consequent arrest and execution of several Tudeh members, the Hessami and Bloorian wings of the KDPI adopted a policy of armed struggle against the Islamic Republic.[84] With the improved relations between Gorbachev's Soviet Union and Iran, the Hessami and Bloorian factions became marginalized within the vortex of the Kurdish struggle in Iran.

INTRA-FACTIONAL POLITICS IN
CONTEMPORARY IRANIAN KURDISH GROUPS

Throughout the 1980s, Ghassemlou refused to modify KDPI's demands for Kurdish autonomy, which led to a deadlock with the Islamic Republic. Despite the strong stand, Ghassemlou's negotiating with the Islamic Republic divided the KDPI into hostile subfactions and may have led to his assassination. The non-Tudeh left in the KDPI accused Ghassemlou and the Kurdish bourgeoisie of betraying the Kurdish cause by abandoning KDPI's ideals in favor of a policy aimed at national reconciliation with the Iranian bourgeoisie (the Islamic Republic).[85] Further schisms developed within the KDPI, and the ensuing power struggle among the factions carried into the KDPI's Eighth Congress in 1988, resulting in the expulsion of fifteen prominent members of the party's executive committee. The left coalesced around the expelled members of the KDPI and established a new movement: the Kurdish Democratic Party of Iran-Revolutionary Leadership (KDPI-RL).[86] With its stridently Marxist orientation and its dogmatic sectarianism, the KDPI-RL has been unable to appeal to a large segment of the Kurdish population.

The KDPI was dealt a major blow when Dr. Ghassemlou was assassinated on July 13, 1989, while meeting with representatives of the Iranian government in a Vienna apartment. Two of Ghassemlou's Kurdish companions, Abduïlah Ghaderi-Azar (the KDPI's deputy leader) and Mahmoud Fadil Rasoul (a member of the Iraqi Patriotic Union of Kurdistan), were also gunned down. In addition, Mohammad Ja'far Shahroudi, an Iranian diplomat, was wounded in the jaw. The timing of Ghassemlou's assassination, when his KDPI was negotiating with the Islamic Republic, raised many unanswered questions about the motives for the assassinations.

Shahroudi, who returned to Iran to recuperate from his injury, gave a televised interview from his hospital bed in Tehran on July 27, 1989, in which he denounced the killers as terrorists and vowed to cooperate with the Vienna police until they were apprehended.[87] The Iranian government revealed that Shahroudi had met with Ghassemlou on two previous occasions, and Iranian state television announced that the third fateful meeting between Ghassemlou and Shahroudi took place at the KDPI's request to discuss an amnesty program for the *peshmergas* who had fought against government forces.[88] The KDPI quickly issued an announcement condemning the Islamic Republic as the main culprit in the assassination, and Ghassemlou's Czechoslovakian-born widow, Helena, charged that the meeting had been a trap set by the Islamic Republic to kill her husband.[89] The Vienna police also began to suspect the Iranian government because of Shahroudi's hasty departure from Vienna and the Iranian Embassy's refusal to allow officials in the Austrian criminal justice system to interview Amir Mansour Bozorgian. Bozorgian, who had arranged the meeting between Ghassemlou and the Iranian officials, remained inside the Iranian Embassy.

Bozorgian, an Iranian Kurd, was present during the third meeting. The Vienna police later stated that Shahroudi, after being injured in the attack, fled the apartment and met Bozorgian outside, where he allegedly handed Bozorgian an envelope containing $9,000 in cash. This version of the story was hotly contested by the Iranian government, which accused the "enemies of Iran" of fabricating stories about Ghassemlou's assassination. The Islamic Republic received some support for its innocence from a highly unlikely source, the Marxist-Leninist Revolutionary Organization of the Kurdish Toilers of Iran (Komala), which had been fighting both the Iranian forces and KDPI *peshmergas*. In the opinion of a Kurdish Komala supporter, the party with the most to lose from cooperation between the KDPI and the government was the mujahidin.[90] Supporters of the Komala also alluded to infighting within the KDPI that might have led to Ghassemlou's demise.

The Iraqi government, as expected, blamed the Islamic Republic for Ghassemlou's assassination. Throughout much of the 1980s, the KDPI received aid from the Ba'thi regime of Saddam Hussein, but Ghassemlou broke with Baghdad in 1988 after Iraq used chemical weapons against Kurds in Halabja and then forced Kurdish villagers to resettle away from the Iranian border.[91] The acrimonious relations between the KDPI and Baghdad since that time may have motivated Iraq to eliminate Ghassemlou.

The mujahidin, Ghassemlou's erstwhile ally in the National Council of

Resistance, offered its own theory about the assassination. The mujahidin claimed that Shahroudi, the wounded Iranian negotiator, was a senior intelligence officer and previously served as deputy commander of the Fifteenth Revolutionary Guard Regiment stationed in Kurdistan. According to the mujahidin, Shahroudi used the pseudonym Mohammad Rahimi while in Kurdistan, was a chief contact between Iran and anti-Iraqi Kurds,[92] and was in a unique position to hire "Kurdish mercenaries" to kill Ghassemlou.

While it condemned the Islamic Republic for "orchestrating the murder of Ghassemlou," the dissident wing of the KDPI used the occasion to offer a blistering critique of the KDPI's "collaborationist" policies toward the central government in Tehran. In a memo published on July 18, 1989, the dissidents stated:

> The choice of Dr. Ghassemlou as a target of elimination by the Islamic Republic was not accidental. In recent months, he had chosen the path of negotiations and compromise (at a great cost to the Kurdish cause) over the path of armed struggle. He had even betrayed his own past by declaring that there was no military solution to the Kurdish problem in Iran. Unfortunately, Dr. Ghassemlou became a tragic victim of his own political mistakes and compromising stance toward the reactionary terrorists who govern the Islamic Republic. Any compromise with such a regime would delay the realization of the democratic rights of the Iranian people. . . . We hope that Dr. Ghassemlou's death would teach a lesson to those who sanctioned the policy of compromise over armed struggle at the Eighth Congress of the Kurdish Democratic Party of Iran.[93]

The mystery surrounding Ghassemlou's murder remains and his unidentified assassins remain at large. The KDPI did move swiftly to appoint Dr. Sadeq Sharafandi to replace Ghassemlou as the party's new secretary general, but it is doubtful that the KDPI can recover from the loss of Ghassemlou in the near future. He was an adept politician who developed contacts within a large cross section of Iranian society and established an extended political network in Europe. There is no doubt that Dr. Ghassemlou was the most recognizable political leader with the widest appeal within the Iranian Kurdish population.

The misfortunes of the KDPI, both before and after Ghassemlou's assassination, allowed the Komala to emerge as the most dynamic organization fighting for Kurdish autonomy in Iran. As a Marxist-Leninist movement, the Komala was as critical of the Kurdish bourgeoisie as it was of the Islamic Republic. It was able to expand its appeal by securing the support of Shaikh Ezzedin Husseini, the popular religious leader of Mahabad. Shaikh Husseini, however, never officially joined the Komala. Unlike the KDPI, the Komala judged the success of the Kurdish struggle within the context of a Marxist revolution throughout Iran.[94] Therefore, the Komala viewed itself from the outset as an organization that transcended ethnic boundaries. This feature has distinguished the Komala from other leftist or Marxist Kurdish groups in the country.

The Komala's origin can be traced to the Kurdish uprisings of 1967–1968, which were organized by Kurdish Communist activists such as Ismail Sharifzadeh and Sulayman and Abdullah Moini. Although these activists were concerned about the plight of the Kurdish masses, they were "equally interested in promoting class consciousness and Marxist revolutionary thought among all Iranian workers."[95] A group of Kurdish university students in Tehran and Tabriz were inspired by these goals and organized the Komala in 1969 as the vehicle for the Kurdish and Iranian proletariat.

The Komala's organizational and leadership structures were informal until the early 1980s. However, in September 1983, the Komala undertook major changes when it patterned itself after other orthodox Communist parties and became the Kurdish wing of the newly established Communist Party of Iran. The restructured Komala announced that the party's Founding Congress gave its approval to the changes and elected Abdullah Mohtadi as its first secretary general.[96] The Komala also announced that an official commemorative celebration was held in the village of Gavishan on the Kamyaran-Sanandaj road to celebrate the founding of the Communist Party of Iran-Komala.

Unlike other Kurdish movements that sought to strengthen Kurdish ethnicity through psychological ties to Kurdish history and past struggles, the Komala attempted to establish grass-roots support among the Kurds by paying particular attention to political education and by teaching "village boys and girls the principles of class and guerrilla warfare."[97] The Komala also emphasized decentralization "throughout the organization, armed operations included. The central committee is viewed as a coordinating body rather than a center of decision-making and planning for the entire organization."[98] Moreover, the party's policy of extending operations beyond the Kurdish region helped the Komala recruit new members and maintain a broader base of support than its rivals.

During its first ten years, the Komala's ideological orientation within the Marxist-Leninist line was predominantly Maoist. However, at its First Congress in 1979, the Komala renounced Maoism as inappropriate to Kurdish conditions in Iran.[99] In an analysis published in the party's theoretical journal, *Besooye Socialism*, the Komala argued that the process of urbanization had transformed the socioeconomic structures of Kurdistan dramatically, and the region could no longer be viewed as a rural society dominated by old tribal ties and a traditional peasant way of life.[100] Although acknowledging that Kurdistan remained underdeveloped relative to Tehran, Khuzistan, and other industrial centers of Iran, and that there were fewer industrial enterprises and a smaller proletariat in Kurdistan, the Komala contended that the predominantly rural composition of the area had changed since the mid-1960s.

The Komala attributed the urbanization of Kurdistan in the midst of the region's underdeveloped economy to two factors. First, the Shah's land reform program destroyed the old peasant-landlord relationship, and its social support network, without replacing it with another suitable system. Furthermore, the land reform program did not benefit the vast majority of impoverished peasants, who were unable to purchase the nationalized lands. Consequently, a large segment of the peasantry was uprooted and forced to move to the cities and join the large wage-earning proletariat. Most Kurdish peasants were initially forced to seek employment in other regions of the country; the major Kurdish cities could not absorb them economically. However, with the increase in the price of oil in the 1970s and its impact on the country's economic growth rate, Kurdish cities witnessed a revival that attracted more peasants to fill the need for labor, especially in the construction sector. These factors led to the creation of a wage-earning, low-skilled labor force among the Kurdish peasantry.

The second factor contributing to the urbanization of Kurdistan was the success of the Iranian Revolution and the resulting military conflict between the Islamic Republic and Kurdish *peshmergas* and the eight-year Iran-Iraq War. The destructive impact of the war on Kurdish villages pushed many Kurds to move to areas away from the fighting, usually to major cities.[101] By 1977, about 54 percent of the Kurdish work force was employed outside the agricultural sector. This figure, according to the Komala's analysis, has increased to the extent that by the early 1990s the class structure in Kurdistan reflects the existence of two distinct classes: a large wage-earning proletariat and a small capitalist class.[102] It is the emergence of this new capitalist class structure that has made orthodox Maoist analysis superfluous when dealing with the Kurdish situation in Iran.

Notwithstanding the Komala's early success in expanding its membership, it has not been able to exercise effective control over any area of Iranian Kurdistan for a sustained period. Furthermore, since the government's capture of rebel-held areas in 1986, the Komala's military effectiveness has been reduced substantially. Many Komala activists have died in confrontations with their adversaries, and some have been assassinated abroad. For example, in August 1989, gunmen shot at two Komala officials in Cyprus and killed Bahman Javadi, who had flown from his exile home in Sweden to meet with relatives. Although no suspects were arrested and the Cypriot police would not attribute a motive to the killing, the Komala office in Sweden immediately blamed "Iranian agents" for assassinating Bahman Javadi.[103]

An additional factor that has debilitated the effectiveness of the Komala and the Kurdish struggle within Iran has been the internecine fighting between the KDPI and the Komala *peshmergas*. After bloody confrontations between the two Kurdish groups, the Komala's central committee in 1987 sought to end this conflict. It called for an immediate cessation of hostilities between the KDPI and the Komala and the establishment of a united Kurdish front against the Iranian army and Revolutionary Guards.[104] However, the proposed united front was never formed as both the Komala and the KDPI failed to reconcile their ideological incompatibility.

The only visible manifestation of cooperation between the Komala and the KDPI was in the loose alliance formed between the Komala and the breakaway wing of the KDPI, the KDPI-RL. As the Komala's first secretary, Ibrahim Alizadeh, stated, as soon as the split within the KDPI became finalized, the Komala and the KDPI-RL forged a close working relationship. The establishment of a link between a movement whose primary activities focused on nationalistic themes and the Komala, which eschewed ethnic nationalist rhetoric in favor of a class-based Marxian internationalism, had not, in Alizadeh's words, led to "our compromising our position. We [Komala] will pursue our work and they [KDPI-RL] will do theirs as long as both of us struggle to achieve democratic rights for the Kurdish masses and as long as they do not object to our stance in defense of workers' rights throughout the country."[105] Alizadeh expressed hope that the mainstream KDPI would follow the same principle and forge a tactical alliance with the Komala.

The Komala's apparent accommodationist stance toward the KDPI-RL and KDPI created a schism within the party that came to a head during the Sixteenth Plenum of the Central Committee of the Communist Party of Iran in November 1989. At this meeting, the members of the central committee attacked the "rightist, deviationist and nationalistic" tendencies that had developed within the Komala and asked that those responsible for such a development be removed from their posts.[106] The Sixteenth Plenum became a turning point in the brief history of the Communist Party of Iran in that it led to the purging of the "undesirables" from the Komala and brought back ideological uniformity to its leadership.[107]

Despite the conflicts within the Komala and its changing relationship with other Kurdish movements, the Komala's political platform and its objectives have remained unchanged, as reflected in a document published by the party in September 1984. This document outlined a fourteen-point program for the Komala:

1. The free and unhindered right of political participation is an inherent right of every individual. Every male and female over the age of 16 should be given the voting right, and every individual, male or female, over the age of 18 should be able to run for any office. Kurdistan should be governed at all levels by freely elected representatives of its people.

2. Everyone should be free to express his or her own views. No power on earth should be allowed to deny this basic right to the people.

3. The Kurdish people should be allowed to determine the structure of their own government. The people have an undeniable right to revolt against

any authority that attempts to impose its will and form of government on the Kurdish people.

4. Every individual should be able to freely choose his or her religion, or not to choose any religion. Discrimination based on an individual's religious preference should be strongly rejected. Religion should be viewed as a private domain of an individual and the government should not interfere in this matter.

5. Freedom of press, assembly, and speech is an inalienable right of all people, especially the deprived masses. By the same token, freedom to join any political, trade and professional organization should be guaranteed.

6. Every worker, whether employed or unemployed, should be guaranteed a decent living. The right to a decent living standard and the right to work should be viewed as basic human rights.

7. Women should have equal rights with men in all facets of life, and women's servitude by the ruling classes should be terminated. We demand equal pay for equal work for men and women.

8. No one should be forced to marry any other person, nor should recognized marriages be restricted to those conducted by religious authorities. Family laws should be amended to reflect equality between men and women, husbands and wives.

9. An individual should be free from unwarranted intrusion into his/her life. No authority should be allowed to intrude in the private life of another person. The right to travel freely and choose one's place of residence should be guaranteed by law, and no one should be forced to live in exile against his/her wishes.

10. All individuals are entitled to proper health care. Access to health facilities should be available, free of charge, to all individuals irrespective of in what part of the country they live and how much they make.

11. Free public education should be made available to all citizens. Illiteracy, the scourge of imperialism and dependent capitalism, should be uprooted from the country.

12. The right to bear arms should be recognized for all Kurdish toilers who have had to resort to arms to defend their families and homes. No one has the right to disarm the militant toilers of Kurdistan.

13. The religious and reactionary laws of the Islamic Republic should not be implemented in Kurdistan. All trials must be open to the public, and the judges should be elected by the people. Everyone should be considered innocent until proven guilty. No physical or psychological force should be used to extract a confession from an accused, and due process of law should be observed at all levels of legal proceedings. No one should be incarcerated more than twenty-four hours without specific charges. Speedy arraignment should be a nonnegotiable right of every individual accused of commission of a crime.

14. All laws that reflect ethnic chauvinism and oppression must be

14. All laws that reflect ethnic chauvinism and oppression must be revoked. We consider all cultural, political, and economic discriminatory laws and regulations against the Kurdish people null and void. The Kurdish people have the right to strengthen their cultural ties by using their local vernacular in official business and in school.[108]

Compared with the autonomy demands of the KDPI, the Komala's objectives are not only ambitious but also vague. The document is silent on the extent of autonomy demanded and on the relationship between the central government and Kurdistan should an autonomous province be established. The document is also silent on the all-important issue of internal trade and defense and foreign policy matters. Faced with its Marxist and secessionist appearance, the Islamic Republic has not taken Komala's demands seriously. Furthermore, the KDPI and other "mainline" Kurds have found the Komala's program for Kurdish autonomy to be unrealistic and utopian and have not given serious attention to it. It is obvious that, whatever hopes the Kurds and the Islamic Republic may have for mutual accommodation, they will have to be realized outside of the Komala's proposed framework.

The Iran-Iraq War and the US-led war against Iraq provided opportunities and pitfalls for improving the Kurdish situation in Iran. The implications of these two wars for the Kurds will be discussed in Chapters 3 and 5. Suffice it to say that the outlook for Kurdish autonomy in Iran, at least along the lines advocated by the Komala, or even the KDPI, remains bleak. As Charles MacDonald noted, Kurdish armed struggle against the Islamic Republic will continue indefinitely.[109] The tide of the struggle will change based on domestic political developments in Iran and the vagaries of regional and international politics.

3

THE KURDISH
CONDITION IN IRAQ

THE KURDS, THE BRITISH,
AND THE IRAQI MONARCHY

The country of Iraq is a twentieth-century creation. Although Mesopotamia is a recognized center of civilization and the city of Baghdad has a long history of contribution to Islamic civilization, modern Iraq is a byproduct of the defeat of the Ottoman Empire and its disintegration after World War I. Consequently, Kurdish nationalist movements predate the British creation of the Iraqi state in the twentieth century.

Kurdish nationalist movements of the nineteenth century developed along "parallel lines with the similar movements of the other subject races of the Ottoman Empire in Asia, the Arabs and the Armenians."[1] The first Kurdish ethnonationalist was Badr Khan of Botan, whose exploits in the 1840s included daring raids against rival tribes and non-Turkish neighbors. In the nineteenth-century milieu of nascent Kurdish nationalism, the Kurdish poet Haji Qadir should also be mentioned as a catalyst in raising Kurdish consciousness. He implored Kurdish tribal leaders to put their differences aside, transcend regionalism and narrow provincialism, and unite for the greater cause of Kurdish nationalism.[2] Haji Qadir castigated the Kurdish elite for writing in Persian or Turkish, instead of their own Kurdish vernaculars, and accused Kurdish shaikhs and mullahs of being too accommodating to the wishes of Persian and Turkish overlords. He relied on the seventeenth-century Kurdish national epic, *Mem u Zin* (the Kurdish *Romeo and Juliet*), to evoke nationalist sentiments among the Kurdish masses.

During World War I, Britain seized control of the Ottoman *vilayets* (provinces) of Baghdad and Basra, the heart of what later became Arab Iraq and the area that the British promised to give to Sharif Hussein of Mecca in return for generating an Arab revolt against the Turks. On October 24, 1915, in response to Sharif Hussein's demands, the British agreed to aid in the establishment of an Arab state comprising the *vilayets* of Baghdad and Basra. No mention of Kurdish-inhabited Mosul was made in this agreement, and it was not until the armistice between the Allied powers and the Ottoman sultan, which was agreed upon at Mudros on October 30, 1918, that the British occupied Mosul.[3] The British occupation of Mosul violated the

Mudros Treaty, but because of their military weakness, the defeated Turks had no option when British forces under General Marshall occupied Mosul. In November 1918, the British forced Turkish General Ali Ihsan Pasha to sign a capitulating agreement, which led to the total withdrawal of Turkish forces from the *vilayet* of Mosul. (Mosul's final status was not settled until 1925.)

Before control over Mosul was established, British forces occupied such Kurdish-inhabited cities as Kirkuk and Sulaymanieh. British policy favored the appointment of local leaders to administer, under the supervision of British advisers, the area under British control. One of the most prominent local leaders was Shaikh Mahmoud of the Barzinji tribe. Although Shaikh Mahmoud had rival shaikhs, Kurdish notables in Sulaymanieh agreed to accept him as leader of a Kurdish government. The British subsequently appointed him governor of Sulaymanieh and promised their support.[4] The British High Command first assigned Major E. W. Noel to act as the chief adviser to Shaikh Mahmoud and, in effect, control his activities. Despite Shaikh Mahmoud's efforts to project a united Kurdish front, it became evident that his authority was contested by other Kurdish notables.

Furthermore, the British policy of exercising tight control over the activities of Shaikh Mahmoud began to irritate the Kurdish leader. In order to test his staying power, the British extended his authority beyond Sulaymanieh, which brought him into conflict with chiefs of other tribes in Zakho, Irbil, Barzan, Kirkuk, Panjwin, and Halabja. The opposition of some of these tribal chiefs to Shaikh Mahmoud's authority was so intense that in one case, involving the Jaf tribe of Halabja, the British sanctioned a revolt against Shaikh Mahmoud's authority.[5] Shaikh Mahmoud suspected that the British were playing the old colonial game of divide-and-rule by playing one tribe against another. Unable to overcome traditional tribal and clan rivalries among the Kurds, Shaikh Mahmoud revolted against the British and declared independence in May 1919.

The British sent a small expeditionary force from Kirkuk to Sulaymanieh to challenge Shaikh Mahmoud, but the British force proved inadequate and had to retreat to Kirkuk. The British then dispatched a full division to Sulaymanieh, and after fierce and bloody battles with the Kurds, they defeated Shaikh Mahmoud and took him to a prison in Baghdad. According to some accounts, Shaikh Mahmoud was later exiled to India.[6] According to another account, the British condemned him to death but later commuted his sentence.[7] It is believed that Shaikh Mahmoud escaped from captivity and fled to Sardasht, in Iran, where he continued his military challenge to British authorities. After Shaikh Mahmoud's defeat and the reimposition of British military authority over Kurdish areas, there were numerous uprisings. These uprisings were partly fueled by the Turks, who wanted to drive the British out of Mosul, and partly by the Kurds, who feared permanent or long-term domination by an outside force.[8]

In the meantime, a number of important developments occurred that affected the status of the Kurds. On May 1, 1920, the League of Nations gave Britain mandatory power over Iraq and Palestine. Amir Faisal, who earlier was expelled by the French from Syria and who was the second son of Sharif Hussein of Mecca, was installed by the British on the throne of the new Hashemite monarchy in Iraq in August 1921. Thus the British became more interested in buttressing a strong pro-British monarchy in Iraq than they were in pressing the issue of Kurdish autonomy. In order to give Faisal's government an aura of legitimacy, the British organized a referendum to approve the accession of Amir Faisal to the throne. The Kurds either boycotted the referendum or voted against Faisal.

In the process of forging a new governing entity in Iraq, the British sought to integrate the Kurds into the new Iraqi society by convincing the Iraqi Arabs to reserve some senior positions in the government for the Kurds. The Arabs, however, opposed this scheme as they did not trust the Kurds. Furthermore, the British were divided over the issue of Kurdish integration into the new Iraqi society. As one observer noted, the British authorities in Kurdistan "supported Kurdish participation in high office while those in Baghdad took a dim view of the Kurds."[9]

On the international front, the Kurdish struggle for a homeland received a major boost in August 1920, when delegates of the victorious Allied powers and the defeated Ottoman sultan signed the Treaty of Sèvres. This treaty called for the creation of an independent Kurdistan and Armenia, as well as independent Arab states of Hijaz, Syria and Iraq.[10] The Treaty of Sèvres contained three articles with respect to Kurdish autonomy and independence. Article 62 dealt with the mechanism for providing autonomy to the "predominantly Kurdish areas lying east of the Euphrates, south of the southern boundary of Armenia as it may hereafter be determined, and north of the frontier of Turkey with Syria and Mesopotamia."[11] Under Article 63, the Turkish government agreed to execute within three months the terms set forth in Article 62 by a three-man commission appointed by the British, French, and Italian governments. Article 64 outlined the conditions for Kurdish independence. It said:

> If within one year from the coming into force of the present Treaty the Kurdish peoples within the areas defined in Article 62 shall address themselves to the Council of the League of Nations in such a manner as to show that a majority of the population of these areas desires independence from Turkey, and if the Council then considers that it should be granted to them, Turkey hereby agrees to execute such a recommendation, and to renounce all rights and title over these areas. . . . If and when such renunciation takes place, no objection will be raised by the principal Allied Powers to the voluntary adhesion to such an independent Kurdish State of the Kurds inhabiting that part of Kurdistan which has hitherto been included in the Mosul *vilayet*.[12]

The provisions of the Treaty of Sèvres with respect to Kurdish autonomy and independence were never implemented. In fact, the treaty was never ratified as

Turkey claimed sovereignty over Mosul as called for in the National Pact proclaimed by the Turkish nationalists in 1920.

A number of factors contributed to British backtracking on the Treaty of Sèvres. First, the victory of the Turkish nationalists over the Greeks, which halted Greek advances toward Ankara, emboldened the Turks to become more aggressive in opposing independence for the Mosul *vilayet*. Furthermore, the rise of Mostafa Kemal Ataturk as a dominant stabilizing factor in Turkish and regional politics compelled the British to take a more serious look at the Turkish position on Kurdish independence and the implications of independence on an emerging pro-Western Turkey. Second, the British were aware of the existence of oil in Kirkuk and other cities in the Mosul *vilayet*. The British reasoned that by incorporating the area into their client state of Iraq, as opposed to allowing the establishment of an independent and unpredictable Kurdish state, they would have a more secure grip on the area's oil reserves.[13] Another explanation for the weakening of British support for the establishment of an independent Kurdish state was the opposition of the British India Office, which guided British political and military policy in the Gulf region during World War I. It concluded that the British protectorate of Iraq would not remain a viable state without the inclusion of the Mosul *vilayet*, and without an economically viable Iraq, British interests would be in jeopardy.[14]

Despite the nonperformance of its provisions, the Treaty of Sèvres represented international recognition of the Kurdish movement and the Kurdish desire for self-determination in the twentieth century. The provisions of this treaty still form the basis of Kurdish claims to establish their own state.

In 1922, Mostafa Kemal succeeded in removing the last vestiges of the government that signed the Treaty of Sèvres. Mostafa Kemal considered the terms of the treaty humiliating for Turkey, as it would have reduced Turkey to a virtual protectorate under European powers, and he demanded that Britain return Mosul to Turkey. In order to stave off Turkish demands, Britain once again played its Kurdish card. Britain asked their client government in Baghdad to join them in issuing the so-called Anglo-Iraqi Joint Declaration, which was forwarded to the League of Nations in December 1922. This declaration recognized the right of the Kurds to establish an autonomous government within the framework of the Iraqi state and confirmed the contested Mosul's inclusion within the borders of Iraq.

The Kurds were not satisfied with the Anglo-Iraqi Joint Declaration as they did not wish to be governed by King Faisal and his British overlords. Shaikh Mahmoud, who had received authorization to return to Sulaymanieh, began to assemble forces immediately upon his return and, after organizing his second government in Sulaymanieh in three years, proclaimed himself the ruler of the area. He undertook measures such as issuing postage stamps and revenue stamps and continued organizing an army independent of Britain and Iraq.[15] Shaikh Mahmoud's increasing independence and his refusal to accept any form of Iraqi suzerainty over his domain threatened British petroleum policies in the region, and British forces were sent to defeat Shaikh Mahmoud. It was not until July 1924, however, that the British army exercised some control in Sulaymanieh. The magnitude of resistance was such that the Royal Air Force (RAF) had to bolster the ground forces by bombing the city in December 1924 to stem the rising tide of anti-Faisal and anti-British Kurdish uprisings.[16]

At a meeting in Lausanne in 1923, an attempt was made to harmonize the emerging realities in the area with the provisions of the Treaty of Sèvres. While the Kurds were not represented at Lausanne, both Lord Curzon and Ismet Inonu, the chief representatives of the British and Turkish delegations, respectively, claimed "deep concern for the interests of the Kurds and presented this as an argument for their respective theses."[17] During the course of the negotiations, it became clear that the fate of the Kurds was not a stumbling block nor even a central issue of concern. What mattered to both Turkey and Britain was the status of Mosul.

The Lausanne meeting did not resolve the issue of sovereignty over Mosul, but it did result in the signing of the Treaty of Lausanne in July 1923. This treaty, in effect, replaced the Treaty of Sèvres. Although it included provisions that obligated Turkey to respect the linguistic and cultural rights of the country's non-Turkish minorities, the treaty made no mention of an independent Kurdistan. However, Britain, as the mandatory power in Iraq, was to negotiate with Turkey over the final status of the contested Kurdish-inhabited province of Mosul. The British-Turkish negotiations proved futile, and the issue was referred to the League of Nations. The Council of the League of Nations decided in December 1925 to give control of Mosul to Iraq on the condition that certain guarantees for the protection of the Kurdish minority be given. To this effect, Iraq's prime minister gave a speech in early 1926 declaring that Arabic and Kurdish would be the official languages of Mosul and that Kurdish children would receive their education in Kurdish. He affirmed his government's commitment to staff government bureaucracies in the region only with Kurdish civil servants. These commitments were formalized when the Local Languages Law was enacted in Iraq, and although the provisions were not fully carried out, it marked the first time that the Iraqi government legally recognized Kurdish cultural rights and separate identity.

Kurdish disenchantment with Iraqi rule led to renewed uprisings in Sulaymanieh under Shaikh Mahmoud's leadership. In the winter of 1927, an Iraqi expeditionary force supported by British firepower was sent to Sulaymanieh, and the Kurdish forces were once again defeated. Shaikh Mahmoud fled to Iran and joined forces with Mahmoud Khan Kanisanani, a tribal chief in Marivan who was fighting the Iranian government. When this rebellion was put down by the Iranian army, Shaikh Mahmoud escaped to

Iraq, where he was arrested and sent into internal exile in southern Iraq.

The last major revolt by Shaikh Mahmoud against Iraqi and British authorities began after the British announced they would grant independence to Iraq in 1932. When it became clear that the treaty granting Iraq's independence did not contain guarantees for the rights of the country's minorities, Shaikh Mahmoud organized an offensive against Iraqi forces in the spring of 1931. Shaikh Mahmoud was defeated once again and could no longer muster any opposition to the Iraqi government. With hopes of creating an independent state of their own dashed, the Kurds initiated a series of minor revolts. Although these revolts were aimed primarily against the Iraqi government, they had crossborder implications as the Kurdish fighters crossed into neighboring Turkey and Iran to seek shelter and use the territories of these two states as bases of operation. Consequently, Iraq, Turkey, and Iran signed the Treaty of Sa'dabad in 1937 with the ostensible purpose of coordinating their defense policies. Although the treaty did not specifically deal with the Kurdish revolts and crossborder incursions, it was widely understood that containing Kurdish rebellions was discussed very seriously among the Iraqi, Turkish and Iranian authorities as part of their defensive arrangements.

Meanwhile, another nucleus of opposition developed among Barzani tribal leaders, and as a result, Shaikh Ahmad Barzani became the next torchbearer for Kurdish autonomy. (Shaikh Ahmad's great grandfather moved his tribe from a village near Irbil and settled in an area near Zibar in northeast Iraq. This area was later named Bar Zan [place of migration], and thus the clan became known as the Barzani tribe.) Shaikh Ahmad proved to be an adept military leader, but his eccentricities, especially in his unorthodox Islamic practices that combined Christian and Islamic elements, caused other Kurdish tribal leaders to oppose the Barzanis. One prominent tribal leader, Shaikh Rashid of Bardost, particularly objected to Shaikh Ahmad's practice of allowing his sect to consume pork, which is against Islamic dietary laws.

Although Shaikh Ahmad reverted to the practices of orthodox Islam, he was never able to acquire the needed assistance of other Kurdish tribes in confronting Iraqi and British troops. Another, and perhaps more serious, cause of the failure of Shaikh Ahmad's revolt was his opposition to the spring 1932 British plan to settle the Assyrian Christians, who had left or been expelled from Turkey, on or near Barzani tribal lands. In the fighting that ensued, the Iraqi army suffered heavy casualties, which led to RAF bombing of Kurdish villages and outposts. After intensive ground fighting and aerial bombardment by the British, Shaikh Ahmad and his followers were driven into Turkey. The British and Iraqi governments thereafter issued a general amnesty to Shaikh Ahmad and his family and allowed them to return to Iraq. However, upon his return, Shaikh Ahmad was apprehended and sent to Nasiriyeh in southern Iraq, along with his family and principal supporters. They were later transferred to Sulaymanieh where they were kept under close scrutiny.[18] For all practical purposes, this brought

Shaikh Ahmad's rebellion to an end.

Shaikh Ahmad's younger brother, Mullah Mostafa Barzani, escaped from Sulaymanieh in 1943 and returned to Barzan to assume leadership of the tribe. Mullah Mostafa became the most celebrated and enduring modern Kurdish nationalist and remained the most visible symbol of Kurdish ethnonationalism up to his death in 1979. Mullah Mostafa's success was a result of his ability to engage Iraqi forces in protracted battles and withstand their onslaught for many years; it was also a result of his ability to combine secular and religious power into a highly charismatic leadership. No other Kurdish leader in the twentieth century could "so rally rank and file Kurds as could he, to the chagrin of those Kurds who wished to do away with the old order along with Turkish and Iraqi rule."[19]

After his escape from Sulaymanieh and upon his arrival in Barzan, Mullah Mostafa organized a small fighting force and began to attack police stations and other symbols of governmental authority. By the end of 1943, Mullah Mostafa's small force had grown large enough to keep Iraqi forces at bay. In response, Iraqi Prime Minister Nuri Sa'id tried to convince Mullah Mostafa to surrender by ordering Barzani's older brother, Shaikh Ahmad, who was still under surveillance and control in Sulaymanieh, to send a message and persuade him of the futility of armed struggle as a means to attainKurdish autonomy. Mullah Mostafa disregarded this message and intensified his attacks on the Iraqi positions, inflicting heavy casualties and causing the defection of many Iraqi soldiers of Kurdish descent.

Fearing the disintegration of their client state Iraq, the British strongly advised Nuri Sa'id to negotiate with Mullah Mostafa and settle the Kurdish problem peacefully. Nuri Sa'id dispatched a delegation headed by Majid Mostafa, the minister of state who was also a Kurd, to negotiate with Mullah Mostafa.[20] The negotiations between the Iraqi government and the Kurds were conducted primarily through Iraqi army officers of Kurdish origin. One concrete result of these negotiations was the removal of surveillance restrictions on Shaikh Ahmad in 1944. In addition, Mullah Mostafa submitted a list of demands that included the establishment of a Kurdish province (which included oil-rich Kirkuk) under elected Kurdish leaders. A new minister of Kurdish affairs in the Iraqi cabinet would act as the chief liaison between the government and Kurdish authorities in the new province. The province would maintain autonomy in cultural, agricultural, and economic affairs. With the exception of control of the army and police, the provincial authorities in Kurdistan would have complete autonomy in running the affairs of the province. Moreover, each Iraqi cabinet ministry would have to add a Kurdish deputy minister to its ranks.

The demands became the subject of heated debate within the Iraqi cabinet. While Prime Minister Nuri Sa'id declared he was ready to accept some of the Kurdish demands, Arab nationalists in his cabinet objected because they feared acceptance would invariably lead to further concessions and the establishment of an independent Kurdistan. Nevertheless, the government expressed its willingness to continue negotiations with Mullah Mostafa in order to achieve a political settlement of the Kurdish problem. As negotiations proceeded, the government fell, and with the coming to power of Hamdi al-Pachachi as prime minister, the government's willingness to negotiate with the Kurds ended.[21]

With the breakdown of negotiations, fighting resumed between the two sides. In late 1945, Iraqi forces and Britain's RAF forced Mullah Mostafa's forces to retreat across the border into Iran. As was discussed in Chapter 2, Mullah Mostafa joined the rebellion in Mahabad, and his forces lent support to the newly established Kurdish Republic of Mahabad. With the defeat of the Mahabad republic, however, Mullah Mostafa and his forces were compelled to retreat, eventually seeking refuge in the Soviet Union. They stayed in the Soviet Union for the next twelve years and did not return to Iraq until the overthrow of the Hashemite monarchy in 1958. While living in the Soviet Union, Mullah Mostafa received the honorary title of "General" and used this title intermittently until his death.

Aside from military and tribal uprisings, a number of nationalistic parties emerged to provide intellectual sustenance for the development of Kurdish ethnonationalism in Iraq. In particular, two nascent groups, the *Heva* (Hope) Party and the Freedom Group, paid homage to Mullah Mostafa as the living symbol of Kurdish aspirations. Headquartered in Baghdad, *Heva* operated in many Kurdish cities, with strong branches in Kirkuk, Sulaymanieh, and Irbil. The party's orientation was leftist, and in articles and analyses appearing in its principal publication, *Azadi* (Freedom), *Heva* was equally critical of Kurdish feudalism and Western imperialism. Although recognizing Mullah Mostafa's leadership of and his importance to the Kurdish movement, *Heva* remained suspicious of his "dictatorial and theocratic attitude, and intended to use him for the time being and to discard him once the objective of independence or autonomy was attained."[22] In the end, Mullah Mostafa proved more durable than the *Heva* Party. The Freedom Group was formed in Barzan by a group of petit bourgeois nationalists whose loyalty to Mullah Mostafa was unquestioned. However, the leadership core of the Freedom Group remained nontribal and consisted primarily of urbanized Kurds and Iraqi army officers of Kurdish origin. Notwithstanding the ideological incompatibility of the *Heva* Party and the Freedom Group, they worked harmoniously to further the cause of Kurdish autonomy.

More crucial than either the *Heva* Party or the Freedom Group to the advancement of the Kurdish cause was the Kurdish Democratic Party of Iraq (KDP), founded in 1946 by a group of intellectuals led by the Kurdish lawyer Hamzah Abdullah. The genesis of the KDP can be traced to a group calling itself the *Rizgari Kurd* (Kurdish Liberation) Party, which was formed in January 1946 with an overwhelming communist membership. In a memorandum prepared for the United Nations in early 1946, the *Rizgari Kurd*

Party appealed to the president of the United Nations General Assembly to remedy past mistakes in Kurdistan:

> It was undoubtedly the greed and interests of [the old] imperialist policy which led the world to so many unimaginable grievances and troubles in the two great world wars. The Party . . . has a great reason to believe in your good intentions, and in your unshakable will to put an end to the forces of aggression and imperialism. It will be quite useful here to draw your attention to the fact that it will be impossible to establish world peace and rescue humanity from the terrible and distressful grievances of wars as long as some nations are exploited and humiliated by hateful imperialism. Our Party in the name of the Kurdish Nation who [sic] has been humiliated and subordinated to foreign rule, demands the extermination of imperialism in our country and the removal of the persecution and injustice of the governments to which it has been subordinated and divided.[23]

Copies of the memorandum were sent to the US, Chinese, and Soviet Legations and British Embassy in Baghdad for the purpose of transmitting it to the United Nations. It is interesting to note that Edwin Schoenrich, the interim US chargé d'affaires in Baghdad, passed on a copy of the memorandum to the secretary of state on January 23, 1946, and informed him that the Legation was unable to obtain specific information on the *Rizgari Kurd* Party and its objectives,"either through its Iraqi political contacts, or British intelligence. . . . It may be of some significance that the memorandum is often critical of what is deemed British and American interference in the internal affairs of other countries, and is strongly pro-Soviet in tone."[24] In the emerging atmosphere of the Cold War, accusations of pro-Soviet sympathies did not endear the *Rizgari Kurd* Party to the United States and Britain.

After a series of defections of its rank-and-file members to the Iraqi Communist Party (ICP), the *Rizgari Kurd* Party in August 1946 transformed itself into the Iraqi Kurdish Democratic Party (KDP), with Mullah Mostafa as its president and Hamzah Abdullah as its secretary general. The founding of the KDP augured a major split, albeit a short-lived one, in the Kurdish ranks because a branch of the Kurdish Democratic Party of Iran already existed in Sulaymanieh under the leadership of Ibrahim Ahmad. He viewed the new KDP as a threat to Kurdish unity and the authority of Qazi Mohammad and his nascent Kurdish Republic of Mahabad, which for Ibrahim Ahmad and many other Kurds "constituted the most viable vehicle for Kurdish national aspirations at the time."[25] This schism, however, became a nonissue with the downfall of the Mahabad republic, and Ahmad's organization lost its relevance.

In fact, after the defeat of the Mahabad republic, Ibrahim Ahmad joined the Iraqi KDP and in a power struggle ousted Hamzah Abdullah and managed to have himself elected as the KDP's new secretary general in 1951. Under

Ahmad's stewardship, the KDP moved to the left and was unable to attract support among the conservative Kurdish peasantry and tribal leaders.[26] After obtaining KDP documents and the party's manifesto, the US Legation in Baghdad concluded that it was a well-organized entity with strong Communist influences. As such, the United States viewed the emergence of the KDP with apprehension.[27]

On September 17, 1946, the KDP issued a statement signed by Mullah Mostafa asking the Iraqi people to join forces with the Kurds and unite in the common struggle to liberate their country from "imperialism and its agents, so that each may lead on with his own land a free and happy life in brotherly cooperation with the other. . . . Long live the Arabs and Kurds as brothers in the country!"[28] This statement was followed by a series of documents in which the KDP outlined its plan for the creation of a federal and binational state. However, the KDP's notion of federalism was different from what the term "federalism" normally implies. In essence, the KDP was advocating independence from Iraq. In September 1946, the party called for the creation of a federated state of Kurdistan that would be free to enter into treaties with any other country. It would also have complete freedom in choosing members of the executive, legislative, and judicial branches of its government and would be free to establish economic ties with other countries. All social, political, and economic affairs of Kurdistan would remain the exclusive domain of that state.[29] Although the KDP's platform was vague on the issue of national defense, it was presumed that this thorny issue would be worked out between Iraqi and Kurdish representatives.

REPUBLICAN IRAQ AND THE KURDS

By the mid-1950s, nationalist ferment in Iraq was strong enough to jeopardize the long-term survival of the pro-British Hashemite monarchy. In July 1958, a group of military officers, the so-called Free Officers, under the titular leadership of Abdul Karim Ghassem staged a successful but bloody coup against King Faisal and his government and declared the establishment of a new republican political system in Iraq. Most opposition groups welcomed the overthrow of the monarchy and pledged their support to the republican government with the hope that a new era in Arab-Kurdish relations was beginning. Although the young officers who came to power in 1958 had no clear vision of Iraq's future and had not demonstrated a commitment to the Kurdish cause, their attitude toward the Kurds was "friendly, if not in any way actively sympathetic."[30] As a goodwill gesture toward the Kurds, the newly established three-man Sovereignty Council, which was to act as the country's collective ceremonial presidency, included a Kurd, Khalid al-Naqshbandi. He was a former governor of Irbil and came from a prominent landowning and religious family.

The new regime promised to drastically transform the condition of the Kurds. A provisional constitution was promulgated in 1958 that for the first time acknowledged the Kurds as a distinct ethnic group with national rights. The new Iraqi Constitution reaffirmed the country's place as an integral part of the Arab nation while stating unequivocally that "Arabs and Kurds are considered partners in this nation."[31] Ghassem, whose mother was purportedly a Shi'a Kurd, was apparently intent on improving the situtation of the Kurds and appointed several Kurds to high-level positions in his government.

In the early years of the Ghassem regime, a symbiotic relationship developed between the government and the Kurds. Both Ghassem and Mullah Mostafa—who had returned to Iraq as a hero after twelve years in the Soviet Union—found it necessary to cooperate with each other in order to neutralize their respective adversaries. Ghassem's internal adversaries included the Communists, the Ba'thists, the Nasserites, and other Arab nationalists, all of whom wished to shape the sociopolitical structures of the new Iraq in their own image. An early divisive issue in the aftermath of the overthrow of the Hashemite monarchy revolved around Iraq's position vis-à-vis the recently established United Arab Republic (UAR). The UAR was formed in February 1958 with the merger of Egypt and Syria under Egyptian president Gamal Abdul Nasser's leadership. Because of Nasser's nationalistic credentials and his immense stature in the pantheon of Arab nationalism, there was increasing pressure on Ghassem to make Iraq part of this union. The Kurds were opposed to this move, reasoning that in a union whose basic philosophy was to promote Arabism and Arab nationalism their condition would not improve. In fact, their sociopolitical and cultural demands probably would be ignored. There were indications that Arab-Kurdish relations had deteriorated in Syria after Syria joined the UAR, as manifestations of non-Arab ethnicity were considered counterproductive to the furtherance of the overriding cause of Arab unity.[32]

Kurdish opposition to Iraqi membership in the UAR led the KDP to work closely with both the ICP and Ghassem. The Kurds and the ICP had already established a close association when the July 1958 coup (which later became known as the Revolution) occurred.[33] In particular, in the period 1949–1955, at the height of anti-Communist and anti-Kurdish military campaigns, a number of Kurds became leading members of the ICP. For example, the head of the party's central committee from 1949 to 1953 was Baha ed-din Nuri, the son of a religious teacher in Sulaymanieh.[34] Other Kurdish members of the ICP during this period included Hadi Sa'id and Bilal Aziz, both from Irbil, and Abdullah Omar Mohiadin, who was from Kirkuk. Baha ed-din Nuri was an unlikely ICP leader as he had little revolutionary experience and his "grasp of theory was none too solid. His sentiments were rather simple—love for the Kurds and an unquestioning faith in the future of communism."[35]

ICP opposition to membership in the UAR, unlike that of the Kurds, did not stem from the Party's fear of greater Arab unity. The ICP was opposed to a union of Arab countries dominated by bourgeois nationalism and anticommunism. The ICP viewed the UAR as the "very hurried and ill-thought-out product of the Syrian Ba'th Party's fears that it would be overtaken in popularity in Syria by the Syrian Communist Party, which had gained greatly in strength throughout the 1950s, particularly after the Syrian government had begun to forge closer military and diplomatic ties with the Soviet Union."[36] Although the ICP softened its initial opposition, the KDP found an important ally in opposing Iraq's membership in the union in the early months of the revolutionary regime.

Abdul Karim Ghassem opposed Iraq's joining the UAR because his political ambitions would have suffered operating in the shadow of Egypt's Nasser, a vastly more charismatic and dominant personality in the Arab world than Ghassem. Thus, a triangular alliance was formed between Ghassem, the ICP, and the KDP to prevent Iraqi membership in the UAR, despite support for this idea both at the popular level and in the inner circles of the Free Officers. By the fall of 1958, Ghassem had gained the upper hand in the Free Officers group, and he managed to keep the pro-UAR sentiments in check. This led the disaffected pro-unionist Free Officers to attempt to overthrow Ghassem in March 1959. This attempted coup originated in Mosul with Syrian backing. Mullah Mostafa gave his unqualified support to Ghassem and sent thousands of his *peshmergas* to Mosul to fight on the side of the government. The ensuing battle not only pitted pro-and anti-unionist forces against each other but also pitted landlords against peasants and one Kurdish tribe against another.[37] The eventual victory of the forces loyal to Ghassem led to closer cooperation between Mullah Mostafa and Ghassem.

The alliance between Ghassem, the ICP, and the KDP began to fall apart, however, in July 1959 when fighting broke out between Turkoman and Kurdish residents of Kirkuk. Prior to 1958, Turkomans held dominant positions in the political and economic arenas in Kirkuk. With Ghassem's accession to power, this began to change; a number of important government positions in the city were given to the Kurds. As a result, the Turkomans began to see themselves in a disadvantageous position vis-à-vis the more recent Kurdish residents of Kirkuk. Moreover, the conservative Turkomans began to fear the close relationship between the Kurds and the ICP. Tensions between the two ethnic groups in Kirkuk exploded into a major battle on the eve of the first anniversary of the Iraqi Revolution, resulting in the deaths of thirty-one people with 130 people injured during the fighting.[38]

The government reacted swiftly to the incident, which it referred to as a "massacre." Ghassem issued a scathing denunciation and promised to punish those responsible as "individuals," but not to punish the political organizations to which they belonged. It was clear that the organization Ghassem had most in mind was the ICP. As already mentioned, the ICP had established a close relationship with the KDP and, therefore, supported the Kurds and blamed Turkoman nationalists for the savagery that ensued.[39] However, the government-controlled media blamed the Communists, so Ghassem proceeded to purge Communist or pro-Communist members of his cabinet and suppress the ICP. Despite the ICP's support for the Ghassem regime—and Ghassem's alliance with the ICP—Ghassem had always remained wary of the intentions of the Iraqi Communists; he relied on them only to bolster his position within the ruling regime and to weaken the position of those who favored Iraqi membership in the UAR. With the "massacre" at Kirkuk, Ghassem found the opening to distance himself from the Communists and purge suspected Communists from government bureaucracies and the armed forces.

Notwithstanding Mullah Mostafa's support of the Ghassem regime in its early months, the Kurds were not unified on the issue of the KDP's support of the new government and the Free Officers. For example, the KDP's secretary general, Ibrahim Ahmad, opposed Mullah Mostafa's position on Iraqi membership in the UAR. Ahmad supported Iraqi membership because he thought it would strengthen the country's stature, Arab and international, and make it easier for Iraqi leaders to grant concessions to the Kurds. This was viewed as a challenge to his presidency of the KDP so Mullah Mostafa removed Ahmad from his post in 1959 and replaced him with Hamzah Abdullah.[40] At the same time, the more left-wing operatives in the KDP and on its central committee convinced the party to sign a pact with the ICP, which resulted in the publication of a divisive manifesto in May 1959. The tone and content of the manifesto indicated that Mullah Mostafa was either not involved or did not participate in the drafting of this document.

The KDP's May 1959 manifesto strongly attacked the existence of reactionary social structures in Kurdistan and those people responsible for maintaining a feudal system. As a tribal chief and a major landholder, Mullah Mostafa feared that this left-wing drift of the KDP would make it possible for the government to extend the provisions of the September 1958 land reform program to Kurdistan. Genuine land reform, although popular with the peasantry, was anathema to Kurdish shaikhs, khans, and aghas; they knew that land reform would undermine their power base among the Kurdish peasantry. Thus, it was not surprising that Mullah Mostafa and his peers were alarmed by the May manifesto. Changes in the land tenure system threatened their political survival.

Furthermore, Hamzah Abdullah, Mullah Mostafa's hand-picked secretary general of the KDP, became too supportive of the Communists in Mullah Mostafa's view. As a result, in early 1960, he dispatched a group of his supporters to the KDP's headquarters to physically remove Abdullah from his post. In October, Ibrahim Ahmad and his supporters were welcomed back to the party, and Mullah Mostafa engineered Ahmad's re-election as KDP's secretary general.[41] Mullah Mostafa's antireformist moves coincided with

Ghassem's anti-Communist thrust. This allowed him to turn on his former allies within the Communist camp, at Ghassem's bidding, in the hope that Ghassem's regime would be more amenable to Kurdish autonomy demands than was the Hashemite monarchy.

During the early years, the Ghassem regime did allow Kurdish cultural activities to flourish and rewarded Mullah Mostafa with the legalization of the KDP in January 1960 and the return of his land, which had been confiscated by the monarchy and given to pro-Hashemite Kurdish tribal leaders.[42] Mullah Mostafa's increasing power and his alliance with Baghdad allowed him to settle old scores with other Kurdish tribes, "especially the Bardosts, who had helped the Iraqi government in the 1930s and 1940s against Barzani."[43] Many of the anti-government Kurdish tribes were also bitter enemies of the Barzanis. For example, the Zibari tribe had been feuding with the neighboring Barzani tribe for almost a century. Others, such as the Bardost and Surchi tribes, became enemies of the Barzanis when they helped the monarchy turn back Mullah Mostafa's challenge in the 1930s and 1940s. As Martin van Bruinessen noted, a traditional dividing line in Kurdish society in Iraq has been whether a tribe is fighting for or against the government. Similarly, urban Kurdish politicians have, at times, "turned against the mainstream of the Kurdish movement and reached agreements with the central governments under pretexts that were unintelligible and unacceptable to the tribesmen. Both groups suspect the other of inherent tendencies to betrayal— and both have a few convincing instances to cite."[44]

As Mullah Mostafa Barzani's power increased, at the expense of other Kurdish tribes and political forces in the region, his relations with Ghassem deteriorated. In 1960, when Mullah Mostafa succeeded in assassinating his old rival, the chief of the Zibari tribe, Ghassem found it necessary to counterbalance Mullah Mostafa's authoritarian hegemony in Kurdistan by providing arms to his rivals. Mullah Mostafa traveled to the Soviet Union to ask the Kremlin to put pressure on Ghassem to change his policies, but to no avail. In March 1961, Sadeq Miran, a Kurdish associate of Ghassem, was murdered. The government charged the KDP with complicity and arrested Ibrahim Ahmad for allegedly ordering Miran's assassination. Although Ahmad was later released for "lack of evidence," his arrest was a signal to the KDP that Ghassem was determined to curtail the power of the party.

In mid-1961, fighting between the Barzanis and two of their traditional Kurdish enemies, the Surchi and Herki tribes, intensified. By September, Mullah Mostafa's forces occupied areas, such as Zakho, that had traditionally been outside their sphere of influence. Ghassem retaliated by bombing the village of Barzan and initiating the first major Iraqi-Kurdish fighting during the Ghassem regime.[45] In July 1961, relations between Mullah Mostafa and Ghassem were further strained when Mullah Mostafa demanded that the Kurds be granted virtual autonomy.

As mentioned earlier, the new Iraqi Constitution recognized the Kurds as equal partners with the Arabs and guaranteed Kurdish ethnic and cultural rights within the Iraqi state. Furthermore, the Iraqi government had appointed several Kurds to senior positions in the government and had allowed the publication and dissemination of Kurdish materials and the teaching of Kurdish in schools. The Iraqi government, therefore, rejected the demands for total political autonomy for Kurdistan, fearing that it would lead to chaos and could induce the majority Iraqi Shi'as to demand rights similar to the Kurds, which would lead to the dismemberment of the country. As a result, renewed fighting erupted between Iraqi forces and Mullah Mostafa's *peshmergas* in the fall of 1961; it continued intermittently until 1963, when a cease-fire agreement was signed.[46]

After their final break with Ghassem, the KDP sought to forge alliances with other opposition groups in Iraq. Their erstwhile partners, the Communists, no longer seemed a viable option, and the Ba'thist and other nationalists seemed to be the only alternatives. However, neither the Ba'thists nor the other nationalists had demonstrated any commitment to the Kurdish cause, nor were they interested in promoting any cause aside from that of Arab unity and Arab nationalism. Nevertheless, the KDP contacted an assortment of Ghassem's rivals within the Free Officers group, promising them a cease-fire if they succeeded in overthrowing Ghassem.[47] The KDP even approached the Communists in November 1962 with an offer to join forces to overthrow Ghassem. The ICP rejected the offer; the Communists did not think that a KDP-ICP coalition would be strong enough to mount a credible challenge to Ghassem's rule given that a large number of pro-Communist officers or sympathizers had already been purged by Ghassem. The KDP then made an about-face and ordered its followers to support the Ba'thists in the hope of helping them overthrow the government.[48]

The ICP, fearing the strong possibility of a successful coup, issued a statement warning Ghassem to guard against the activities of "the agents of imperialists" in the armed forces and government bureaucracies. They also appealed to Ghassem to undertake an immediate and wide-ranging purge of the army. Although the Communists did not have precise information about an impending coup, they called upon the masses to be "vigilant and ready" to respond to the threat.[49] The ICP's prediction of a military coup came true in February 1963 when a violent coup overthrew Ghassem's regime.

The period between the end of Ghassem's honeymoon with the KDP in 1961 and the overthrow of his regime witnessed savage fighting between the Kurds and the Iraqi government forces, interrupted by brief periods of negotiations.[50] By 1963, Mullah Mostafa's *peshmergas* had inflicted heavy casualties on Iraqi forces and had succeeded in keeping their primary Kurdish adversaries and pro-Baghdad tribes at bay. Mullah Mostafa's guerrilla tactics in the mountainous terrain of Kurdistan had apparently frustrated and fatigued Ghassem's forces.[51] Consequently, in January 1963, the two sides agreed to sign a cease-fire, much to the relief of Ghassem, who wanted to extricate himself from the Kurdish quagmire and concentrate on neutralizing his adversaries among the Ba'thists, Nasserites, and other nationalist groups.[52]

THE FIRST BA'THI REGIME AND THE KURDS

Shortly after the cease-fire, Ghassem was overthrown by Ba'thists, on February 8, 1963. After capturing power and executing Ghassem, the Ba'th Party inaugurated a reign of terror against its adversaries, particularly the ICP and its alleged sympathizers. The Ba'thists accepted Mullah Mostafa's offer of a truce in order to put the Kurdish issue on the back burner so that they could focus on their more immediate policy of physically exterminating their primary rivals. Between five and seven thousand "Communists" were executed by the new regime in a matter of days in early February 1963.[53] In Baghdad alone, the death toll reached fifteen hundred. Many of these executions were conducted by or under the auspices of the National Guard, the Ba'thist paramilitary force.[54]

The Communists had been aware of Ba'thi machinations to stage a coup against Ghassem's government, but they took no practical steps to protect themselves, and could not have anticipated the efficiency and speed with which they were rounded up by the Ba'thists. It was clear that the Ba'thists had a detailed list of names of Communists and sympathizers before they seized power. In a startling interview with Mohammad Hassanein Heikal, the influential editor of Cairo's *Al-Ahram* newspaper, King Hussein of Jordan charged that the US Central Intelligence Agency (CIA) had been in touch with influential members of the Ba'th Party and had supplied the names and addresses of alleged Communists to the coup makers.[55] As Hanna Batatu observed, it is difficult to determine the accuracy of King Hussein's assertion, or why the staunchly pro-American monarch would implicate the United States in the Iraqi bloodbath. Perhaps he wanted to deflect criticism of his own regime amid revelations that he had been on the CIA's payroll since 1957.[56]

The Ba'thi junta called itself the National Council of the Revolutionary Command (NCRC) and appointed Colonel Abdul Salam Aref, a non-Ba'thist, as the new president. However, neither Aref nor any other individual or group had a firm grip on power, and the political climate in the country remained chaotic, contributing to the overthrow of the regime in November. On February 15, 1963, Colonel Aref promoted himself to the rank of field marshall and asked the Kurds to support his regime. In the new cabinet, the Ba'thists held twelve of the twenty-one seats; the Kurds held two. Baba Ali, a landowning member of the Barzinji tribe and son of Shaikh Mahmoud, was given the agriculture portfolio, while Brigadier Fuad Aref was appointed minister of state.

Despite Mullah Mostafa's wait-and-see attitude toward the new regime, there were groups that wanted the Ba'thists to grant immediate and wide-ranging concessions to the Kurds as a sign of their commitment to the Kurdish cause. For example, the Committee for the Defense of the Kurdish People's Rights, an organization based in Lausanne, Switzerland, issued a statement on February 12, 1963, demanding that Kurdish-Arab relations in Iraq be based on the establishment of an "autonomous Kurdish government, the evacuation of Kurdish territory by Iraqi troops and an equitable division of state revenues, especially oil royalties, between Kurd and Arab."[57] Mullah Mostafa, however, thought that such radical demands would jeopardize prospects at the impending talks between the KDP and the government and distanced himself from the statement.

The KDP's central committee appointed Jalal Talabani to be the chief Kurdish negotiator at the talks, which began on February 19, 1963. Two days later, both Talabani and his Iraqi counterparts departed for Cairo to participate in ceremonies commemorating the formation of the UAR. In Egypt, President Nasser promised Talabani he would pressure Iraq into granting cultural concessions, but said he could not support total autonomy for the Kurds. After returning from Cairo, the two sides resumed talks in high spirits. However, problems developed over the question of autonomy and the exact meaning of the term "decentralization." In a press conference held on February 28, a gloomy Talabani made it clear that the success of the cease-fire between the Ba'thi government and the KDP depended upon the government's willingness to grant the Kurds total autonomy in all areas, with the exception of foreign policy and defense matters.[58]

On March 10, the NCRC announced that a compromise had been reached and that the government was prepared to grant the Kurds autonomy within the framework of the Iraqi state. According to the deputy prime minister, Ali Saleh Sa'di, the compromise would allow the Kurds to develop self-governing internal political and social institutions while remaining "attached to the central government for foreign, economic and military affairs."[59] A joint committee of Kurdish representatives and government officials would be formed to work out the details.

As the negotiations proceeded, news of a proposed federation of Iraq and Syria disturbed the Kurdish side; they feared that in such a federation the Kurds would constitute a small percentage of the total population of the country and their bargaining position would be substantially weakened. Even though the merger of Iraq and Syria did not happen, the Kurds began to increase their demands. For example, they insisted that the autonomous province of Kurdistan must include Irbil, Sulaymanieh, Kirkuk, and those parts of Mosul and Diyala where the Kurds were in the majority. This was unacceptable to the government because it would have placed a substantial number of oil fields under Kurdish control, damaging the economic viability of Iraq. The Kurds also demanded that a Kurdish vice president and deputy chief of staff of the armed forces be appointed, that one-third of central government posts be allocated to the Kurds, and that Kurds be granted privileged positions in the defense and foreign ministries. President Aref accused the Kurds of negotiating in bad faith and hardened his position. The government negotiators now said they would only grant the Kurdish language concessions and would not compromise on any other issue with the KDP. This left the two sides no realistic option but to resume fighting.

By the end of May, Aref had moved the bulk of the Iraqi army to the northern part of the country in anticipation of a major war with the Kurds. Just prior to the resumption of full-scale fighting in June, Aref issued an ultimatum, accusing the KDP of "asking for impossible conditions" and making war inevitable. He blamed the Soviet Union for agitating the "pro-Communist" KDP and accused the United States, UAR, Israel, and the People's Republic of China of providing arms to the Kurds.[60] As fighting ensued, the NCRC sought to enlist the services of several anti-Barzani Kurdish tribes. By October 1963, the Sharafi, Zibari, Bardost, Berati, and Herki tribes had organized several hundred fighters in support of government forces. In addition, the Iraqis organized an irregular brigade, the *Salah-ed-din Ayyubi,* to engage Mullah Mostafa's *peshmergas* in the mountains. This brigade was to be composed of detribalized Kurds and Arabs from the Mosul and Jabal Hamrin regions. However, Kurdish participation was negligible.[61] The Kurds again proved to be adept at fighting Iraqi forces and inflicted heavy casualties. Along with the deteriorating political and economic conditions in Iraq, this led Aref to conspire with a group of non-Ba'thi officers to overthrow the government on November 18, 1963, and become the uncontested ruler of Iraq.

THE NON-BA'THISTS AND
THE KURDISH DILEMMA: 1963–1968

After the overthrow of the Ba'thi government, Mullah Mostafa sent a message to President Aref asking for a cease-fire. Aref, who needed time to consolidate his power and wanted to focus his attention on persecuting his Ba'thi rivals, responded positively to Mullah Mostafa's overtures, and a cease-fire became effective on February 10, 1964. He then ordered a five-thousand-man Syrian contingent, which had been sent to fight alongside the Iraqi forces, to leave the country, and announced his government's intention to resume negotiations with the Kurds for the purpose of granting them "special rights" in Iraq. His government also announced its intention to disband the irregular militias and anti-Barzani Kurdish forces that had been assembled in the last two months of the Ba'thi regime. Finally, the government lifted the blockade of the Kurdish region after the cease-fire began.

The announcement of the cease-fire between Mullah Mostafa and Aref caught many members of the KDP's politburo by surprise and caused a rift in the party's leadership. Disenchanted politburo members objected to Mullah Mostafa's negotiations with Aref, which were undertaken without the KDP's approval, and thought that he had betrayed the goals of Kurdish autonomy, for which they had been fighting. Consequently, the KDP's politburo, led by Ibrahim Ahmad, Jalal Talabani, Lieutenant Colonel Nuri Ahmad Taha, and Omar Mostafa, issued a document criticizing Mullah Mostafa and declaring that military operations against the government should continue until Kurdish autonomy was achieved.[62] Mullah Mostafa, however, was more interested in immediate reconstruction aid and the rebuilding of Kurdish schools, roads, and towns, which had been severely damaged in the fighting with Iraqi forces. He felt that Kurdish autonomy demands should be soft-pedaled until the social and economic infrastructures of Kurdistan were rebuilt.

The rift threatened the whole fabric of the party and led to major clashes between Kurdish forces loyal to Mullah Mostafa and those supporting the KDP dissenters. The government sent a military contingent to support Mullah Mostafa; and the KDP, in turn, began to reject his leadership, accusing him of being a traitor to the Kurds and a "sell out" to the Iraqi regime. The rift was symptomatic of a deeper malaise that plagued the Kurdish movement. The urban bourgeoisie and leftists, who dominated the KDP's leadership, developed an uneasy relationship with "tribal-feudal" leaders like Mullah Mostafa. They accepted his leadership not out of any deep ideological compatibility, but because his leadership was essential in obtaining the confidence and loyalty of the majority of Kurdish tribes and he was the most recognizable figure among the Kurds. Without Mullah Mostafa's towering presence, it is unlikely that the KDP would have survived the Iraqi onslaught.

Mullah Mostafa's older brother, Shaikh Ahmad, endeavored to reconcile the KDP dissenters with his brother, but to no avail, and inter-Kurdish fighting continued. The February 1964 cease-fire between Mullah Mostafa and Aref, however, remained operative until April 1965. Then, because of internal pressures from the KDP and because the 1964 Iraqi Constitution did not recognize the equality of Kurds and Arabs in Iraq, the truce broke down.[63] Furthermore, because of the split in the ranks of the KDP, Aref felt no compulsion to grant concessions to Mullah Mostafa. In April 1965, the Iraqi army was sent north to re-establish the government's authority in the Kurdish region, and Mullah Mostafa had no realistic alternative but to resume fighting.

Faced with fighting an overwhelming force of fifty thousand men, Mullah Mostafa accepted large quantities of arms from the Iranian government, leading Aref to charge him with being a stooge of the Shah of Iran and an enemy of Iraq. The KDP dissenters took advantage of the situation and arrived at a kind of modus vivendi with Aref. They also helped anti-Barzani tribes fight with the government forces against Mullah

Mostafa's *peshmergas*. Fierce fighting continued until mid-April 1966. On April 13, President Aref was killed in a helicopter crash, and his brother, army chief of staff General Abdul Rahman Aref, replaced him. Upon assuming the presidency, Abdul Rahman Aref issued a statement declaring that under his administration the Kurds would finally be granted self-rule (he did not use the term "autonomy"), guaranteeing "their national identity, traditions, and language."[64] Mullah Mostafa proposed a cease-fire. He was eager to start negotiations with the government, aware that Jalal Talabani, one of his rivals and a KDP politburo member, was seeking to negotiate a separate peace agreement with Abdul Rahman Aref. So, when Prime Minister Abdul Rahman al-Bazzaz offered a twelve-point peace plan on June 29, 1966, Mullah Mostafa accepted his offer, despite misgivings.

Prime Minister Bazzaz was one of the few high-level Iraqi authorities who had a genuine interest in resolving the Kurdish issue. He believed that as long as the Kurdish problems remained unsolved, Iraq would not be able to emerge as a stable and prosperous country. Although Bazzaz did not stay in power long enough to implement his Kurdish plan, it has provided the framework within which many subsequent peace initiatives in Kurdistan have been formulated. The Bazzaz peace plan was radical in its content and breadth as it accepted the principle of Kurdish autonomy. Among other things, it called for: use of Kurdish as an official language in local government and in schools; release of all Kurdish political prisoners; a general amnesty for those who had fought against the central government; free elections for a Kurdish legislative assembly; and use of Kurdish forces for the maintenance of internal law and order and security.[65]

Bazzaz's removal from office in August 1966 and his replacement with Naji Taleb was a blow to the prospects for Kurdish-Iraqi peace. Unlike his predecessor, Prime Minister Taleb did not hold positive views of Mullah Mostafa and did not favor granting extensive autonomy rights to the Kurds, fearing it would result in sectarian polarization and possibly the disintegration of Iraqi society.[66] Nevertheless, Mullah Mostafa and President Aref met in October to try to recharge the stalled negotiations. Opposition to implementing the Bazzaz peace plan from members of his government, especially those in the army, however, frustrated Abdul Rahman Aref's attempts to deliver peace. In the interim, Mullah Mostafa consolidated his position in Kurdistan with Iranian assistance and Israeli aid, which was funneled to Iraqi Kurdistan via Iran.

THE SECOND BA'THI REGIME
AND THE UPRISING IN KURDISTAN

In July 1968, another Ba'thi-led coup overthrew Abdul Rahman Aref's government. This coup returned the Ba'thists to power after their brief tenure was ended in 1963 by Abdul Salam Aref's coup against them. The July 1968 coup was a two-tiered process. On July 17, Ba'thi officers cooperated with non-Ba'thists to overthrow Abdul Rahman Aref. On July 30, a coup within a coup occurred when the Ba'thists purged the non-Ba'thists from their ranks. Contrary to popular perceptions, in both of these stages the Ba'thists prevailed primarily by "stratagem rather than through force."[67] The Ahmad-Talabani faction of the KDP supported Aref's overthrow, and it apparently provided some material and logistical help to the Ba'thists. Mullah Mostafa also welcomed the coup, although he remained cautious about the new regime based on his experience with the first Ba'thi government in 1963.

The second Ba'thi regime sought to expand its base of support by including representatives from different political and ethnic groups in the cabinet. For example, four Kurds were given cabinet positions. Mohsen Diza'i, a personal representative of Mullah Mostafa, became minister for the reconstruction of the north (Kurdistan). Other Kurds in the cabinet included Mosleh Naqshbandi (minister of justice), Abdullah Naqshbandi (minister of economics), and Ihsan Shirzad (minister of works and housing). However, the fifteen-member Revolutionary Command Council (RCC), set up by the Ba'thists as the ruling body and highest decisionmaking institution in the country, was dominated by Sunni Arabs, although it did include Abdul Karim Shaikhli, an Arabized Kurd who was originally from Sulaymanieh.

On August 3, 1968, the country's new president, General Ahmad Hassan al-Bakr, and Iraq's ruling RCC announced that they were ready to discuss the Kurdish problem on the basis of the twelve-point plan negotiated with the previous regime. On August 4, the RCC announced that as a goodwill gesture the government would implement the language and cultural autonomy provisions of the plan as soon as possible. On August 5, the government announced a general amnesty for all Kurds, including army and police deserters. Moreover, the government's announcement indicated that deserters would not be required to surrender their weapons as a condition of the amnesty.[68] As talks between the government and Mullah Mostafa got under way, the Bakr government insisted that Jalal Talabani be included on an equal basis with Mullah Mostafa in all Kurdish autonomy talks so that all factions of the KDP would be represented. Talabani had already developed a cordial relationship with the Ba'thi government, and the RCC perhaps wanted to use Talabani as a counterweight to Mullah Mostafa, who viewed the RCC's insistence on including Talabani as an attempt to weaken his negotiating position.

This inauspicious beginning was followed by a series of skirmishes in September and October 1968 between Mullah Mostafa's *peshmergas* and those loyal to the Ahmad-Talabani faction of the KDP. Although Mullah Mostafa's forces were far superior, Talabani managed to hold on to some areas of Kurdistan through air support provided by the Ba'thi regime. In November, the Iraqi air force bombed several villages under Mullah Mostafa's control, prompting him to send a memorandum to the United Nations asking for the appointment of a UN mediator to prevent a "genocide" in Kurdistan.[69] However, the UN did not send a mediator to Kurdistan when it became clear that Talabani was in cahoots with the government in the latest rounds of fighting. In early January 1969, twelve Iraqi brigades, numbering some sixty thousand troops, were dispatched to Kurdistan. Although this mission was aborted after a few weeks due to the harsh winter climate and the heavy losses on both sides, the Iraqis captured vast areas, from Sulaymanieh to Rowandiz in the north, and permitted Talabani's forces to occupy certain areas that the Iraqi army had "liberated."

On February 4, President Bakr made the surprising announcement that his government had implemented most of the provisions of the twelve-point plan and that he was "looking forward to seeing an increasing number of our Kurdish brothers believe in a peaceful settlement as a result of the course the progressive Government is asking."[70] Nobody, including members of Bakr's government, took this seriously, as nothing had been done to implement any provisions of the plan. Another surprising move by the Bakr government was its January 19, 1969, announcement of the discovery of a major conspiracy against the Ba'thi regime. In addition to a number of prominent Iraqi politicians and military officers who were implicated in the plot, the government accused Iran, Israel, and the CIA of seeking to destabilize Iraq.[71] With respect to Kurdish participation in the conspiracy, the Bakr regime accused Mullah Mostafa of becoming an agent of the Shah of Iran, Israeli, and US intelligence. As revealed in the 1976 report of the House Select Committee on Intelligence (the Pike Report), Mullah Mostafa was, in fact, the recipient of massive military aid from Iran, and the Israeli and US governments were deeply involved in a secret arms transfer program to Mullah Mostafa through the Shah's regime.[72]

The Ba'thi regime followed its verbal offensive with a major military campaign in August 1969, aimed at Kurdish targets throughout northern Iraq. Despite its limited military success, the offensive terrorized Kurdish villages because they were randomly targeted by the Iraqi army. The Bakr government offered to reopen negotiations with Mullah Mostafa when it became clear that a military solution to the Kurdish problem would not work. Likewise, Mullah Mostafa realized that continued fighting would be disastrous for Kurdish civilians.

Negotiations began in mid-December 1969 and continued in earnest until March 1970, culminating in the publication of the March 11, 1970, Manifesto. The manifesto had a number of themes in common with the twelve-point Bazzaz plan. However, it even went beyond that plan in recognizing Kurdish national rights.[73] In its final form, the March Manifesto became the most extensive plan that any Iraqi government had adopted to accommodate Kurdish national aspirations. It dealt with three major themes: autonomy, the structure of autonomous governing bodies, and the relationship between the central government and the local autonomous administration. These were elaborated on in fifteen articles.[74] In past agreements between the Kurds and the central governments, disagreements over the definition of the term "autonomy" undermined whatever had been achieved. As Lee Buchheit noted, the most "accurate assessment that can be made about the Kurdish definition of autonomy is that it has changed over the years in response to the Kurds' sizing up of their own chances for complete independence and the capability of the Iraqi military to preserve the union."[75] In the words of a Kurdish leader, the Kurds "have never given a definition [of autonomy]. It depends on our strength and that of our enemy."[76] The March Manifesto was partly intended to force the Kurdish leadership into accepting specific parameters for autonomy.

Major provisions of the March Manifesto included: recognition of the Kurdish language in areas with a Kurdish majority; self-rule; appointment of Kurds to high-level positions in the central government (including a Kurdish vice president); creation of national administrative units in the Kurdish region; monetary and other assistance to help Kurds return to their villages; implementation of a genuine agrarian reform program; promotion of Kurdish cultural rights and educational advancement opportunities; establishment of a Kurdish academy of letters and a Kurdish university in Sulaymanieh; and an amendment to the constitution recognizing the equality of Kurds and Arabs in a binational Iraq. In addition, the manifesto required Kurdish rebels to turn in their heavy weapons and all broadcasting equipment used in clandestine radio stations and to desist from carrying out armed aggression against the state.

Both the Kurds and the Iraqi government displayed great enthusiasm for the March Manifesto, and during 1970, many of the provisions of the manifesto were implemented, including passage of the constitutional amendment and appointment of senior Kurdish officials to administrative posts at both provincial and national levels. The government also located new factories in the region and hastened the pace of agrarian reform. Within a few months, "construction had begun on hospitals and schools and over 2,700 houses had been built or rebuilt in the area."[77]

Aside from explicit provisions in the agreement that the Kurds found satisfactory, there were other motives for Mullah Mostafa's initial enthusiastic support of the March Manifesto. Because of the evolving cordial relations between the Ahmad-Talabani faction of the KDP and the Ba'thi government, Mullah Mostafa feared that, in the absence of a peace accord between the Kurds and the central government, the Ba'thists would aid his rivals in their power struggle with him. (In fact, after Mullah Mostafa signed the agreement, Ba'thi authorities began to isolate Jalal Talabani and Ibrahim Ahmad. Talabani's activities were sharply curtailed, and Ahmad left Iraq for London to receive prolonged medical treatment for an unspecified illness.) Furthermore, the heavy losses suffered since 1961 by the Kurds in fighting Iraq placed a moral burden on Mullah Mostafa to find an honorable way out of this quagmire. Based on past experience, he had to view the extensive sociopolitical and cultural concessions promised the Kurds in the March Manifesto with caution; nevertheless, he was confronted with an offer he could not refuse. As Mullah Mostafa later stated: "How can you refuse self-rule for the Kurdish people?"[78]

Despite its auspicious beginning, adherence to the March Manifesto began to come unglued by the summer of 1972. Mullah Mostafa began to demand revisions in the manifesto to allow him more military and political latitude. As later revealed, the United States, Israel, and the Shah's Iran were partly responsible for Mullah Mostafa's new demands because they promised to increase financial and military support to him in exchange for his continuing to challenge the Ba'thi government.[79] The selection of a Kurdish vice-president created problems when the Iraqi government refused to accept the candidacy of the KDP's nominee, Habib Mohammad Karim. Ostensibly, Karim's Iranian origin made him suspect in the eyes of the Iraqi government, and the two sides could not agree on another candidate.[80]

The major drawback of the March Manifesto, however, and its principal undoing, was its failure to define the precise geographic boundaries of the area to be covered by the autonomy provisions. The manifesto had specified that within a four-year period—by March 11, 1974—the laws of the autonomous region should be enacted. However, the contours of the autonomous region had to be determined before the governing institutions of the region could be structured and the necessary elections held. According to Article 14 of the March Manifesto, a census would determine the areas where the Kurds were in the majority, and the autonomous region would include those areas. This census was scheduled for December 1970 but was postponed, apparently by mutual consent, until the spring of 1971 so preparations could be made to organize the census taking.

The census was postponed a second time because Mullah Mostafa, for good reason, thought that the results of the census might show that the Kurds were in the minority in certain areas. He was adamant that Kirkuk, and other oil-producing regions in the north, be included in the Kurdish autonomous area. While it was a foregone conclusion that the census would show a clear Kurdish majority in the provinces of Irbil, Sulaymanieh, and Dahuk, because of large-scale population shifts, Mullah Mostafa believed the census would not reflect realistically the Kurdish presence in Kirkuk. As he emphatically stated, "Kirkuk is part of Kurdistan. If the population census shows that the majority of its inhabitants are not Kurds, I will not recognize this. I will not bear, before the Kurds, the responsibility for relinquishing Kirkuk. Maybe this can take place after me."[81] The government, meanwhile, insisted that only the results of an official census could be used in determining the size of the Kurdish population in a particular area.

The deadlock did not result in the complete breakdown of talks between the two sides, but it did result in the realization by the Ba'thists that perhaps they erred in limiting negotiations to Mullah Mostafa, and not including other Kurdish factions in the negotiations. In addition, an increasing number of Iraqis questioned the wisdom of reducing the Iraqi presence in the proposed autonomous region, lest it lead to further challenges to the authority of the state by the Kurds.[82] The deadlock also resulted in further polarization within the Kurdish camp. For example, some prominent members of the KDP, including Mullah Mostafa's eldest son, Obaidullah, and Aziz and Hashem Aqrawi, split with Mullah Mostafa, accusing him of obstinacy and collaboration with the Shah of Iran, Israeli Mossad, and the CIA. Despite these defections, there was little doubt that Mullah Mostafa still commanded the largest Kurdish force and remained the most dominant Kurdish figure in Iraq. In fact, the Kurdish ministers in the Iraqi cabinet, in order to show their solidarity, left their posts en masse in February 1974 and left Baghdad to join Mullah Mostafa. The government responded by replacing them with the trio of Aziz Aqrawi, Hashem Aqrawi, and Obaidullah Barzani. These three, joined by two other Kurds, Abdullah Ismail and Abdul Sattar Taher Sharif, founded the pro-Ba'thi Kurdish Revolutionary Party (KRP) in early 1974.

The Arabization of Kurdish areas by the Ba'thi regime, which was opposed by the Kurdish resistance, was a detriment to Kurdish-Ba'thi rapprochement and helped lead to the demise of the March Manifesto. The process of Arabization predated the Ba'thi government in Iraq and really began after the creation of Iraq as a nation-state in 1921 by the British. Before 1921, education was within the purview of religious authorities, and children attended schools based on their religious affiliation. While Christian and Jewish children attended their own denominational schools, Muslim children were educated in *madrassahs*, traditional institutions run by Muslim clerics. In the *madrassahs*, emphasis was placed on quranic teachings and Muslim universalism, as opposed to ethnic particularism.

However, after 1921 and under British guidance, the educational curriculum began to change, with the emphasis placed on Arab history rather than on the Muslim Ottoman Empire. In fact, Arab culture and language were overemphasized, with the principal aim of infusing a sense of Arab nationalism into the minds and hearts of schoolchildren. A negative byproduct of this new educational curriculum was the exclusion of the study of the culture and language of an important segment of Iraqi society, namely, the Kurds. Thus, not only did the new government-run education system overemphasize the study of Arabic culture and language at the expense of other subject matter, but it also contributed to the myth of regional and ethnic homogeneity in Iraq.[83] Furthermore, the Kurds felt that they did not receive an equitable share of the education budget.

By 1926, there were only twenty-five primary schools in Kurdish areas, sixteen of which used both the Kurdish and Arabic languages for instruction. (Kurdish schools represented 2 percent of all primary schools in the country.) The British-mandated authorities contended that it was necessary to rely on

Arabic instruction in Kurdish primary schools because the Kurdish language "provided too narrow a basis for secondary and higher education."[84] After the termination of the British mandate and the emergence of a sovereign Iraq, new emphasis was placed on providing educational opportunities for all Iraqi citizens, irrespective of religion or ethnic origin. Nevertheless, not until 1957, a year prior to the overthrow of the Hashemite monarchy, were Kurdish books made available to primary schools in the region.

The neglect of Kurdish educational needs was a major impetus for the 1943 Kurdish uprisings.[85] This stimulated the Iraqi monarchy into issuing proclamations promising more funding for Kurdish schools and Kurdish-language books. The government's sincerity could not be tested, however, as it faced mounting internal challenges, leading to its overthrow in 1958. Under various republican governments, occasional attempts were made to accommodate Kurdish language needs. In 1960, with much fanfare, Ghassem's regime established a directorate general office for Kurdish studies. Both the twelve-point plan of Bazzaz in 1966 and the 1970 March Manifesto included extensive provisions for meeting Kurdish cultural and linguistic needs. However, political obstacles prevented the implementation of any meaningful educational reform in the Kurdish areas. Furthermore, the Ba'thi government's strong promotion of Arab nationalism, and its preoccupation with becoming the leading practitioner of Arab unity, inherently negated the promotion of another, potentially destabilizing form of nationalism in Iraq.

Population transfer has been another vehicle through which Arabization in Kurdish regions has been promoted and practiced. In fact, William Westermann, in his pioneering study of Kurdish independence movements— originally published in the July 1946 issue of *Foreign Affairs* and excerpted in its Summer 1991 issue—concluded that in no part of Kurdistan "does the Kurdish element form more than a strong minority of the local population."[86] This is a highly debatable assertion, given the fact that census data have, for the most part, either been unavailable or inaccurate in Iraq. Iraqi governments and the Kurds have always acknowledged that the Kurds constituted the majority in Irbil and Sulaymanieh. It is the status of Kirkuk and other areas that has been problematic. It is probably safe to assert that without population transfers, the Kurds would have constituted a slim majority in Mosul and Kirkuk and would have had a strong presence further south in the two districts of Khaneqain and Mandali. Because both Irbil and Sulaymanieh are located deep in the heart of Iraqi Kurdistan, Arabization and population transfer have not affected these areas as much as they have affected other Kurdish regions.

A variety of methods were used to Arabize Kurdish regions. Intimidation by the military and the transfer of Kurds who resisted Arabization sometimes resulted in the wholesale transfer of populations. The main areas to which the Kurds were transferred included Nasiriyeh, Diwaniya, al-Mothanna, and al-Ramadi in the southwestern desert region of the country.[87] The government also established numerous "cluster villages" in Kurdistan, and many Kurdish peasants were removed from their traditional villages and housed in these newly established cluster villages. The government's justification for this program was to provide better and more modern housing for the Kurds. However, the design of these villages allowed for easy surveillance of the houses and for the villages to be easily sealed off. Therefore, the Kurds charged that the principal purpose for the cluster villages was to prevent contact between the inhabitants and the *peshmergas*.[88] In this respect, the cluster villages resembled the "strategic hamlets" that were created in South Vietnam to "pacify" the peasantry and prevent their contact with Viet Cong guerrillas during the Vietnam War.

In some areas under the guise of implementing a new land reform program, the government confiscated land from semifeudal Kurdish landholders. The government then offered loans and credits with favorable terms to Arab peasants to purchase parcels of the confiscated land. The favorable loan and credit terms were generally unavailable to Kurdish peasants, who had no option but to leave their villages in search of work elsewhere. In other areas, especially in Kirkuk, Khaneqain, and Sinjar, the Kurds were forbidden outright to purchase land or obtain title to new land.[89] In yet other areas, the Ba'thi regime redrew administrative boundary lines in order to create Arab majorities. As a result of this "redistricting," many Kurdish villages were placed outside the boundaries of the autonomous region. For example, the villages of Kalar (population 33,000), Kifri (population 50,000), and Cham Chamal (population 51,000) were no longer considered part of Kirkuk.[90] All in all, the provinces of Mosul and oil-rich Kirkuk and the districts of Khaneqain and Mandali became the main focus of the government's Arabization program.

Throughout 1972 and 1973, intermittent skirmishes continued to prevent implementation of the March Manifesto. Faced with the possibility of a protracted war it could not win, the Ba'thi government on December 12, 1973, offered a new plan for Kurdish autonomy, but it fell short of the KDP's expectations. The principal objection of the KDP to this revised autonomy plan was the government's insistence that the 1957 census be used to demarcate the boundaries of the Kurdish autonomous region. This had been rejected previously by Mullah Mostafa and was at variance with Article Fourteen of the March Manifesto, which called for a new census to determine the size of the Kurdish population.[91] Nationalization of the Iraqi Petroleum Company in 1972 further complicated Kurdish-Iraqi relations because it affected the status of the Kirkuk oil fields. Mullah Mostafa pressured the government to agree to a proportional distribution of petroleum revenues. The government, mindful of Kurdish claims over the status of Kirkuk, refused to give in on this issue and stated that only the national government could make decisions on the distribution of national assets such as oil revenues.

By 1974, the Ba'thi government concluded that the talks with Mullah Mostafa over the implementation of the provisions of the March Manifesto would not allow the government to make the plan operational within the required four-year time limit. Consequently, the government unilaterally amended the plan and announced a new plan for Kurdish autonomy on March 11, 1974. It gave the Kurds fifteen days to accept the plan or forfeit any chance of gaining self-rule in the future. The 1974 Autonomy Law dealt with the same areas of self-rule as the 1970 March Manifesto. In addition, the Autonomy Law provided for the establishment of a Kurdish legislature and an executive council and delineated the responsibilities these organs had to the local population and the central government.[92] The members of the legislature would be elected directly by the Kurdish electorate, and the executive council would be chosen by the legislature. The Autonomy Law left determination of the boundaries of the region to a census, but it was clear that Kirkuk would not be included. Sulaymanieh, Irbil, and Dahuk became the component parts of the autonomous region, with Irbil designated as the regional capital of Kurdistan. As Uriel Dann noted, it is important to note that Sulaymanieh, which had long served as the center of Kurdish intellectual and cultural life, was bypassed in favor of Irbil when the central government selected the regional capital. Insofar as the Kurdish national movement was concerned, Irbil had had minimal historical significance.[93]

The Kurdish leadership was caught by surprise when President Ahmad Hassan al-Bakr announced Iraq's new autonomy plan for the Kurds. As before, the exclusion of Kirkuk remained a major stumbling block for the Kurds, and when the government rejected Mullah Mostafa's request to designate Kirkuk and not Irbil as the administrative center of the Kurdish autonomous region, the Kurds rejected the plan. Another equally important reason for rejection of the 1974 Autonomy Law was the promise of more aid from the United States, Israel, and the Shah of Iran if Mullah Mostafa continued to put pressure on the Baghdad government. As he later lamented, without promises from these parties, "we would not have acted the way we did. Were it not for American promises, we would never have become trapped and involved to such an extent."[94]

Buoyed by the promise of more aid, Mullah Mostafa and his allies in the Kurdish movement intensified their fighting against the Iraqi regime. Despite the success enjoyed by the Kurds in keeping the Iraqis at bay, the government forces managed to retake some major towns, such as Zakho, by the summer of 1974. This led to increased Iranian support for the Kurds, including long-range artillery equipment and "possibly Iranian troops dressed as Kurds. . . . [By early 1975], the war reached a point where Iraq could not win unless Iranian support was cut off, and failing that faced the prospect of all-out war with Iran. Neither country wanted this."[95] The sustainability of the Kurdish movement against Iraq was now, to a large extent, a function of Iranian largess.

By February 1975, Iraq had indicated to some Arab countries that it wished to settle its disputes with Iran peacefully and was willing to settle its boundary disputes with Iran. On March 6, 1975, the Shah and the Iraqi vice president, Saddam Hussein, met in Algiers and signed an agreement terminating hostilities between the two countries. Under the terms of the Algiers Agreement, which were made public on March 15, Iraq agreed to accept the midchannel (Thalweg Line) of Shatt al-Arab as the boundary between the two countries. In the past, Iraq had insisted on total control of this waterway that separated the two countries at their southern extreme at the entrance to the Gulf. In return, the Shah agreed to cease all aid to the Kurdish resistance in Iraq.

The Algiers Agreement was a bitter blow to the Kurdish dream of autonomy and destroyed Mullah Mostafa's ability to pursue the war. After meeting with the Shah, he issued a declaration on March 23 ordering his forces to give up their fight and lay down their arms. The Iraqi government then offered a general amnesty to Kurdish *peshmergas* if they surrendered by April 1, 1975. At the same time, the Iranian government informed Kurdish fighters and civilians who had taken refuge inside Iran that the border between Iran and Iraq would be sealed along the Kurdish region, and those willing to accept Baghdad's amnesty offer should do so prior to the April 1 deadline. The Shah offered to allow Mullah Mostafa and some of his *peshmergas* and members of his tribe to settle in Iran. After moving to Iran, they were housed in camps away from Kurdistan in areas where their movements could be easily monitored by Iranian authorities. Suffering from cancer, Mullah Mostafa left for the United States shortly after his arrival in Iran. He died in 1979 in Washington, D.C., and was buried in the Iranian city of Oshnoviyeh.

Because of the short deadline and fear of the Iraqis, many Kurds did not return to Iraq before April 1. Some of those who returned within a few weeks of the amnesty deadline were allowed to resume their "normal life." Others, particularly army deserters, were moved to southern provinces away from their homeland. Furthermore, the Ba'thi government tried to establish a buffer zone by destroying some fifty Kurdish villages along the Iranian and Turkish borders and resettling their inhabitants elsewhere. Estimates on the number of Kurds resettled in the immediate aftermath of the Algiers Agreement vary widely, ranging from 40,000 to 300,000 people.[96]

THE KURDISH STRUGGLE
AFTER MULLAH MOSTAFA BARZANI

The Algiers Agreement generated heated debate among the Kurds about the direction of the Kurdish struggle in Iraq. The KDP began to splinter into several groups. Mullah Mostafa's sons, Massoud and Idris, regrouped loyal supporters of their father in Iran and established the Kurdish Democratic Party-Provisional Leadership. This group has continued to fight the Iraqi government, but with little success. The KDP-Provisional Leadership remains, nonetheless, an important component of the Kurdish resistance, seeking to negotiate a settlement of Kurdish autonomy demands. With the death of Idris in July 1987, apparently from a heart attack, the KDP-Provisional Leadership faced a crisis of leadership. However, with help from Iran and Massoud's cordial relations with the Islamic Republic, the Party was able to function effectively. As an ally of Iran during the eight-year Iran-Iraq War, the KDP-Provisional Leadership forces occasionally engaged the *peshmergas* of the KDPI and the Komala, opponents of the Tehran government. By fighting fellow Kurds, the KDP-Provisional Leadership lost some legitimacy as the "puppet" of the Islamic Republic.[97] However, after Saddam Hussein's military defeat by the US-led coalition forces in the Gulf War of 1991, Massoud has emerged as a spokesman and chief negotiator for the Kurds with the Iraqi government.

Another group of Mullah Mostafa's allies, led by Hashem Aqrawi, opted to accept Baghdad's 1974 Autonomy Law and ceased hostilities against the Ba'thi government. Under the banner of the Kurdish Democratic Party-Ba'th, this group has taken an active role in the administration of the Kurdish autonomous region and has become the Kurdish component of the Ba'th Party in Iraq. Because of the KDP-Ba'th's close association with the central government, this fragment of Mullah Mostafa's KDP has lost legitimacy in the eyes of most Kurds and is no longer considered to be representative of Kurdish autonomy demands.

A more serious schism within the Kurdish movement occurred in November 1975 when a group of radical KDP members and former associates of Mullah Mostafa accused him of betraying the Kurdish cause by striking a Faustian bargain with the United States, Israel, and the Shah of Iran that caused the collapse of the Kurdish resistance. Subsequently, these disenchanted Kurds, under the leadership of Jalal Talabani, formed a new political party—the Patriotic Union of Kurdistan (PUK). Talabani formally announced the establishment of the PUK in June 1976 from his refuge in Damascus. In its early years, the PUK represented three different movements: the "Green Line," consisting primarily of Talabani's personal followers, the Marxist-Leninist Komala (not to be confused with the Iranian Komala), and the Socialist Movement of Kurdistan. The leadership of the PUK, however, has always been under the firm authority of Talabani.[98]

Talabani's leadership has been marked by a series of unlikely alliances between the PUK and other countries and groups in the region. Talabani has maintained cordial relations with Syria since the founding of the PUK. In 1979, the PUK provided support to the Iranian Komala when it was put under siege by Iranian forces. However, the staunchly Marxist-Leninist Iranian Komala has remained aloof from the PUK in recent years because of ideological differences. In 1981, Talabani formed a loose alliance with Ghassemlou's KDPI, primarily to offset the support given to the KDP-Provisional Leadership by the Islamic Republic. This resulted in major clashes between the KDP-Provisional Leadership and PUK *peshmergas* and substantially weakened Kurdish unity in Iraq.

In 1983, in the midst of the Iran-Iraq War, the Islamic Republic, in collaboration with the KDP, launched a major attack against Iraqi positions inside Iraqi Kurdistan. In response, Talabani declared the PUK's readiness to fight these outside "invaders" because Talabani wanted to improve his relations with Saddam Hussein. In a major turnaround, the PUK announced that it had accepted a cease-fire with the Iraqi regime and would entertain the idea of accepting Saddam Hussein's limited autonomy under the existing circumstances. The PUK justified its astonishing about-face by stating: "At least we can talk to Saddam Hussein. . . . Khomeini has killed 20,000 Iranian Kurds and sees all minorities as agents of Satan."[99]

Relations between Talabani and Massoud and Idris Barzani remained adversarial until mid-1986. However, Talabani's disenchantment with Saddam Hussein, and the PUK's exasperating attempts at signing a meaningful autonomy agreement with the Ba'thi regime, brought about another shift in Talabani's alliance pattern. In November 1986, the KDP-Provisional Leadership and the PUK announced their intention to set aside their differences, and in a meeting between Talabani and the Barzani brothers in Tehran, they signed an agreement to coordinate their activities against their common adversary, Ba'thi Iraq.[100] This was a victory not only for the Kurdish movement but also for the Islamic Republic of Iran in its war against the Iraqi government. The PUK's sudden warming toward Iran was explained by Talabani in the following terms: "The affiliation [with Iran] is necessary, constructive, and legitimate, . . . and in the interest of the Kurdish people. . . . [It is] a determining factor in liberating Kurdistan."[101]

The rapprochement between the PUK and the Iranian-backed Barzani forces led to the formation of the Iraq Kurdistan Front (IKF) in 1988. As will be discussed in Chapter 5, under the leadership of Jalal Talabani and Massoud Barzani, the united Kurdistan Front, which includes all anti–Saddam Hussein Iraqi Kurdish groups, has taken the lead in negotiating an autonomy agreement with Saddam Hussein in the post–Gulf War atmosphere that has given the Kurds greater leverage in dealing with Baghdad.

Another close associate, Mahmoud Osman, broke with the KDP after Mullah Mostafa's defeat and established his own organization under the banner of the Preparatory Committee of the KDP. Originally based in Syria, this group moved its headquarters to Iraqi Kurdistan in 1977 and developed a working relationship with the PUK, particularly with its Socialist Movement group and its leader, Rasoul Mamand. Disenchanted with what he viewed as Talabani's authoritarian and erratic leadership style, Mamand and his group broke with the PUK in the spring of 1979 and joined forces with Osman's movement. This union resulted in the creation of yet another Kurdish opposition party—the United Socialist Party of Kurdistan. At its first congress in 1981, the party changed its name to the Socialist Party of Kurdistan-Iraq (SPKI).[102] In subsequent years, relations between the PUK and the SPKI deteriorated, and the latter group has lost a significant number of its supporters in fights with Talabani's group. The SPKI's current position as a member of the Kurdistan Front is marginal.

Divisions within the Kurdish resistance movement in Iraq in the wake of Mullah Mostafa's departure resulted in the deterioration of the Kurdish position vis-à-vis the Ba'thi regime in Iraq. However, the Iran-Iraq war of 1980–1988 and the 1991 Gulf War following Saddam Hussein's invasion of Kuwait, have profoundly affected the Kurdish struggle, and have offered opportunities and constraints that have affected the course of the Kurdish struggle. These developments will be analyzed in Chapter 5.

4

THE "MOUNTAIN TURKS":
THE KURDS IN TURKEY

KURDISH UPRISINGS IN
THE EARLY TWENTIETH CENTURY

The defeat of the Ottoman Empire, its dismemberment after World War I, and the emergence of modern Turkey ushered in an era of intense Turkish (as opposed to Ottoman) nationalism, at the expense of the rights of other ethnic minorities in the country. The post–World War I Treaties of Sèvres and Lausanne, described in Chapter 3, heightened modern Turkey's fear of further dismemberment and intensified the desire of the country's leadership to suppress all non-Turkish ethnic identities. No country has been as preoccupied with the eradication of Kurdish national identity as Turkey in the twentieth century. Consequently, the Turkish government coined the term "Mountain Turks" to refer to the country's Kurdish population. Republican Turkey's Kurdish policy was outlined by Mostafa Kemal Ataturk, the nationalist founder of modern Turkey, and has been followed by his successors. One of Ataturk's most loyal associates, Turkish Prime Minister Ismet Inonu, encapsulated Kemalist Kurdish policy: "Only the Turkish nation is entitled to claim ethnic and national rights in this country. No other element has any such right."[1] This view was reiterated in September 1930 by the country's minister of justice, Mahmut Esat Bozhurt: "We live in a country called Turkey, the freest country in the world. . . . I believe that the Turks must be the only lord, the only master of this country. Those who are not of pure Turkish stock can have only one right in this country, the right to be servants and slaves."[2] This has made the status of the Kurds in Turkey markedly different from that of the Kurds in Iran and Iraq, where their ethnic identity and equality have been recognized by law, if not always by practice.

At the end of the nineteenth century, several Kurdish uprisings occurred in the Ottoman Empire. The most significant of these revolts was led by Shaikh Obeydullah of the Hakkari province in 1880. Obeydullah's objective was to establish a greater Kurdistan by unifying Kurds in Iran and the Ottoman Empire. In pursuit of this goal, he launched military attacks inside Iran, which led to cooperation between Iranian and Ottoman authorities in suppressing Shaikh Obeydullah's rebellion. He was subsequently arrested and exiled to Mecca, where he lived until his death. Shaikh Obeydullah's rebellion was significant in that it augured the emergence of twentieth-century Kurdish uprisings with nationalistic, as opposed to feudalistic, tribal, or religious, overtones. For Obeydullah, the Kurds possessed unique characteristics that made them different from the Persian and Turkish peoples under whom they lived. In a letter to a British diplomat, written in 1878, Shaikh Obeydullah said the "Kurdish nation is a people apart. . . . The chiefs and rulers of Kurdistan, whether Turkish or Persian subjects, and the inhabitants of Kurdistan one and all are united and agreed that matters cannot be carried on in this way with the two governments."[3]

At the end of the nineteenth century and the beginning of the twentieth century, a number of sociopolitical and literary organizations advanced the cause of Kurdish ethnonationalism. In 1897, the first Kurdish newspaper, *Kurdistan*, was founded by the prominent Badr Khan family. It served as a conduit for the dissemination of Kurdish culture and nationalistic activities. This publication appeared irregularly for several decades in Cairo and some European capitals.[4] In 1908, the Badr Khan family and General Sharif Pasha of Sulaymanieh formed a number of Kurdish literary clubs and an educational society that functioned effectively during a brief honeymoon between the Kurds and the Turks. The Kurdish school in Constantinople (Istanbul) educated Kurdish children until it was closed by the authorities in 1909.[5] In addition to Constantinople, other centers of Kurdish culture and language were established in Diyarbakir, Mosul, and Baghdad. The Kurdish intelligentsia and their activities, however, had minimal impact outside the major urban areas. In the countryside, Kurdish intelligentsia educated in Western liberal thought were viewed disfavorably by the Kurdish aghas and khans, who regarded them "with hostility and suspicion as carriers of ungodly and revolutionary ideas."[6]

In addition to the urban-rural dichotomy that undermined development of unified Kurdish nationalist organizations, intense rivalry among prominent feudal families also undermined Kurdish unity. For example, distrust between the prominent Badr Khan and Abdul Qader families was so intense that they continually spied on each other and provided information to the Turkish authorities.[7] This type of information proved invaluable to the Turks as they sought to contain the emerging Kurdish rebellion in their crumbling empire.

The onset of World War I presented the Kurds with an opportunity to press the Turkish authorities for concessions. However, the Ottoman Sultan portrayed the war as a holy war, and the majority of Kurds responded to the Sultan's call to defend the Muslim Ottoman Empire. The Sultan was also adroit at exploiting Kurdish-Armenian tensions and recruited Kurds in his war against the Armenian minority. When the Russian forces entered Kurdistan during the war, many Armenians welcomed them as liberators and aided the Russians in their slaughter of the Kurds. With the signing of the Treaty of Mudros in October 1918, however, World War I came to an end for Turkey, and the Kurds and Armenians found common ground for cooperation as both wanted to establish their own independent states.

The potential for Armenian-Kurdish conflict still existed, as they had overlapping territorial claims. For example, the Ottoman *vilayets* of Diyarbakir, Kharput, and Bitlis were claimed by both groups. In order to avoid future misunderstandings, General Sharif Pasha, representing the Kurds, and General Boghos Pasha, representing the Armenians, signed an agreement on September 20, 1919, in Paris.[8] This agreement influenced the Allies to call for the establishment of an independent Kurdistan and Armenia when they signed the Treaty of Sèvres in 1920 with the Turks. However, the provisions of the Treaty of Sèvres were never implemented.

The abolition of the Caliphate in 1924 undermined the old Ottoman concept of a Muslim *umma* (community) and allowed the Kemalist secular notion of a Turkish nation to emerge. Because Kurdish religious and tribal leaders had derived their authority from the twin institutions of the Sultanate and Caliphate, the abolition of these institutions removed the temporal and spiritual basis of their legitimacy, which led the Turkish republic to outlaw all public manifestations of Kurdish identity. This Kemalist threat to Kurdish identity and sociopolitical structures brought Kurds with competing, and sometimes diametrically opposed, viewpoints together in a common struggle against republican Turkey. In this regard, three Kurdish nationalist movements are worth noting.

The first was the revolt of Shaikh Sa'id of Piran, which started in February 1925 with a Kurdish rebel force numbering an estimated fifteen thousand men.[9] Shaikh Sa'id, a resolute Muslim, was the son of a hereditary chief of the Naqshbandi dervishes. Shaikh Sa'id's rebellion was influenced by the activities of a Kurdish nationalist organization called *Ciwata Azadi Kurd* (Kurdish Freedom Society), which later changed its name to *Ciwata Kweseriya Kurd* (Kurdish Independence Society), or *Azadi*—freedom or independence.[10] Although this organization was founded in secret in Anatolia sometime between 1921 and 1924, the Turks were aware of and concerned about the existence of the *Azadi*. In order to neutralize its activities and discourage Kurds from joining it, the Turkish government routinely dismissed Kurdish officers who were suspected of having sympathy with, or being members of, the *Azadi*. The government also threatened to severely punish any Kurd whose membership in the *Azadi* became known. As Robert Olson stated, the *Azadi*'s objectives were threefold: "to deliver the Kurds from Turkish oppression; to give Kurds freedom and opportunity to develop their country; and to obtain British assistance, realizing Kurdistan could not stand alone."[11]

The *Azadi* played an important role in planning a Kurdish officers' rebellion at the Beyt Sebab garrison in September 1924. The rebellion failed because the *Azadi* leaders were unable to coordinate the Kurdish officers' rebellion with the anticipated uprisings of tribal leaders. Moreover, word reached the commander of the Beyt Sebab garrison in time for him to suppress the rebellion and arrest suspected Kurdish officers. The leaders of the rebellion, however, managed to flee to Iraq. The British were impressed with the ability of the Kurdish officers involved in the rebellion, but they had no intention of giving full-fledged support to a potentially secessionist Kurdish movement. They did realize that the *Azadi* could be used as a "very powerful weapon against Turkey in case of war,"[12] and as a diplomatic bargaining chip in peacetime.

The *Azadi* was apparently responsible for giving impetus to Shaikh Sa'id's rebellion and, perhaps, for the premature rebellion on February 8, 1925, in the village of Piran, which led to a series of battles between the Turkish army and the forces under the leadership of Shaikh Sa'id. Shaikh Sa'id's religious background, and his disenchantment with the emerging secular institutions of the Kemalist republic, led him to make a strong appeal to Kurds and Turks to rise up against the Turkish government in a holy war to restore the Caliphate.[13] However, it is a mistake to interpret Shaikh Sa'id's rebellion as a purely religious uprising against modernization and secularization. Sa'id was a staunch Kurdish nationalist, and a principal aim of his movement was the establishment of an independent Kurdish state. He represented a type of Kurdish leader who was "simultaneously an ardent nationalist and a committed believer. . . . For the average Kurd who participated in the rebellion, the religious and nationalist motivations were doubtless mixed."[14] Most Kurds did not consider religious identification and Kurdish nationalism as antagonistic concepts, nor did they view them as being mutually exclusive.

A major drawback of Shaikh Sa'id's rebellion was that it drew support primarily from the *Zaza*-speaking Kurdish tribespeople, although it was supported by several notable tribal chiefs. Urban support was also relatively weak. The important Kurdish city of Diyarbakir, for example, did not join the uprising. In other Kurdish cities, such as Elazig, the Kurdish populace turned against the rebels due to "their excessive looting and pillage."[15] The rebellion was finally put down by the stronger Turkish army, and by the end of April 1925, the Turks had recaptured areas under Shaikh Sa'id's authority. Shaikh Sa'id and nine of his top associates were arrested, tried for treason, and hanged on June 29.

Despite its short duration, Shaikh Sa'id's rebellion marked a watershed in Turkish-Kurdish relations. It caused the Turkish government to adopt harsh measures against Kurdish cultural manifestations and Kurdish nationalism. This compelled many Kurds in the Mosul *vilayet,* which was claimed by both Turkey and the British Mandate of Iraq, to express a definitive desire to become part of Iraq. This helped convince the League of Nations, after its inquiry mission to determine popular sentiments concerning the status of Mosul, to award Mosul to Iraq. While Shaikh Sa'id's rebellion led to the suppression of Kurdish ethnonationalism in Turkey, the League of Nations' decision, and the Anglo-Turkish Treaty of June 1926 regarding the status of

Mosul, it also led to an understanding between Britain and Turkey: they would oppose the emergence of an independent state or an autonomous area in Turkey, while allowing for such an entity to emerge in Iraq.[16]

The second noteworthy early twentieth-century Kurdish rebellion in Turkey was led by Ihsan Nuri Pasha, a former officer in the Ottoman army. This rebellion, which broke out shortly after Shaikh Sa'id's ended, was particularly strong in areas near Mount Ararat in the northern region of Turkish Kurdistan. The rebellion was supported by a group of Kurdish intellectuals who, from their exile centers in Syria and Lebanon, had organized a new movement, the *Khoyboun* (Independence), for Kurdish independence. The principal goal of this movement was to forge a united front of all Kurdish forces and lend support to Ihsan Nuri's rebellion. Ihsan Nuri's rebellion was significant because it marked the first time that a secular nationalist organization led a Kurdish rebellion. The rebellion obtained the tacit support of Reza Shah's government in Iran, and as a result, Ihsan Nuri's forces were able to freely cross into Iran and receive equipment and supplies from sources in Iranian Kurdistan and Azerbaijan.[17] Reza Shah apparently was intent on using his "Kurdish card" to force Turkey to settle some of its territorial disputes with Iran.

By 1929, Ihsan Nuri's movement was in control of a large expanse of territory spreading through Bitlis, Van, Ararat, and Botan. Unable to keep the Kurdish revolt from spreading to other areas of Kurdistan, the Turkish government lodged numerous protests with Reza Shah's government, demanding that Iran prevent the Kurds from using its territory as a military launching base against Turkish forces. By early 1932, both Iran and Turkey were eager to settle their territorial disputes and establish cordial relations. On January 23, the two countries signed an agreement whereby Turkey was given an area around Mount Ararat and Iran gained territorial concessions around Van to the west of Uromiyah.

Turkish-Iranian rapprochement had started well before the signing of the 1932 agreement. Two years earlier, the Turkish government finally convinced Reza Shah to cut off Ihsan Nuri's Iranian sources and allow Turkish forces to enter Iranian territory in pursuit of Kurdish rebels. By the summer of 1930, the Kurdish forces were surrounded by a Turkish force of forty-five thousand men, and by the end of the summer, the revolt had been defeated. Some of the leaders, including Ihsan Nuri, escaped to Iran. Many others were captured and executed. Turkish retaliation against Kurds was particularly severe in areas where Ihsan Nuri's rebellion had its strongest support. For example, the Turkish military authorities reportedly arrested some one hundred Kurdish intellectuals in Van, sewed them into sacks, and threw them into Lake Van to die an agonizing death.[18]

Turkish policy in the aftermath of the Ihsan Nuri rebellion emphasized the mass deportation of Kurdish villagers, the exiling of Kurdish shaikhs and aghas, and the forceful recruiting of young Kurds into the Turkish army. The government also condoned acts of vigilantism against the Kurds during this period of repression, and in some cases legally sanctioned such behavior. For example, Article 1 of Law No. 1,850 read:

> Murders and other actions committed individually or collectively, from the 20th of June 1930 to the 10th of December 1930, by the representatives of the state or the province, by the military or civil authorities, by the local authorities, by guards or militiamen, or by any civilian having helped the above or acted on their behalf, during the pursuit and extermination of the revolts which broke out in Ercis, Zilan, Agridag (Ararat) and the surrounding areas, including Pulumur in Erzincan province and the area of the First Inspectorate, will not be considered as crimes.[19]

The passage of this law was instrumental in the "pacification" of the area of the First Inspectorate, including the major Kurdish areas of Diyarbakir, Bitlis, Hakkari, and Mardin.

The third major Kurdish revolt of the first half of the twentieth century was Shaikh Sayyed Reza's rebellion in Dersim (now called Tunceli) in the northwestern region of Turkish Kurdistan. Shaikh Reza's revolt began in 1937 and lasted until the end of 1938, when it was crushed by the Turkish army. Dersim established a tradition of revolting against Turkish hegemony when a Kurdish nationalist rebellion took place in November 1920 among the Kocgiri tribes in support of the provisions of the Treaty of Sèvres and the establishment of a Kurdish homeland.[20] By April 1921, the Kocgiri rebellion had been defeated by the Turks.

Shaikh Reza's rebellion in Dersim cut across tribal boundaries and proved more durable than the earlier revolt. In addition to the support of his own Abbasushaghi tribe, Shaikh Reza succeeded in gaining support from at least two others—the Yusufkhan and Demenan tribes. After assembling a guerrilla force of up to fifteen hundred men, Shaikh Reza began attacking visible symbols of Turkish authority, such as the gendarmerie posts in Dersim, and forcing rural Turkish police to abandon their posts. Shaikh Reza's rebellion later spread to other regions and was joined by a contingent of veterans of the Shaikh Sa'id rebellion from Syria. Unlike Shaikh Sa'id's and Ihsan Nuri's rebellions, the Dersim revolt did not involve conventional warfare between two opposing armies. In Dersim, the Turkish army faced a small but determined force that relied on the hit-and-run tactics of guerrilla warfare.

Shaikh Reza, his two sons, and several other tribal leaders were captured, tried, and condemned to death in November 1937. However, the revolt continued for several months. It was finally put down in October 1938 after a long period of sustained attacks on Dersim by Turkish forces, which included reliance on the "massive use of poison gas, artillery and air bombardment."[21] Unable to replenish their supplies and facing total eradication, the Kurdish forces had no choice but to terminate their uprising. The repression that followed was extensive. Entire villages were depopulated or massacred. The destruction of Dersim was so thorough that it evoked apocalyptic visions. The Turkish government sought to erase the memory of this bloody episode by replacing the name Dersim with Tunceli and putting the area under a total state of siege until 1950.[22] The use of the words "Kurdistan" and "Kurds" was banned and references to them were removed from Turkish history books and publications.

The trauma of Dersim augured a new quiet phase of Kurdish struggle in Turkey, which lasted until the early 1960s, when the emergence of democratic and leftist movements contributed to the revival of Kurdish nationalism. Until 1950, Turkish politics had remained the exclusive domain of the Republican People's Party (RPP), but in the late 1940s, Ismet Inonu, Ataturk's successor, decided to move the country toward a more liberalized political and economic system by encouraging the development of a more competitive and democratic ambiance in the country. As a consequence, new political movements began to emerge in anticipation of challenging the monopoly of the country's dominant political party—the RPP.

The parliamentary election of 1950 marked the first time that competitive multiparty elections were allowed in republican Turkey. The election resulted in the defeat of Inonu's RPP and the victory of the newly formed Democratic Party (DP), and the coming to power of one of DP's founders, Adnan Menderes, as the new prime minister. The DP's support came from an assortment of groups that had become alienated from the country's increasing political authoritarianism. As a strong opponent of Turkey's state-centered economic system, and as a self-described champion of a laissez faire economy, the DP succeeded in attracting support from large industrialists, merchants, and major agrarian interests. Urban intellectuals, journalists, and the educated middle class also welcomed the prospect of more democracy and supported the DP.

The Kurds voted overwhelmingly for the DP in reaction to the suppression of the Kurds by Kemalist policies.[23] A number of Kurds were elected to the Turkish National Assembly and obtained cabinet seats. More important, the DP allowed exiled aghas, shaikhs, and khans to return and co-opted them into the new system. In return for being allowed to assume their traditional authority, these Kurdish leaders acted in the way political machines in big US cities had operated. That is, they "controlled large numbers of local votes, in exchange for which they received spoils to distribute among their followers. Thus the positions of these traditional leaders were reinforced, both vis-à-vis the central government and vis-à-vis the local population."[24]

At the same time, an increasing number of Kurds, particularly Kurds from wealthy families and Kurds who had benefited from the government's laissez faire approach to Kurdish economic development, moved to towns and provided the background for what became known as *Doguculuk*, or

"Eastism." This referred to a philosophy based on the advocacy of economic change and development in the "East," as Turkey's Kurdistan has been officially called. Although the leaders of *Doguculuk* took pains to work within the system and avoid public politicization of their movement, the government eventually became suspicious of their ultimate motives and ordered the arrest of some fifty leaders of the movement in December 1959. This severely tested the limits of Turkish democracy with respect to the country's Kurdish minority.

Some Kurdish intellectuals argued that the government's suppression of the *Dogucu*, or "Eastists," was mainly due to the deteriorating economic situation in Turkey, which caused Prime Minister Menderes to seek scapegoats and devise diversionary tactics.[25] Furthermore, the Turkish army, which had lost political influence as a torchbearer of Kemalism and whose members had experienced economic deprivation because of inflation and higher prices, became increasingly impatient with the Menderes government. The Turkish army was also apprehensive about Mullah Mostafa's uprisings in neighboring Iraq spilling into eastern Turkey, and questioned the ability of the civilian government to contain a similar revolt in Turkey.

On May 27, 1960, the Turkish military staged a coup and overthrew Adnan Menderes, executing him a year later. Although the Kurds had become victims of Menderes's authoritarianism in the latter part of his tenure in office, they feared the new military junta more than the Menderes administration, and in fact, one of the first measures undertaken by the Committee of the National Front (the ruling junta) was to intern a number of prominent Kurds and send many others into internal exile in western Turkey. Forced Turkification of Kurdish children was also undertaken, as was Turkicization of the names of Kurdish villages. In November 1960, the junta's leader, General Cemal Gursel, warned Turkish Kurds not to support or emulate Mullah Mostafa's uprisings in Iraq. If they did, the Turkish armed forces would not "hesitate to bomb their towns and villages into the ground."[26]

Nevertheless, the military junta did take specific measures to ameliorate the authoritarian trends that had developed during the previous regime. For example, it purged obdurate officers from its ranks or sent them away to be diplomats in remote capitals. The junta also convened a constituent assembly and promulgated a new constitution in 1961 that provided more democratic freedoms than had previously existed. It promised to turn over power to an elected civilian government—and did in 1961—and prevented two right-wing coup attempts from succeeding against the new civilian government.[27] Under the new and expanded constitutional guarantees of freedom of press, assembly, and association, the Kurds were once again able to express their desires, albeit through Turkish associations and publications. A few publications even emerged that dealt with Kurdish history and culture, though they still used the Turkish name for the eastern region when referring to Kurdistan. Although these publications were eventually suppressed, the 1961 constitutional freedoms did allow for experimentation, with a limited degree, of Kurdish cultural self-expression.

THE GROWTH OF THE KURDISH
MOVEMENT AND THE TURKISH LEFT

In the 1961 elections, no political party was able to obtain a majority, but the candidates of the Justice Party received a plurality of votes cast. In Kurdistan, the Justice Party's main rival was the New Turkey Party, and the voting in Kurdistan resulted in an even split between these two parties. Although the Justice Party was better financed and had powerful business backing throughout Turkey, many Kurds thought that their interests would be better served if the New Turkey Party came to power because one of its leaders, Dr. Yusuf Azizoglu, was a Kurd and had close contacts with the *Dogucu* in Diyarbakir. Since no political party dominated the elections, a coalition government came to power with the RPP's Ismet Inonu becoming the new prime minister.

The coalition government broke down in June 1962 because of the intense rivalry between its two major components—the Justice Party and the RPP. The Justice Party withdrew from the coalition and a new coalition government was formed on June 25, dominated by the RPP and including the New Turkey Party and the Republican Peasant's National Party. Inonu maintained his post in the new cabinet. Dr. Azizoglu of the New Turkey Party was appointed minister of health. During his brief tenure, Azizoglu paid particular attention to improving health standards in the eastern areas of the country and built more hospitals in Kurdistan than "all previous governments put together, which gained him considerable popularity."[28] Dr. Azizoglu eventually ran afoul of his Kemalist colleagues in the cabinet, who forced his resignation by accusing him of promoting Kurdish ethnonationalism and separatism.

The relative political freedom that characterized the Turkish political scene during the 1960s and 1970s allowed for the emergence of various leftist groups among the Turkish and Kurdish intelligentsia. A significant segment of the Turkish left organized itself under the banner of the Workers' Party of Turkey (WPT) in the 1960s and began to contest elections. In the 1965 parliamentary election, fifteen WPT candidates won seats in the National Assembly. The WPT included a number of Kurds, and through the efforts of its Kurdish members, it began to gradually recognize the importance of the Kurdish issue in Turkey. At its Fourth Congress in November 1971, the WPT issued a resolution which read, in part: "There is a Kurdish people in the East of Turkey. . . . The fascist authorities representing the ruling classes have subjected the Kurdish people to a policy of assimilation and intimidation which has often become a bloody repression."[29] This was a revolutionary statement, marking the first time in modern Turkey that a Turkish political party had openly recognized the existence of the Kurds as a persecuted minority. However, it cost the WPT its legal status, and its leaders were sentenced to long prison terms for undermining the unity of the nation. They were eventually released through the government's amnesty program of 1974.

Kurdish intellectuals took advantage of this period of Turkish glasnost and in 1969 organized the Revolutionary Cultural Society of the East (DDKO) as the first legal Kurdish organization. The DDKO generated antipathy among the Kemalist bureaucrats and functionaries because it sought to publicize the suppression of Kurdish dissent and the economic under-development of the Kurdish regions.[30] Kurdish membership in the WPT and DDKO, which somewhat overlapped, represented what Martin van Bruinessen has called the "left wing of the emerging Kurdish movement" in Turkey.[31] During the 1960s, the emerging Kurdish left found itself confronted with a rival bourgeois nationalist group within the Kurdish movement in Turkey. The nationalist wing of the Kurdish movement identified itself with Mullah Mostafa's party in Iraq and became a "sister" to the Iraqi KDP.

Tensions between the more conservative and traditionalist pro-KDP wing and the Kurdish left threatened to undermine the Kurdish movement in Turkey. While the pro-KDP wing called only for the establishment of Kurdish autonomy, the Kurdish left demanded not only cultural rights but also the socioeconomic restructuring of Kurdistan and the transformation of the hierarchical Kurdish society into a more equitable society. A schism then developed within the ranks of pro-KDP Kurds. Under the leadership of Dr. Sivan, a more radical faction withdrew and went to Iraqi Kurdistan to prepare for armed struggle against the Turkish government. This placed Mullah Mostafa in a quandary because he was making overtures toward the Turkish and Iranian governments for support against the Iraqi regime. The other faction in the pro-KDP wing, under the leadership of Sait Elci, remained in Turkey until the military coup of 1971 forced Elci to flee to Iraq. The rivalry between Sivan and Elci continued in Iraq leading to the assassination of both of them under mysterious circumstances. According to one account, Elci was killed by Sivan. In retaliation, Mullah Mostafa condemned Sivan to death and ordered his execution.[32] Other popular theories have blamed Turkish intelligence (MIT) for masterminding the assassinations. In any event, the elimination of Elci and Sivan prevented both factions of the pro-KDP from exerting any significant influence on the Kurdish movement in Turkey.

In March 1971, the Kurdish movement suffered yet another setback when, once again, the military intervened in Turkish politics and installed a government headed by Nihat Erim. The WPT and DDKO were outlawed, their leaders and activists were imprisoned, and the military initiated a new round of sustained attacks on Kurdish villages, resulting in their destruction and/or the deportation of their residents. It was not until the restoration of parliamentary democracy, and the coming to power of an elected civilian prime minister, Bulent Ecevit, in January 1974, that the Kurds were able to reorganize themselves politically. The rejuvenated Kurdish movement had a broader social base and was "more radical in its demands" than the 1960's Kurdish movement.

A number of factors contributed to the radicalization of Kurdish political parties in the 1970s. As van Bruinessen noted, the most significant factor in the radicalization of the Kurdish movement was Kurdish urbanization—the massive voluntary and involuntary migration of Kurdish villagers to cities— and the inability of the strained Turkish economy to absorb them into mainstream life.[33] Kurdish migrants to the cities of western Turkey became aware of the great disparities that existed between the western region of the country and their own eastern region—in living standards, economic development, educational opportunities, access to health care facilities, and overall quality of life.[34] Although agriculture remained a major source of revenue for the eastern region, Kurds also became acutely aware of their region's importance to Turkey as the only producer of oil. For all intents and purposes, the region did not benefit from petroleum production, as the bulk of petroleum production revenues were exported to other parts of the country. In 1971, petroleum production generated $2.5 million, and the following year it generated $10 million.[35] Less than 5 percent of revenues generated, however, were spent for the development of the Kurdish region.

Moreover, as the number of Kurdish secondary-school and university students increased, students became more politicized and sensitive to legal and social discrimination against Kurds. Leftist student radicalism pervaded Turkish educational institutions, and younger Kurdish migrants became the conduit through whom awareness of issues of class struggle, underdevelopment, exploitation, and imperialism "spread outside narrow intellectual circles. . . . Urban educated teachers and students returning to their villages brought new political ideas, in simplified form, to the countryside and attempted to mobilize the peasants."[36] Kurdish mobilization faced new dangers in the 1970s, however. Revision of the country's penal code and constitution in 1971 made it easier to prosecute those who were active in the Kurdish movement. Nevertheless, until the imposition of martial law in Kurdish regions in 1979, various coalition governments that ruled Turkey during much of the 1970s were relatively ineffective in implementing a sustained and efficient repressive policy toward their Kurdish minority.

Another factor contributing to the leftward drift of the Kurdish movement in Turkey was the alienation of the Kurdish population from the "progressive" ruling circles. For example, before becoming Turkey's prime minister in January 1974, Bulent Ecevit campaigned in the east and promised the Kurds that if his RPP won the elections, he would address the underdevelopment of Kurdish areas. However, when Kurds, including his supporters, raised the issue of Kurdish autonomy, Ecevit reacted harshly, in the same fashion as his predecessors. The Turkish left was the only segment of society that recognized the Kurdish predicament and called for an end to the Kemalist policy of forced assimilation and oppression. Differing objectives and tactics, however, strained relations between the Kurdish and Turkish left. For Kurds, the goals of socialist revolution and Kurdish nationalism were not incompatible; they had to be pursued simultaneously. The Turkish left, on the other hand, considered Kurdish insistence on ethnic recognition as counterproductive, divisive, and ultimately detrimental to the survival of the political left. They contended that ethnic recognition would be achieved under the proletarian leadership of a socialist Turkey. The two sides parted company and the Kurdish left sought to organize separate political parties.

During 1974–1975, former members of the banned DDKO reorganized it into the Revolutionary–Democratic Cultural Associations (DDKD). The DDKD was supposed to provide the glue that brought disparate Kurdish organizations together, but ideological differences and personality clashes caused schisms within the DDKD, leading to the development of new groups. One group that emerged was *Ozgurluk Yolu* (The Road to Freedom), which published a monthly journal under the same name from 1975 to 1979. Many of its members were activists in the banned WPT. They advocated an alliance with the Turkish proletariat to end Kurdish oppression. *Ozgurluk Yolu* did not penetrate a large segment of the Kurdish population, but maintained some appeal among intellectual and trade union circles. In 1979, it adopted a more formal structure and became the Socialist Party of Turkish Kurdistan (SPTK).

Because of its roots in the WPT-DDKO alliance, the SPTK remained optimistic about the prospects for Kurdish-Turkish coexistence within a democratic, socialist system. The SPTK predicted that the socialist revolution in Turkey would take place in two stages:

> [Since] Kurdistan has not got its national independence yet and done away with feudalism, the character of the revolutionary stage facing the Kurdish people is the national democratic revolution. This revolution is going to take the colonial fetters off the people, wipe out the foreign domination, and liberate the Kurds. . . . Our Party knows very well that only socialism can put an end to exploitation and backwardness. [Therefore], the national democratic revolution should be brought to perfection by the socialist revolution.[37]

The 1980 military coup in Turkey, which decimated the country's political structure and party organization, led to the imprisonment or exile of many SPTK members. The exiled leadership has operated principally from Sweden, where Kemal Burkay, the party's secretary general, relocated.

Another leftist group was organized in 1976 and became known by the name of its journal, *Rizgari* (Liberation). Unlike *Ozgurluk Yolu*, the leaders of *Rizgari* viewed Kurdish overtures toward the Turkish government, even if led by a moderate like Ecevit, as unproductive. They did not support Ecevit and his RPP in the 1977 elections, arguing that the Kurds, as a colonized nation in Turkey, should focus on their own problems instead of getting mired in the political machinations of the colonizing nation. The *Rizgari* contended that only a socialist revolution led by the Kurdish proletariat would guarantee the rights of the Kurdish nation in Turkey.[38]

Disagreements over ideological and strategic issues led to a schism within the *Rizgari* in 1979. The splinter group, *Ala Rizgari* (Flag of Liberation), questioned the practicality of the Kurdish proletariat leading a socialist revolution. *Ala Rizgari* reasoned that the Kurdish proletariat was too small and weak to initiate such a major undertaking and win against the overwhelming power of the Turkish state. Instead, it called for adoption of a less rigid ideological stand that took notice of the Kurdish reality and made the necessary adjustments in Marxist doctrine to fit that reality. It also criticized the Soviet Union and its role vis-à-vis the Kurds, which caused some of the group's detractors to label it a Trotskyite organization. However, this claim cannot be sustained by empirical evidence.

Anti-Sovietism was a strong component of a Maoist Kurdish movement organized in 1976. *Kawa* was named after Kaveh-e Ahangar, a heroic figure in the Iranian poet Ferdowsi's major epic, *Shahnameh* (The Book of Kings). (Ahangar fought the diabolical tyrant Zahak-e Mar Doush and defeated him against all odds.) *Kawa* carried out a number of daring attacks against Turkish outposts throughout the latter half of the 1970s. The group's membership, however, did not extend beyond a small group of students and urban dwellers. In 1978, a split occurred in *Kawa*'s leadership over disagreements about Chinese foreign policy and the prevailing Three Worlds Maoist foreign policy paradigm.[39]

As mentioned earlier, the assassinations of Elci and Sivan substantially weakened the Turkish branch of the Iraqi KDP. The demise of Mullah Mostafa's revolt in 1975 further debilitated the Turkish branch. However, in 1977, a younger, and more militant, segment organized a new party called the National Liberation of Kurdistan (KUK). Its center of support was in the province of Mardin in southeastern Turkey near the Iraqi and Syrian borders. The KUK supported the KDP-Provisional Leadership in Iraq after its formation by Mullah Mostafa's two sons. The KUK sought to forge an alliance with other Kurdish groups, particularly with the SPTK, in a "theoretical United Democratic Front" in the 1980s.[40] The KUK's ranks have been severely decimated in clashes with another radical leftist party—the Workers' Party of Kurdistan (PKK). The remnants of the KUK have broken with the "feudal" elements of the Iraqi KDP and their supporters in Turkey, and claimed to have embraced Marxism-Leninism.

The most prominent and effective Kurdish organization to emerge during the leftist "renaissance" of the 1970s was the PKK. The PKK originated in 1974 when a small group of Kurdish university students in Ankara organized the Ankara Democratic Patriotic Association of Higher Education. Their original activities focused primarily on gaining official recognition for Kurdish language and cultural rights. The principal leader and driving force behind the association was Abdullah (Apo) Ocalan, a former student in political science at Ankara University. In addition to Ocalan, ten other individuals were present at the first meeting of this group, including Kesire Yildirim, the only female, who later married Ocalan and became an influential leader of the PKK. Yildirim, however, became estranged from Ocalan when she began questioning his policies and tactics and left him in 1988 to join a PKK breakaway faction in Europe.[41] The Turkish press reported that Ocalan took up with Gonul Tepe and made her the chief organizer of PKK operations in Tunceli and Bingon.[42]

The PKK, like the Komala in Iran, blended Marxism-Leninism with a strong dose of Kurdish nationalism. It advocated the establishment of a Kurdish Marxist republic in southeastern Turkey, with the ultimate aim of creating an independent Kurdistan that unites Kurdish regions throughout the Middle East.[43] What separated the PKK from other Kurdish organizations was the party's unequivocal advocacy of total Kurdish independence. Other Kurdish groups in the Middle East either called for Kurdish autonomy (KDPI, Iraqi-KDP), or equivocated on the issue of total independence (SPTK, KUK).

After its formation in 1974, the Ankara Democratic Patriotic Association of Higher Education expanded its membership beyond university circles and became involved with other segments of Kurdish society. In 1977, the group met in Diyarbakir and issued a document reflecting its analysis of the Kurdish situation in Turkey. This document provided the framework within which the PKK has functioned since its formation as a Marxist-Leninist Kurdish political party in 1979. The document was distributed clandestinely throughout Turkey under the title "*Kurdistan Devriminin Yolu,*" or "The Path of the Kurdish Revolution." It described Kurdistan as a classic colonial entity, where Kurdish feudal landlords and "comprador bourgeoisie" collaborated with the ruling classes in the colonial countries, especially in Turkey, to perpetuate the exploitation of the Kurdish peasantry and the working class. The document was highly critical of Kurdish intellectuals for becoming Turkified in their outlook and behavior, thus forsaking their Kurdish cultural heritage.

The document recommended a two-tiered revolution to solve the Kurdish problem—national, then democratic. The national phase of the Kurdish revolution would entail the establishment of an independent Kurdistan as a sine qua non for attainment of Kurdish rights. The democratic phase of the revolution would "clear away the contradictions in society left over from the Middle Ages, [such as] feudal and comprador exploitation, tribalism, religious sectarianism and the slave-like dependence of women."[44] The document asserted that the transformation of Kurdish society could be achieved only through a Marxist-Leninist revolution whose final aim would be to create a classless society. Armed struggle was advocated as the only method by which these goals could be achieved, and the PKK tried to practice what it preached. In the semi-anarchic conditions prevailing in Turkey in the late 1970s, when the government was paralyzed by its inability to contain violent clashes between the extreme right and left, the PKK launched a number of major attacks on Turkish targets throughout the southeastern part of the country and established a strong presence in the region.

The PKK's activities, as well as those of other political parties and movements, came to a stop with the military coup in September 1980. Under the leadership of the chief of staff, General Kenan Evren, the Turkish military announced on September 12 that it had seized all executive and legislative power and would restore order and democracy to the country. The coup marked the third time that the Turkish military had intervened in politics since the late 1940s. Unlike the previous two interventions, however, the military did not give up control of the legislative and executive branches of the government easily. In fact, it was not until the elections of late 1983 that a civilian cabinet and parliament were established.[45]

Although the coup was ostensibly staged to "restore democracy, not to destroy it,"[46] the Turkish military suppressed political activity and opposition. Political parties were banned and their leaders were arrested, including the overthrown prime minister, Suleyman Demirel of the conservative Justice Party, and his chief rival, Bulent Ecevit of the RPP. Interestingly, Turgut Ozal, who was the chief economic planner in the deposed Demirel government, was not arrested. Instead, he was given wide leeway to restructure the Kurdish economy for the purpose of integrating it into the international capitalist market. This involved a redirection of economic resources away from the traditional smaller industries toward "those sections of capital most able to adapt to this reorientation."[47]

Implementation of the new economic order required a docile labor force. Therefore, as one of its first measures, the military junta suspended all trade union activity. In particular, the junta targeted the militant Confederation of Progressive Trade Unions (DISK) for suppression. By March 1983, the junta had acknowledged the arrest of about twenty thousand "suspects," the overwhelming majority of whom were activists or sympathizers in leftist groups. Kurdish activists who were arrested in the immediate aftermath of the 1980 coup and charged with promoting separatism numbered about three thousand individuals. Over half of those arrested for "separatist activities" were members of the PKK.[48] However, the total number of Kurds arrested and tried exceeded three thousand, as many of them held membership in banned political and labor groups and were charged under various categories of crimes committed against the state. After the coup and the subsequent mass arrests of Kurdish and leftist activists, the Kurdish struggle, particularly that staged by the PKK, took a decidedly different and more violent turn.

The junta also endeavored to further impede the promotion of Kurdish language and culture. In 1982, the military junta convened a civilian constituent assembly to draft a new constitution. The 1982 constitution, which was approved by a referendum, placed a number of restrictions on the use of the Kurdish language. Articles 26, 28, and 89 of the constitution were particularly clear on this issue:

Article 26 No language prohibited by law shall be used in the expression and dissemination of thought. Any written or printed documents, photograph records, magnetic or video tapes, and other media instruments used in contravention of this provision shall be confiscated.

Article 28 Publications shall not be made in any language prohibited by law.

Article 89 No political party may concern itself with the defense, development, or diffusion of any non-Turkish language or culture; nor may they seek to create minorities within our frontiers or to destroy our national unity.[49]

In addition to the constitutional prohibitions against the use of the Kurdish language, the Turkish penal code was revised to criminalize expressions of Kurdish ethnic identity. These, along with the existing ban on the use of the terms "Kurd" or "Kurdish," further radicalized the Kurdish movement and its most visible supporter, the PKK.

Turkey's penal code, which was formulated in 1938, was used extensively to suppress free speech and political activity, and was used very effectively against the Kurds. The penal code contained a number of draconian measures. Articles 141 and 142, for example, prohibited organizing "communist" and/or "separatist" organizations and disseminating ideas about communism and separatism. Articles 158 and 159 prohibited "insulting" the president of the republic, the Parliament, and government and military authorities. The Kurds were routinely prosecuted for violating these articles.[50] Even lawyers who defended Kurds accused of promoting separatism were prosecuted. For example, Huseyin Yildirim, a Kurdish lawyer representing PKK defendants, was arrested by the military in October 1981 and held in the Diyarbakir military prison until July 1982, during which time he was physically tortured under degrading conditions simply because he refused to stop defending his clients in court.[51] During their tenure in office, both the junta leader and president, General Evren, and his prime minister, Admiral Bulend Ulusu, repeatedly warned the Kurds about the danger of violating the country's penal code.

A new emphasis was placed on reviving the scientifically unsubstantiated theory that the Kurds were simply another Central Asian Turkic tribe and were, therefore, of Turkish origin. A spate of articles in magazines and academic journals appeared using this line of thinking. The writings of Sukru Mehmet Sekban, a Kurdish propagandist for Ataturk's nationality policy, were also resurrected. Sekban developed a "pseudo-history of the Kurds, complete with a set of pseudo-linguistics, 'firmly' embedding the Kurds among the Turkic family of peoples."[52] However, no serious scholar of Kurdish or Turkish history found Sekban's theories credible, nor was the average Kurd influenced by them.

The junta's suppression of manifestations of Kurdish ethnicity affected a wide segment of society. For example, in March 1981, Serafettin Elci, who served as minister of public works under the Ecevit administration in 1978–1979, was sentenced to two years and three months in prison for "making Kurdish and secessionist propaganda."[53] The former cabinet minister's conviction was the first against a high-level politician of Kurdish origin since the military junta came to power, and it was designed to demonstrate the government's determination to eradicate all forms of Kurdish nationalism. Elci's conviction was based on published statements that were critical of the government's neglect of the socioeconomic needs of the southeastern region, and on his open challenge of the ban on recognition of the existence of Kurds in the country. In a document used as major evidence against him, Elci was quoted as having said, "I am a Kurd. There are Kurds in Turkey."[54]

Elci's conviction paved the way for the show trials of a large number of Kurdish nationalists and militants in April 1981. The junta prepared the public for these trials by airing a ninety-minute television program on March 30 denouncing Kurdish activists. The program featured numerous testimonies by captured Kurdish militants and peasants denouncing the goals, programs, and activities of the PKK. In a dramatic plea, an elderly peasant charged that the PKK was worse than the European invaders, and that the militants had "forced his son to murder his mother and sister."[55] The program was also aimed at gaining some support among Kurds for the government's policies by portraying the Kurdish guerrillas, particularly the PKK forces, as terrorists bent on aggrandizing their own fortunes at the expense of the Kurdish population.

THE RETURN TO CIVILIAN RULE: THE POST-1983 ERA

In 1983, the junta began to prepare for the return of civilian rule and laid the foundation for parliamentary elections. The November 1983 elections resulted in the victory of Turgut Ozal's Motherland Party. Ozal's assumption of power as the new civilian prime minister did not remove the military's influence. In fact, General Evren continued to serve as president, and the military remained in full control of internal and foreign security matters, with the civilian prime minister given a freer hand in economic matters. Even after the 1989 elections, which transferred the presidency to Turgut Ozal and resulted in the establishment of a civilian-dominated executive, the military's dominating influence in running the affairs of the Kurdish provinces remained unchallenged.

Dankwart Rustow has contended that democratic institutions in Turkey have been strengthened since 1983, and greater opportunities for political participation have been made available to the Turkish citizenry. He has furthered asserted that the 1970s pattern of parliamentary deadlock and political paralysis were reversed following the 1980 coup.[56] Although there is empirical evidence to support Rustow's analysis in some instances, the Kurds have not benefited from the political reforms that have been instituted in Turkey since the return of civilian rule. A formidable obstacle to the granting of Kurdish demands is the pervasive presence of Kemalist ideology within the ruling circles and within a sizable portion of the population. As Anthony Hyman noted, the persistent lack of public sympathy for the demands of Kurdish nationalists in Turkey is due largely to the fact that the grandparents of over 50 percent of urban, middle-class Turks came from the Balkans, Egypt, the Crimea, Central Asia, the Caucasus, and other adjacent regions. Given this reality in today's Turkey, the preservation of the territorial integrity of the Kurdish state remains the top priority, and the Turks are painfully aware of the "disruptive effect of non-Turkish nationalism" and view it as anathema to their country's survival.[57]

Since restoration of civilian rule in late 1983, the Turkish approach to the Kurdish insurgency has been two-pronged. On the one hand, the government has sought to "pacify" the Kurdish population by directing more economic aid to southeastern Turkey to revive its economy, especially agriculture, and by integrating the local Kurdish economy into the mainstream Turkish economy. The massive Ataturk Dam project was initiated in the 1980s for this purpose. Improvements in the region's infrastructure, particularly in the government's efforts to modernize regional communications facilities and roads, have been pursued seriously by the Turkish government.[58] On the other hand, the government has continued to implement harsh measures against those promoting ethnic nationalism in an effort, in the words of the human rights group Helsinki Watch, to destroy Kurdish ethnic identity.[59]

Stepped-up measures against Kurdish activism by the Ozal government coincided with the revival of the PKK's activities in 1984. After the 1980 coup and the arrest of several thousand Kurdish militants and nationalists, many remaining PKK members left Turkey and set up cells inside the neighboring countries of Syria and Iraq. During the summer of 1984, the PKK announced the formation of the Kurdistan Liberation Brigades (HRK) and, from bases in northern Iraq, carried out a number of attacks against Turkish army units and police stations located in villages in southeastern Turkey.

The Turkish army reacted by immediately dispatching heavy armored units into Kurdistan but, for the most part, failed to capture the PKK guerrillas who launched the attacks. The PKK's guerrilla attacks intensified, and in May 1985, the PKK announced the formation of a broad coalition of forces called the Kurdish National Liberation Front (ERNK).[60] This organization was dominated by the PKK and, according to one analyst, included only the PKK with a few other individuals joining as independent activists and not as representatives of other organizations.[61] From June through November 1985, ERNK guerrillas conducted some fifty operations against Turkish forces and their Kurdish collaborators. According to ERNK, these operations destroyed four army platoons and killed over eighty soldiers and collaborators.[62]

Logistical and political problems hampered PKK's operations inside Turkey. Turkish-Iraqi cooperation in the mid-1980s, as well as PKK-KDP rivalries, made it increasingly difficult for the PKK to continue guerrilla attacks against Turkish forces. With the loss of its freedom to operate out of the rugged, mountainous Turkish-Iraqi border areas, the PKK had to concentrate on building up its operational bases in Syria, where the relatively flat Turkish-Syrian border region made it easier to control guerrilla activities. In July 1987, Turkish prime minister Turgut Ozal signed an agreement with Syria that called for closer cooperation between the two countries on security matters and committed Syrian authorities to stopping the PKK from using its territory as a base of operations against Turkey. Although Syrian authorities curtailed the PKK's activities to a large extent, Damascus found it useful to use its "Kurdish card" to gain concessions from Turkey on the contentious issue of Euphrates River water. Turkey's control of the source of the Euphrates River is a matter of concern for both Syria and Iraq, who depend on it for irrigation. It seems likely that as long as the Euphrates River issue remains unsolved, and as long as Turkey plays politics with that issue, Damascus will allow the PKK or other Kurdish guerrillas to remain "a serious nuisance to Turkey but not to the point of provoking Ankara to take military measures against Syria."[63]

In 1988, the Turkish press began to run stories about the PKK's collaboration with the Kurdish Democratic Party of Iran (KDPI). Having lost its freedom of operation in northern Iraq, and with its movements restricted by the Syrian government, the PKK was said to have moved to Iran under the KDPI's supporting umbrella to hit Turkey from the east.[64] The PKK would be in a good position to hit areas in Van, Kars, and Agri in southeast Turkey. The Turkish press reminded Iran of its obligation under the 1937 Sa'dabad Pact to prevent the Kurds from using Iranian territory as a staging ground for attacks on Turkey.[65] The Sa'dabad Pact, whose signatories included Iran, Iraq, Turkey, and Afghanistan, was a nonaggression treaty in which the parties agreed to refrain from interfering in each other's internal affairs, cooperate on security matters, and maintain the immunity and sanctity of their common borders.

Moreover, the Turkish press in January 1989 published the "confessions" of Emine Gerger, a female PKK activist who was awaiting trial at Diyarbakir, alleging that the Soviet Union was the mastermind of guerrilla operations in southeastern Turkey in a triangular alliance that involved Syria and the PKK.[66] Bulgaria, another neighbor of Turkey, was accused by some Turkish circles of aiding the PKK. The chairman of the Balkan Turkish Cultural Association stated that a thousand PKK militants masqueraded as Bulgarian Turks and infiltrated back into Turkey when the Turkish-Bulgarian border was opened to Bulgarian refugees of Turkish descent in 1989.[67] Turkish authorities also implicated some elements of the Greek military and intelligence in aiding the PKK. Isamil Sezgin, a former PKK member, allegedly informed Turkish authorities of a PKK training camp on the Greek island of Lavrion, and General Matafias, former commander of the Greek Cypriot National Guard, was identified as a trainer of PKK guerrillas in camps inside Syria.[68]

It is interesting to note that these accusations against the PKK were made precisely when the PKK had succeeded in establishing bases deep inside Turkey, and when Turkish military operations against Kurdish villages were at their height. By portraying the PKK as an organization without grass-roots support, the Turkish government hoped to alienate the local population from the *peshmergas* and undermine popular sympathy for them. However, it was evident that without some measure of popular support, the PKK would not have survived the onslaught of the Turkish armed forces. To many Kurds, the government's publication of reports based on the "confessions" of captured PKK activists was an implicit admission by the Ozal government that there was a Kurdish problem in Turkey. In fact, shortly after his victory in the presidential election of 1989, Turgut Ozal, in an unprecedented break with official dogma, recognized not only the ethnic conflict in Turkey but also modern Turkey's multicultural composition. In Ozal's words, the people of Turkey "come from many different origins as the remnants of an empire. A theory of a nation is more correct than one of races. . . . A country that does not think and is locked in by taboos cannot develop."[69]

Some analysts have attributed Ozal's dramatic admission of Turkey's multiethnicity to the government's inability to win the "hearts and minds" of the Kurdish people. For example, according to the mayor of Nusaybin, a sizable Kurdish town near the Syrian border that has been the scene of major antigovernment activities, an overwhelming number of people cooperate with the PKK because of the brutality of the Turkish special operations teams against the civilian population.[70] In Sirnak, a Kurdish town at the foot of the Cudi Mountains in southeastern Turkey, the most revered shrine is the grave of Zaydie, a sixteen-year-old female PKK fighter who was killed in the mid-1980s in a battle with Turkish forces. Kurdish parents bury their children close to Zaydie's grave believing that it is good luck to bury their children near a heroic figure; and women wishing to become pregnant routinely visit her graveside, leaving "flowers and little momentos, beseeching her spirit to bless them with children."[71]

In order to devise a new Kurdish policy that would have the support of the major political parties, President Ozal convened a special summit conference on April 2, 1990, with Erdal Inonu (the leader of the Social Democratic Populist Party), Suleyman Demirel (the head of the right-wing True Path Party), and Prime Minister Yildirim Akbulut (the leader of the Motherland Party). All participants agreed that immediate measures had to be adopted in order to "pacify" Kurdistan. President Ozal presided over an emergency cabinet meeting on April 9 to outline specific steps to be taken to contain the uprisings in the southeast. As will be explained, the governor of Diyarbakir was authorized to take any measure necessary to confront the PKK and its supporters, and severe restrictions were placed on media coverage of the uprisings in Kurdistan.

In July 1990, the opposition Social Democrats, who see themselves as the true heirs to Ataturk's political legacy, put Ozal on the defensive by calling for a policy that would allow the Kurds to speak their own language. In a major criticism of Turkey's language laws, the Social Democrats argued that the "legal mechanism which denies the realities of our country and of our age, has ignored the fact that the peoples of the world as well as our own people speak in their native languages as well as the official language."[72] This prompted negative reactions from the ruling Motherland Party and the other major opposition party, the True Path Party. Esat Kiratlioglu, a senior official of the True Path Party, insisted that there was no language problem in Turkey, and President Ozal stated that Turkey should have one official language.[73] Political rivals of the Social Democrats, as well as many Kurds, thought that the party's advocacy of Kurdish linguistic rights was opportunistic, designed to put it in position to win enough Kurdish votes to capture the majority in the Turkish National Assembly. In fact, a year earlier, the Social Democratics expelled from the party seven National Assembly deputies simply because they attended a conference on Kurdish cultural rights in France.

By 1991, issues relating to the recognition of Kurdish rights had become intertwined with Turkish interparty politics as the ruling and opposition parties vicd for Kurdish votes in the east and southeast. On January 24, 1991, President Ozal, in anticipation of legal changes in the status of the Kurdish language, passed a decree recognizing "languages that are not the primary language of countries with which Turkey has diplomatic relations."[74] After acrimonious debate on January 27, 1991, the Turkish cabinet decided to propose to the National Assembly the repeal of law number 2932, which had been enacted in 1985, banning the use of spoken and written Kurdish in all places. In defending his new position, President Ozal publicly stated that since "one out of six Turks is a Kurd,"[75] his government had to recognize the reality of Kurdish linguistic rights.

Segments of the Turkish press published articles in support of Ozal's proposed linguistic policy, arguing that it would not only help interethnic relations in the country, but would also improve Turkey's image in Europe and help it gain entry into the European Community (EC).[76] Ozal's rivals in the Social Democratic Populist Party and the True Path Party were quick to accuse him of exploiting the issue for political benefit. The Social Democrats' Erdal Inonu expressed satisfaction that Ozal embraced a policy originally recommended by his party but rejected by the ruling Motherland Party. Suleyman Demirel, former prime minister and the head of the conservative True Path Party, asked skeptically: "Are they [the government and the ruling party] going to authorize Kurdish in schools, on the radio and television? Are they going to authorize the use of Kurdish in the administration? It would be misguided, if such is not the case, to exploit this issue in this way."[77]

Much of the Turkish opposition, particularly intellectuals in the Kurdish community abroad, cautiously endorsed President Ozal's language reform proposal. However, Turkish Kurds also expressed distrust of the government's sincerity. Kendal Nezan, president of the Paris-based Kurdish Institute, in an interview with the Turkish magazine *Nokta*, expressed the sentiments of many Kurds when he said that President Ozal would be judged not by his words but by his deeds: "Ozal may figure in history either as a hero like [President] De Klerk who progressively phased out the apartheid system in South Africa, or as an incoherent and opportunistic politician who forgets his promises, and, once the danger has passed, gives in to conservative pressure. The attitude he adopts in the coming months will demonstrate which of the two he really is."[78]

Ozal's proposal also met with skepticism and criticism from the Turkish political right and from some members of his own ruling party. For example, *Tercuman*, an influential conservative newspaper, warned Ozal and the country that liberalization of the language policy would further politicize and radicalize the Kurds, encouraging them to make politically charged secessionist demands in the future.[79] This sentiment was echoed by some members of Ozal's party. Minister of State Cemil Cicek feared that once the language issue was resolved, the Kurds would ask to be given the status of a minority, and then demand either autonomy or statehood. A public opinion poll indicated that 47 percent of the Turks did not think that national unity would be hampered if Ozal's language policy was adopted, while 41 percent expressed the view that Turkish unity would be damaged if the proposal became law.[80]

President Ozal's proposal faced unexpected opposition in March 1991 in the National Assembly. Given the fact that the ruling Motherland Party had a solid majority in the National Assembly and that the Turkish Parliament had normally rubber-stamped Ozal's bills, opposition to the proposed language reform bill indicated deep divisions within the ruling circles over easing restrictions on the use of the Kurdish language. As one observer noted, the memory of the Ottoman Empire's dismemberment is very much alive in modern Turkey, and the Turks do not want to witness a second dismemberment of their country in the twentieth century.[81] Another source of opposition came from those who argued that the impact of Ozal's proposal would be minimal because the bill did not remove restrictions on publishing books or newspapers in Kurdish or teaching Kurdish in schools.[82]

HUMAN RIGHTS ISSUES AND
THE KURDISH STRUGGLE IN TURKEY

The Kurdish struggle in Turkey raises human rights issues as well as nationality issues. As has been the case in guerrilla wars elsewhere in the world, human rights abuses are committed by both sides. The Turkish government has condemned the PKK as a "terrorist" organization, whose victims are generally helpless Kurdish civilians. Although the government's condemnation was made to justify government policies, there is empirical evidence that politically motivated murders have been committed by PKK militants in recent years.

On November 24 and 25, 1989, PKK activists killed twenty-eight Kurdish civilians in the village of Ikikaya in Hakkari, including six women and thirteen children. On February 26, 1990, PKK guerrillas reportedly killed a former village headman, along with his wife and children, in the Silopi district in Mardin; and in mid-March, the PKK kidnapped and killed nine employees of a state-owned plant in Elazig.[83] PKK attacks on village guards, progovernment Kurdish armed militias, have also turned violent. In one particularly gruesome confrontation on June 10, 1990, the PKK forces reportedly killed twenty-six villagers; then they doused the homes of four village guards with gasoline and burned them to the ground while forcing the guards and their families to remain inside.[84] The PKK has consistently denied responsibility for civilian deaths in southeastern Turkey. In an interview with the Turkish newspaper *Hurriyet*, Abdullah Ocalan, the PKK's leader, reaffirmed his party's commitment to minimizing civilian casualties and his readiness to stop the fighting when the government expressed a desire to negotiate.[85] Ocalan's statement was particularly important because it was made in the midst of a major Kurdish uprising throughout the southeast.

The Kurdish *Serhildan* (Uprising) started on March 12, 1990, in the Mardin province in the district of Savur with an encounter between units of the Turkish army and the People's Liberation Army of Kurdistan (ARGK), the "regular army" of the PKK. According to Kurdish sources, more than forty Turkish soldiers and thirteen ARGK fighters were killed during this skirmish. The next day, an estimated six thousand Kurds attended the funerals of the ARGK fighters. As the crowd began to chant "long live the PKK" and "down with Turkish colonialism," the Turkish security forces intervened and clashed with the crowd. Thirty-three people were killed or injured, causing another confrontation with Turkish security forces the following day during the funeral procession for the latest victims.[86] The *Serhildan* spread to other areas in Kurdistan, and major strikes and boycotts of schools and government offices became an integral part of the uprising. The *Serhildan*, which continued through the early part of 1991, was the most serious challenge to Turkish authority in the southeast. Although security forces succeeded in containing the *Serhildan* by mid-1991, sporadic popular uprisings in the area have continued and may, once again, turn into massive *Serhildan*.

The Turkish government has always reacted very harshly and swiftly against any manifestation or promotion of Kurdish rights. Long prison sentences have been given to individuals who never participated in violent actions against the government, but who simply defended Kurdish rights in writings or speeches. The persecution of Dr. Ismail Besikci has become a cause célèbre, attracting international attention to Turkey's human rights abuses. Besikci, a Turkish sociologist, challenged the Kemalist myth about the Kurds in a book published in 1969 entitled *The Order of Eastern Anatolia: Socioeconomic and Ethnic Foundations*. Besikci offered a scathing criticism of Turkey's neglect of its southeastern provinces and analyzed the socioeconomic exploitation and political suppression of the Kurds. The government immediately accused him of being an "enemy" of the Turkish nation and a "communist" agent spreading Kurdish propaganda. Although no academic or scientific refutation of his research findings was offered by Turkish academics and social scientists, Besikci was summarily dismissed from his teaching position at Ataturk University in Erzurum. He was imprisoned in 1971, then released in 1974 when Prime Minister Ecevit declared a general amnesty for political prisoners.

Dr. Besikci published three more studies on the Kurds in Turkey before he was arrested again in 1979, on essentially the same charges that were levied against him a few years earlier. He was imprisoned for three years, released, then reimprisoned within two months. He had written a letter of thanks to the chairwoman of the Swiss Union of Writers and was charged with publishing "in a foreign country baseless and false information about the internal affairs of Turkey in such a way as to diminish the influence and prestige of the state."[87] Besikci was released in May 1987, but he was returned to prison in December 1988 because of an interview he gave to *Ozgur Gelecek* in which he defended Kurdish ethnic rights. He was released shortly thereafter, only to be rearrested in February 1990.

His 1990 arrest was for writing a new book, *Kurdistan: An Interstate Colony*. It is a historical analysis of the Turkish regions of Kurdistan, with detailed analyses of specific Turkish policies to "pacify" the Kurds and why they failed.[88] In a lengthy preliminary statement made to the trial judges on April 18, 1990, Besikci said:

> The Turkish state and its official ideology denies the existence of the Kurdish nation and the Kurdish language. The Kurds are considered to be a Turkish tribe, the Kurdish language a dialect of Turkish. In this way, sociological realities are denied by means of official ideology. Official ideology is not just any ideology. Official ideology implies legal sanction. Those who stray outside the boundaries of official ideology are shown the way to prison. The constraints of official ideology obstruct the development of science [scientific analysis]. This pressure paralyses thought and cripples and blunts minds. . . . I do not share the views expressed in [my] indictment, since these views are an expression of the official ideology and based on a lie and denial of truth. These things may exist in law but they are not legitimate. Whether it is five generals or 450 deputies that pass it makes no difference. Legislation denying the existence of the Kurdish nation, language and culture can have no legitimacy at all. In law, legitimacy is more important than legality.[89]

Ismail Besikci then defended his support for the establishment of a Kurdish state:

> The Kurds have lived in Kurdistan for 4,000 years, whereas the Turks started to move from Central Asia through Khorassan into Iran, Kurdistan, Iraq, Syria and Anatolia in the second half of the eleventh century. . . . They have lived on these lands for less than a thousand years. They have humiliated and degraded the original owners of these lands. . . . To wipe out the Kurdish nation, its language and its culture is barbaric. . . . The Turkish nation does not deserve to be known as the perpetrator of such barbarism. . . . I want to dwell a little upon the concept of "national pride." Wanting the Kurdish people to be free, wanting them to live in equal conditions with the Turkish people is taken to be propaganda undermining the national pride of the Turks. In fact, demanding equality for the Kurdish people, or the removal of bans on Kurdish language and culture, definitely cannot undermine the national pride of the Turks. On the contrary, it would strengthen it since defense of human rights and freedoms strengthens national feelings.[90]

The international publicity given to Ismail Besikci, including his adoption as a "prisoner of conscience" by the human rights organization Amnesty International, has certainly been responsible for his life's being spared. However, international publicity has not deterred the prison authorities from torturing Besikci. As Helsinki Watch, Amnesty International, the Initiative for Human Rights in Kurdistan (a German-based human rights group), and other independent international human rights sources have documented, torture is used extensively on the Kurds in Turkish detention centers and police stations.[91] Any individual accused of aiding Kurdish guerrillas, including medical personnel and defense lawyers, is subject to arrest. For example, Dr. Abdullah Bolca, a medical doctor and director of Cizre Hospital in the Mardin province, was arrested in September 1989 for treating a patient whom the police believed to be a member of the PKK. Dr. Bolca was tortured for fifteen days before being released. He was then dismissed from his position and sent to Yozgat in western Turkey. Upon release from detention, Bolca was quoted as saying: "I have no relations with the PKK. My duty as a doctor is to give medical care to whoever is in need. I cannot know if the patient is a terrorist or not. Furthermore, I am not obliged to verify it; it is not my duty."[92]

Another means of suppressing Kurdish ethnic identity has been the large-scale deportation of people from their ancestral villages. The legal foundation for deportation was laid down in Law No. 2510, promulgated in June 1934. According to this law, a person whose mother tongue is not Turkish may be resettled for military, political, cultural, or security reasons if the Ministry of Interior deems it necessary for the good of the country. Since the mid-1980s, deportation of Kurdish villagers, and resettlement in western Turkey, has been reported with regularity by outside observers and by the Turkish press.[93] Many of the depopulated villages have been located along Turkey's borders with Iran and Iraq, where depopulation is ostensibly carried out for security reasons and for preventing contact between Kurds in Turkey and Kurds in neighboring countries. It is impossible to determine the number of people who have been deported to other areas of the country. Upwards of several thousand people have been deported at any given time, and in one instance, thirty-two villages in Hakkari, with a total population of 10,600, were earmarked for depopulation in early 1990.[94] Many deportees have complained that the military authorities did not inform them in advance of the government's decision to evacuate their villages. They have also complained that they were forced to sign blank forms that were later found to be evacuation orders. When they protested, they were told that their villages had to be burned down for security reasons.[95]

Deportation can be used for punishment as well as for military-security reasons. In one instance, Turkish military authorities deported nine Kurds from their homeland in Tunceli for being involved in "damaging behavior" toward the state. The overwhelming majority of these punitive deportations are done without court orders, and deportees are given only forty-eight hours to leave their homes. In addition, they are charged for travel-related expenses incurred moving them to western Turkey. Punitive deportation might last a few months or be permanent.[96]

The Turkish government has bolstered its position vis-à-vis the Kurdish guerrillas by recruiting Kurdish peasants into progovernment armed militias and paying them regular stipends. By mid-1990, the government had recruited 21,480 "village guards" and organized them into units assisting the Turkish military and local police units.[97] Village guards have been targeted for assassination by the PKK because they are considered collaborators with the "colonial regime." Financial considerations undoubtedly play a part in their deciding to join the village guard, given the depressed state of the Kurdish economy and the high level of unemployment that in some areas of the southeast reaches 50 percent. Sentiments against the PKK, and its use of violent tactics in confronting the Turkish military, may also compel some Kurdish peasants to join the village guards in order to bring tranquility to their lives. In May 1988, Mostafa Kalemi, the minister of interior, stated that membership in the village guards was purely voluntary. In Kalemi's words, the Turkish government never forced anyone to "register as a village guard. We have only volunteers, patriots who are against the separatists."[98]

Independent human rights organizations have collected evidence that contradicts Kalemi's claim. An investigation conducted by Helsinki Watch in May 1990 in the town of Siirt and surrounding villages uncovered numerous examples of Kurdish peasants who had been forced to leave their homes because they refused to join the village guards.[99] Amnesty International, in an "Urgent Action" communiqué released in January 1990, reported on the widespread use of intimidation as a means to recruit village guards. The communiqué also reported that in Cukurca in Hakkari province village guards who turned in their arms and terminated their employment were invariably arrested and subjected to ill-treatment and torture for sympathizing with the PKK and harboring separatist ideas. The Turkish press has also published accounts of torture. The daily *Hurriyet* gave an extensive account of the mistreatment of Ismail Keskin, a Kurdish peasant who was tortured by the army at its headquarters in Hakkari for refusing to become a village guard.[100] The weekly *Tempo* quoted a member of the Turkish National Assembly from Kars who gave a speech in Parliament concerning the government's placement of mines in several villages in Cukurca to punish villagers for refusing to take part in the village guard system.[101] The abolition of the village guard system remains a major demand of Kurdish nationalists and human rights organizations.

A new and all-encompassing legal instrument to combat Kurdish nationalism was devised by the Turkish government. Decree 413, which was issued by the Council of Ministers on April 9, 1990, gave Hayri Kozakcioglu, governor general of the ten southeastern provinces under a state of emergency, carte blanche to deal with the Kurdish uprising. Decree 413 allows the governor general to:

- censor the press by banning, confiscating, and heavily fining publications that "wrongly represent incidents occurring in a region which is under a state of emergency, disturbing its readers with distorted news stories or commentaries, causing anxiety among people in the region and obstructing security forces in the performance of their jobs";
- shut down printing plants that print such publications;
- exile to other parts of Turkey people who "act against the state," the

relocation sites to be chosen by the Ministry of the Interior;

- control or prohibit all union activities, including strikes and lockouts; prevent boycotts, slow-downs, and the closing down of workplaces;
- require State Security Court Public Prosecutors to open cases against people who violate Decree 413;
- evacuate villages "for security reasons" without prior notice; [and]
- transfer "harmful" state employees.[102]

Decree 413 legalized other restrictive measures. The Ministry of Interior and the National Security Council were given the authority to control all radio and television broadcasts from the Kurdish provinces under the state of emergency. Existing penalties under the Turkish penal code for disseminating information that would be injurious to the president, Parliament, judges, cabinet ministers, and other high-level government functionaries were supplemented with additional fines. Thus, if a publication violated Decree 413, not only could the editor receive up to three years in prison, he/she could also be fined up to $40,000. On May 9, 1990, the Council of Ministers gave the governor general of the Kurdish provinces the power to dismiss any judge, prosecutor, or military officer working in the area under his jurisdiction.[103] For all practical purposes, the governor general became unaccountable for his actions, a power the president of the Republic does not possess.

Decree 413 severely curtailed reporting from Kurdish regions. Editors who published stories without the approval of the governor general ran the risk of being imprisoned and having their publications suspended by the government. The left-of-center press was hit particularly hard because the police warned printing houses not to publish certain newspapers and magazines. *2000'e Dogru* (Toward 2000), one of the country's most influential and most-read publications, reported extensively on Kurdish issues. It was forced to cease publication four days after the issuance of Decree 413 when it lost its contract with its printing house; the printer feared that its operations would be shut down if it did not cancel *2000'e Dogru*'s contract. Self-censorship, as well as official censorship, became the order of the day. Foreign press reporting was also restricted. It was only after the massive influx of Kurdish refugees from Iraq in the aftermath of the Gulf War that foreign correspondents were allowed to report from southeastern Turkey. Even then, coverage was limited to the influx of refugees and did not generally include reports on the condition of Turkish Kurds.

The condition of Kurdish refugees in Turkey must also be discussed as a human rights issue. Since the late 1980s, two major waves of Kurdish refugees have entered Turkey from Iraq. The first wave came in 1988, after Iraq used chemical weapons against its Kurdish population during the Iran-Iraq War. The second wave of refugees entered Turkey after Saddam Hussein's attacks on the Kurds in the aftermath of uprisings against his regime in March and April 1991 (see Chapter 5). Although the international community took steps to help Kurdish refugees and aid in their repatriation after the 1991 wave, the 1988 refugees did not receive much international attention. They received little assistance and were left to the mercy of Turkish authorities and Iraqi intelligence operatives, who managed to infiltrate the refugee camps.

Due to the lack of an international registry for Kurdish refugees, it is difficult to ascertain the number of refugees who fled Iraq for Turkey in 1988. On September 6, Turkish Foreign Minister Mesut Yilmaz declared the number of Kurdish refugees to be 63,000. The next day, he adjusted the number to 53,377, while Interior Ministry officials estimated 120,000.[104] By late September, official government figures put the total number of Iraqi Kurdish refugees in Turkish camps at 48,500.[105] Originally, the refugees were placed in five tent camps, located in Diyarbakir, Hakkari, and Mardin. However, by late 1988, all Kurdish refugees were quartered in three camps—one at Diyarbakir, the second near the district town of Mus, and the third at Kiziltepe, some eight miles south of the provincial capital of Mardin.

The refugee camp at Mus, the smallest and most isolated of the three camps set up to house Iraqi Kurdish refugees, housed eighty-five hundred refugees in barracks constructed ten years earlier as temporary quarters for earthquake victims from the town of Varto. According to a study conducted by technical experts from two Turkish universities, the barracks at Mus were unfit for human habitation.[106] The frigid winters made living conditions in these primitive barracks very difficult. The high level of child mortality at Mus was indicative of its uninhabitable condition. According to a March 1989 report by Medico International, a German medical relief organization active among refugee groups, nearly three hundred children died because of the cold climate and shortage of heating fuel at Mus.

The living quarters in Mus resembled prison units, with each unit measuring sixty-five square meters and housing twenty to twenty-five refugees. The movement of the refugees was strictly controlled. With the exception of a few who were allowed to leave camp for a few hours each day, refugees at Mus were not permitted to leave the compound.[107] Conditions at the camp near Diyarbakir were somewhat better than at Mus, but they were still degrading. This camp housed over eleven thousand refugees in cement block apartments that were designed to accommodate four thousand. Thirty to thirty-five refugees crowded into a space measuring sixty square meters with "intermittent electricity and unclean water."[108]

Kiziltepe, the largest and most controversial camp, housed about twelve-thousand refugees in two thousand tents. They were still living in tents more than two years after their arrival in Turkey. The tents did not protect the refugees from the freezing winter cold or the blistering summer heat. Disease and cold weather killed several hundred people, many of whom were children. When international donor agencies offered the Turkish government $14 million in 1990 to relocate the refugees from their tents to more permanent quarters, the government decided to move them to a site in Yozgat province east of Ankara. However, the government unexpectedly canceled this plan because of "local community opposition."[109] In December 1990, the Federal Republic of Germany donated DM 1 million to the Turkish government to purchase weatherproof tents to protect refugees at the Kiziltepe camp from exposure to extreme weather conditions. Nevertheless, living conditions remained appalling at the camp.[110]

Aside from humanitarian issues, the Kurdish refugee problem in Turkey raised some legal issues. The major issue concerned the government's unwillingness to extend legal protection to the refugees. As Amnesty International reported, the absence of legal protection placed the Kurdish refugees at risk of *refoulement* (a legal term referring to the forcible extradition of an individual to a country where he/she may be subjected to human rights violations, including torture and execution).[111] *Refoulement* violates internationally recognized human rights standards. Turkey is a party to the 1951 Geneva Convention on Refugees and has acceded to its 1967 Protocol, but Turkey's accession to the Geneva Convention carries a geographic stipulation in that Turkey has agreed to confer refugee status only on individuals from Europe. Kurdish refugees from Iraq are not considered refugees by Turkey but are "temporary guests." Thus, the Turkish government has only allowed the construction of "temporary shelters" for its "temporary guests."[112] Under this Turkish practice, the Kurdish refugees were denied internationally recognized rights as refugees.

Although the geographic stipulation under the 1951 Geneva Convention and its 1967 Protocol allows Turkey to classify as refugees only those who have fled from Europe, the country is obligated to adhere to the concept of non*refoulement* as a recognized principle of public international law. That is, all nation-states must respect the principle of non*refoulement* regardless of "their specific treaty obligations or of the country of origin of the refugees concerned."[113] Turkey, however, has insisted on adhering to a strict interpretation of its treaty rights with respect to Kurdish refugees, although Turkish authorities have reaffirmed their country's commitment to taking a humanitarian approach to these refugees. Specifically, the Turkish government has insisted that no one was repatriated or extradited to Iraq without his/her consent.

Despite Turkish denials, there have been numerous instances of forced repatriation of Kurdish refugees to Iraq. Amnesty International reported that between March and early June 1990, some 2,548 refugees were sent to Iraq under the terms of a general amnesty announced on March 10 by the Iraqi government. Most of the returnees (1,923) were from the Mus camp, where abject living conditions may have contributed to the decision to return to Iraq. There were, however, many instances where threats, intimidation, beatings, and imprisonment by the Turkish authorities were the primary cause of repatriation.[114]

Repatriation of Kurdish refugees to Iraq was conducted without the involvement of the International Committee of the Red Cross (ICRC), which is the customary practice. Although the Turkish government agreed in September 1988 to allow the ICRC to register the refugees and supervise their return, it balked after the Iraqi government told the ICRC that the Kurdish refugees were an internal matter between the two governments, and that because Iraq and Turkey "enjoyed diplomatic relations, all repatriation would be handled on a bilateral basis, thereby making the involvement of a third party unnecessary."[115] What made the issue of repatriation most disturbing were the consistent reports of abuses committed against returnees by the Iraqi authorities. As will be discussed in Chapter 5, the conditions created after Iraq's defeat in the Gulf War, and the influx of Kurdish refugees into Turkey that followed, resulted in some international supervision of refugee conditions in Turkey. However, any lasting improvements will have to originate from within the Turkish government, and from changes in its domestic laws and regulations dealing with the long-festering Kurdish dilemma.

5

INTERNATIONAL AND REGIONAL CONTEXT OF KURDISH NATIONALISM

In the previous chapters, I discussed international and regional variables that shaped Kurdish politics and affected the status of the Kurds in the twentieth century. I will now examine three regional factors in particular that have impacted Kurdish conditions—Iran-Iraq relations during Shah Mohammad Reza Pahlavi's reign, the Iran-Iraq War of 1980–1988, and the 1991 Gulf War.

IRAN-IRAQ RELATIONS AND GULF SECURITY

Since the seventh-century defeat of Iran by the Arabs, ethnic and religious differences have created tensions in Iranian-Arab relations. Although Iranians adopted Islam, they resisted Arabization and retained cultural and ethnic distinctiveness. Two centuries after the Arab invasion, for example, Iran experienced a major literary, cultural, and sociopolitical revival that strained Iranian-Arab relations. They became particularly strained when the Arabs "forgot Islam's universalist and egalitarian dimensions, viewed its Arab origins as proof of their racial superiority, and discriminated against non-Arab converts."[1] The Iranians' conversion to Shi'a Islam in the sixteenth century further alienated Iran from the predominantly Sunni Arabs.

In the Middle East in the twentieth century, the largely sociocultural conflict between Iranians and Arabs acquired a political dimension as well. As the Ottoman Empire disintegrated and independent, and eventually sovereign, Arab states emerged, Iranian and Arab nationalism began to clash, especially with the growth of pan-Arab nationalism in the Middle East. Pan-Arabists sought to unite all Arabs and encouraged the secession of Arab areas in other countries so they could be part of a unified Arab nation. Iran was considered an obstacle to the realization of Arab unity because the nation some pan-Arabists sought to create included the oil-rich Iranian province of Khuzistan.

The gulf between Iran and the proponents of pan-Arabism widened after the overthrow of Egypt's pro-Western monarchy in 1952 and the emergence of Gamal Abdul Nasser as the champion of Arab nationalism. The new leader's promotion of pan-Arabism projected Egypt into the forefront of Arab politics as the torchbearer of anti-European and anti-imperialist struggles.

With respect to the Gulf, Nasser's bête noire was British military and political presence, especially its domination of its client state of Iraq. Thus, the downfall of the nationalist government of Dr. Mohammad Mossadegh in Iran in a British-US-sponsored coup in 1953, and the pro-Western Shah's accession to the throne, heightened Nasser's fear of Western encirclement of his pan-Arab regime.

After the restoration of the Shah to the Pahlavi throne, the United States "encouraged Iran to establish a variety of formal and informal security arrangements with other US allies in the region in the decades after the 1953 coup."[2] While Dr. Mossadegh had avoided joining either the Soviet or Western camp and wanted to maintain good relations with Arab nationalists, given the Shah's urgent need for Western support to shore up his regime, his fear of Soviet-supported instability, and his apprehension about the impact of radical pan-Arabism, he was very receptive to the idea of joining a Western security alliance. The Shah was particularly attracted to a proposal first espoused by the US secretary of state, John Foster Dulles, to establish an alliance of "Northern Tier" states, including Iran, Turkey, and Pakistan. This proposed security arrangement was designed to allow the "Northern Tier" countries to defend themselves, with US assistance, against the spread of Soviet communism and to prevent "contamination" of Arab nationalism with communist ideology.[3] Great Britain, however, opposed a regional alliance system that did not include its client state of Iraq. The United States, on the other hand, did not wish to offend Egypt and other Arab nationalist forces by including the monarchical Iraq in such an alliance because the Hashemite monarchy was viewed by Arab nationalists as an appendage of British imperialism. Thus, President Dwight Eisenhower was leery of including Iraq in a US-supported security arrangement.

Although Dulles's proposed alliance did not materialize, Great Britain succeeded in establishing a regional security system. In February 1955, Britain pressured Iraq into signing a mutual defense agreement, the Baghdad Pact, with Turkey. There were indications that Pakistan was also being pressured by Britain to join the alliance, which it did in September 1955. After receiving the endorsement of Washington, Iran joined the Baghdad Pact in October. Although the United States did not formally join, it became a driving force behind the Baghdad Pact by becoming a major provider of military aid and equipment to the members of the alliance.[4]

As Mark Gasiorowski noted, the Baghdad Pact was "beset with problems from its inception."[5] President Nasser was disturbed by Iraq's decision to join a pro-Western alliance under the tutelage of Great Britain, whose colonial policies had made it anathema to Arab nationalists. As a result, Egypt initiated a policy to destabilize the Iraqi monarchy and turned to the Soviet bloc countries for arms purchases, after being spurned by the West. Nasser's first purchase was from Czechoslovakia in 1955 to counter what he considered to be growing Western encirclement meant to isolate Egypt in the region. The Shah, in turn, viewed the emerging Moscow-Cairo ties as a threat to Iran's security interests. Thus began the era of the Nasser-Shah cold war.[6]

A number of tactics were used by Nasser against the Shah. One tactic, which infuriated the Shah and injured Iran's sense of nationalism, was Cairo's continuous reference to the "Arabian Gulf" and the "occupied south" when referring to the Gulf and Khuzistan, respectively.[7] Although Nasser had some success in convincing Arabs to ignore the historical name of the region, he was less successful in destabilizing the Shah's regime or gaining a permanent foothold in the Gulf region. Another tactic used by Nasser to heighten Persian-Arab tensions was to draw a parallel between "Iranian immigration to the Gulf states and the Zionists' earlier immigration to Palestine."[8]

Nasser's pan-Arabism did not generate much enthusiasm among conservative Arab regimes in the Gulf, but it did strike a familiar chord with the antimonarchical and anti-British forces that were operating in Iraq. When these forces managed to overthrow the Hashemite monarchy in Iraq in July 1958, the Baghdad Pact was dealt a major blow. The new republican regime in Iraq boycotted meetings of the Baghdad Pact and then formally withdrew in March 1959. The remaining members transferred their membership to a successor alliance, the Central Treaty Organization (CENTO), with new headquarters in Ankara.

Iran's membership in the Baghdad Pact was never popular with the Iranian people, who considered the Shah's regime to be a Western client with no popular legitimacy. However, the Shah was adamant in his decision to remain an active member of the Baghdad Pact, both as a deterrent to a Soviet threat and as insurance against internal upheavals against his regime. After the violent overthrow of the Iraqi monarchy, the Shah's determination to remain a CENTO member became even more pronounced. At the same time, the Shah knew that Iran's membership in CENTO did not automatically oblige the West to intervene on its behalf in case of foreign aggression. Therefore, he pressed for a bilateral defense agreement with the United States, which was signed in March 1959. Under the terms of this agreement, in the case of aggression against Iran, the United States would take appropriate measures to defend Iran, including the use of armed forces if mutually agreed upon.[9]

Iran's CENTO membership continued to heighten Iranian-Egyptian tensions, as well as contribute to the rapid deterioration in Iran's relations with the "radical" regime of Abdul Karim Ghassem in Baghdad. When diplomatic relations between Cairo and Tehran were finally broken in the summer of 1960, President Nasser accelerated public attacks on Iran's pro-Western posture and coordinated these attacks with similar ones emanating from Baghdad. The Shah sought to counter these moves by improving Iran's relations with the conservative Arab states of the Gulf, which felt threatened by Nasser's radical pan-Arabism and Ghassem's support for the goals of Egyptian foreign policy.[10]

Notwithstanding Egyptian and Iraqi fears of encirclement by Western countries and their regional clients, CENTO never developed into an integrated alliance system. More than a decade after its formation, the organization was still unable to draft a contingency plan for conducting limited wars or establishing a joint military command structure. Although US policymakers reportedly developed a plan to use tactical nuclear weapons in the region in the event of a war with the Soviet Union, the planning was done outside of the CENTO framework, and perhaps unbeknownst to the member countries. Furthermore, joint military exercises that were conducted under CENTO's auspices were marginal and did not contribute to the war-fighting or defense capabilities of the member states.[11] CENTO's countersubversion committee did little to develop cooperative schemes in combating internal challenges to member states. The regional members of CENTO, however, did occasionally aid each other in the suppression of tribal uprisings, but such cooperative actions were undertaken under bilateral agreements.[12] Although CENTO continued to function until 1979, when Iran and Pakistan withdrew, it had lost its effectiveness as a military alliance system by the late 1960s. Nevertheless, it remained politically important and continued to create friction in Iran-Iraq relations until the overthrow of the Shah's regime.

Until the overthrow of the Iraqi monarchy, the Kurdish card had not been played by either Iran or Iraq against each other. Although occasional Kurdish cross-border raids and hot pursuits had caused the two sides to protest violations of each other's territorial integrity, both Iran and Iraq, as well as Turkey, sought to enforce the terms of the 1937 Sa'dabad Pact. After the advent of republican Iraq in 1958 and the coming to power of a "pan-Arab nationalist" group, however, playing the Kurdish card became an attractive political and military weapon against the Shah's government.

Shortly after coming to power, Abdul Karim Ghassem declared the 1937 pact between Iran and Iraq, which had demarcated the boundary between the two countries and outlined their sovereignty rights in the Shatt al-Arab, to be invalid. Ghassem then laid claim to the entire waterway, and in 1959, he ordered Iraqi troops to block Iranian oil tankers from using the Shatt al-Arab. As discussed in Chapter 3, Ghassem also endeavored to settle the Kurdish problem by initiating peace talks with Mullah Mostafa Barzani. As a "goodwill gesture," Ghassem even provided Mullah Mostafa with weapons and allowed his *peshmergas* to use Iraqi territory to launch attacks inside Iran. Mullah Mostafa's forays into Iran were militarily insignificant and only resulted in minor disturbances in border towns such as Marivan and Baneh. However, by playing his Kurdish card against the Shah's government, Ghassem opened up a Pandora's box, and perhaps contributed to the shaping of the Shah's strategic calculus with respect to the Kurds. In fact, Ghassem's tactic of using Mullah Mostafa to destabilize the Shah's regime backfired against Iraq as the Shah, in conjunction with Israel and the United States, co-opted Mullah Mostafa into a scheme to destabilize the Iraqi government in the early 1970s.

Iran's security relationship with Israel in the post-1953 period became important for both countries. In fact, with the exception of its bilateral security ties with the United States, no other country managed to forge as close a security relationship with the Shah's regime as Israel.[13] Although the genesis of Iran's relationship with Israel dated back to 1950 when the Shah's regime extended de facto recognition to the Jewish state, military and security relations between the two countries were cemented in 1960, when the first team of Israeli intelligence officers arrived in Tehran to train both military and secret police operatives in Iran.

The military intelligence axis soon developed into the most important aspect of Iranian-Israeli relations. Israel's intelligence network, Mossad, and Iran's secret police/security organization, *Sazeman-e Ettela'at va Amniyat-e Keshvar* (Organization of Information and State Security—SAVAK), collaborated for nearly a quarter of a century. Their cooperation ranged from exchanging information and providing training for SAVAK officials, both in Iran and Israel, to providing funds and weaponry to the Kurdish forces in Iraq in the 1970s. Iran's economic relations with Israel were also quite extensive. By the mid-1970s, Israeli exports to Iran were worth over $70 million per year, and Iran had become the principal supplier of petroleum to Israel.[14] According to one account, a secret clause in the Egyptian-Israeli disengagement treaty of September 1975 stipulated that Iran would undertake appropriate measures to satisfy Israel's future petroleum needs after Egypt regained control of the oilfields of Sinai.[15]

Both Israel and Iran had pragmatic reasons for forging an informal alliance against Iraq and other Arab "radicals" and proponents of pan-Arabism. According to a CIA report, a principal goal of Israeli foreign policy was the development of pragmatic relationships with the non-Arab Muslim nations of the Middle East. The report described the formation in 1958 of a formal trilateral arrangement involving the Israeli Mossad, the Turkish intelligence service, and Iran's SAVAK. The main purpose of this arrangement was to develop an anti-Arab policy among the high-level officials in Ankara and Tehran.[16] With respect to Iran, development of an anti-Arab posture was aided by Israel's transmission of intelligence reports on issues affecting Iran, including developments in Iraq and Egypt, and assistance for the Shah's government in its support of the Kurdish uprising in Iraq.[17]

The CIA report, in effect, was a brief summary of the Periphery Doctrine in Israeli foreign policy, which had been promoted by Prime Minister David Ben Gurion. This doctrine entailed the formation of a "peripheral pact" involving a "bloc of states situated on the periphery of the Middle East, and connected to Israel in a triangle, with Turkey and Iran in the north, and

Ethiopia in the south."[18] The common denominator among these countries was their anti-Sovietism and fear of radical Arab nationalism. An underlying motivation for this arrangement was to promote the Israeli view of the importance of non-Arab elements in the Middle Eastern political scene, a view that was appealing to the Shah of Iran. As Ben Gurion stated: "The Middle East is not an exclusively Arab area; on the contrary, the majority of its inhabitants are not Arabs. The Turks, the Persians and the Jews—without taking into account the Kurds and the other non-Arab minorities—are more numerous than the Arabs in the Middle East."[19] As the Shah indicated to Uri Lubrani, Israel's chief diplomat in Tehran, one of the chief reasons for his country's alliance with Israel was that the Jewish state served as a deterrent to an Iraqi or other Arab attack on Iran. "From the Shah's perspective, Iran's alliance with Israel would serve as a strategic decoy in order to divert Arab attention and resources away from Iran. The Shah believed that his Israeli connection would provide a deterrence to Arab regimes because it would create the impression that if an Arab state were to attack Iran, Israel would take advantage of this pretext to strike Iraq's western flank."[20]

Although the Shah's perception of Israel's reaction to a possible Iraqi attack on Iran may have been different from that of the Israeli decisionmakers, both Israel and Iran concurred on the desirability of using the Kurds to keep the Iraqi forces preoccupied with internal challenges, thus preventing them from exerting pressure on Israel's eastern flank and Iran's border regions. The first concrete Israeli-Iranian cooperation on the Kurdish issue occurred in the early 1960s when SAVAK officials acted as intermediaries between Mullah Mostafa and Israeli military and intelligence officers. The Iranians arranged a meeting between Mullah Mostafa and an Israeli delegation headed by the chief of staff, Lieutenant General Tsvi Tsur. After being driven to the town of Piranshahr on the Iraqi border, the Israeli officials changed into Kurdish costumes and walked across the border into Iraqi Kurdistan. Once inside Iraq, the delegation held talks with Mullah Mostafa and promised to provide weapons and training for his forces that would enable them to conduct a full-scale offensive against Iraqi forces.

Beginning in 1963, Israel started to channel large-scale military aid through the Shah's SAVAK to Mullah Mostafa's forces. Israeli military advisers accompanied the arms shipments to the Kurds, and in August 1965, they set up permanent training camps in the Kurdish mountains to train soldiers.[21] After the June 1967 Arab-Israeli war, the number of Israeli weapons shipments to the Kurds increased dramatically as Mullah Mostafa was supplied with Soviet weaponry captured from the Syrian and Egyptian armies during the war. In pursuit of further military assistance, Mullah Mostafa visited Israel in September 1967, resulting in an Israeli commitment of $50,000 a month to his forces.[22]

An evaluation by the US government's National Foreign Assessment Center regarding the success of Israeli-Iranian involvement in Kurdistan concluded that despite several major Iraqi offensives against the Kurds, Mullah Mostafa's forces were able to withstand the onslaught of Iraqi military actions. The report attributed their success both to the level of Israeli-Iranian military assistance to the Kurds and to the Shah's policy of allowing Iranian territory to be used as a supply route and sanctuary for Kurdish forces. The report further concluded that the Shah was not worried about the spill-over effects that the success of Mullah Mostafa's movement would have on his own Kurdish areas. The Shah argued that there was no real danger of an uprising among Iranian Kurds and that he could afford to play his Kurdish card against the Iraqi regime with impunity.[23]

Israeli-Iranian cooperation was conducted in utmost secrecy. However, in September 1972, US syndicated columnist Jack Anderson reported on the monthly Israeli cash subsidy of $50,000 and the Shah's role in this affair. Anderson's report, which was based on a CIA analysis of the situation in Kurdistan, also stated that Iranian and Israeli motives in supporting the Kurdish uprising in Iraq were based on their mutual desire to keep the Iraqi regime embroiled in an internal conflict.[24] Israeli-Iranian involvement in Kurdish affairs was hotly contested by the parties involved. In an interview given in 1976, Mullah Mostafa contended that he never accepted a monthly stipend of $50,000 from the Israelis because in his view the future of the Kurdish cause was closely tied to the fortunes of the "Arab, Turkish, and Iranian people. What happens to them happens to us."[25] However, Israeli prime minister Menachem Begin admitted that Israel provided Mullah Mostafa with money, arms, and military advisers to sustain his fight against the Iraqi regime.[26]

The role played by the United States in bolstering the Kurdish uprising in Iraq during the 1970s is worth noting. During the 1960s, Mullah Mostafa appealed for support for the Kurdish revolt from a variety of sources. When he approached US authorities in the early 1960s, they did not respond favorably.[27] However, when the second Ba'thi regime came to power in Baghdad in 1968, with its radical rhetoric of pan-Arabism and anti-imperialism, the United States revised its position. Like its two regional allies, Iran and Israel, US authorities began to view the Kurds as a strategic asset to be used in keeping the Iraqi regime at bay. Edmund Ghareeb, quoting a report that appeared in *Al-Ahad*, a pro-Iraqi Lebanese publication, contended that the first US overtures toward Mullah Mostafa occurred in August 1969. According to this report, two US military officers attached to CENTO flew to his headquarters and conducted an extensive discussion, leading to the signing of a secret agreement through which Mullah Mostafa received $14 million from the United States.[28]

The secret agreement outlined the expectations of each side and contained a number of specific points. What follows are some of the highlights of this agreement:

- The subject of US aid must be kept secret from all, including high-ranking members within the Kurdish movement.
- The aim of insurgency was to overthrow the Baath regime.
- The Kurdish movement must not cause any harm to Iran in the future, particularly by supporting Iranian Kurds. In return, the Iranian government would not take any actions hostile to the Kurdish movement.
- Doors would be closed to communists seeking to join the movement; the Kurdish movement must not protect them.
- All Soviet aid offers must be rejected and the United States immediately notified of such offers.
- The United States government considered Barzani the man responsible for the movement and would accept only his objections.[29]

Although the United States denied the existence of the agreement, it soon became clear that the CIA was heavily involved with the Kurdish uprising in the first half of the 1970s.

The details of US involvement in the Kurdish uprising became known during the Pike House Committee hearings (the Pike Report), portions of which were published in the *Village Voice*. According to the Pike Report, when the Shah of Iran met with President Nixon and his secretary of state, Henry Kissinger, in May 1972, he asked them to join Iran in supporting the Kurdish revolt in Iraq. Although the United States had refrained from getting involved in Kurdish affairs, Nixon and Kissinger found the Shah's offer appealing. Consequently, in May 1972, President Nixon approved a plan for the CIA to secretly channel $16 million to Mullah Mostafa over the next three years.[30] Both President Nixon and Henry Kissinger sought to keep this arrangement secret. Even the US State Department was kept in the dark with respect to the evolving CIA–Mullah Mostafa ties.[31]

The question arises: Why did the United States reverse its position against getting closely entangled with the Kurdish uprising in Iraq? One explanation is that both the Shah of Iran and Israel finally succeeded in enticing the United States to help Mullah Mostafa's movement. Although there may be some evidence to support this contention, the timing of the US policy shift needs to be analyzed within the context of changes in Iraqi politics.

By early 1972, the Ba'th Party of Iraq had concluded that closer ties with the Soviet Union would help counter Iranian pressure and, by implication, make it costly for the Shah to play his Kurdish card against Iraq.

> There was little ideology in this decision. Despite the secular socialism advocated by the Ba'th, Saddam [Hussein] had never been a serious student of Marxism-Leninism, and his perception of the Soviet Union had always been purely instrumental. For him, Moscow offered the

> possibility of resolving several conflicts at once. It was an important
> counterweight to the Iranian threat. . . . As long as Iran feared its large
> neighbor to the north, it could not threaten its smaller neighbors. . . .
> The creation of a Soviet-Iraqi axis, Saddam reasoned, was bound to bring
> the Shah back to his senses.[32]

Furthermore, formal Soviet-Iraqi cooperation would allow Baghdad to import major weapons from the Soviet Union and enable the Ba'thi regime to increase its deterrent power against the Shah's regime. Because of the long-established links between Mullah Mostafa and the Soviet Union, the Ba'th argued, closer Iraqi-Soviet ties would also allow Moscow to act as an intermediary between Baghdad and Mullah Mostafa to settle the Kurdish dispute.

An equally compelling reason for Saddam Hussein's overtures to Moscow during the spring of 1972 was to gain support for the Ba'th Party's decision to nationalize the Iraqi Petroleum Company (IPC). Many radical and nationalist elements within the Ba'th were demanding that Iraq lay the foundation for its future economic independence by taking steps to control its own resources, especially its vast petroleum reserves. The Ba'thi leadership was also aware that its ambitious socioeconomic development plans for the country could not be satisfactorily implemented without a major shift in the country's oil policies. It was within this context that the IPC was finally nationalized on June 1, 1972.

Prior to formal nationalization of the IPC, the Ba'thi government succeeded in signing a cooperation agreement with the Soviet Union. The Iraqi-Soviet Treaty of Cooperation and Friendship, which was signed in April 1972, marked the second time that the Soviets had signed such a treaty with a Middle Eastern country. The first time was a similar treaty with Egypt that had been signed at Moscow's behest at a time when Egyptian-Soviet relations were exhibiting signs of strain. The treaty with Iraq, on the other hand, was signed at the urging of Baghdad in order to provide, among other things, the psychological and political shield that Iraq needed to proceed with nationalization of its petroleum resources. The Ba'thi government was well aware of the British-US coup that was organized in Iran after that country's petroleum resources were nationalized by Dr. Mossadegh's government in 1953.

Despite the fanfare and radical rhetoric that preceded nationalization of the IPC, the act itself had no more than symbolic value; it did not alter Iraq's dependence on Western oil companies.[33] For example, Compagnie Française des Pétroles (CFP), the French company participating in the IPC, was offered "special treatment" in the postnationalization era, and Saddam Hussein agreed to sell France 23.75 percent of the oil produced by the Iraqi Company for Oil Operations (ICOO), as the nationalized IPC was now called. This represented the CFP's share in the old IPC.[34]

Both the signing of the friendship treaty with the Soviet Union and the impending nationalization of the IPC were instrumental in alerting the Nixon-Kissinger team to the possible danger of increased Soviet influence in the region, and led to a major commitment by the United States to join the Tehran–Tel Aviv axis in supporting the Kurdish insurgency. Shortly after nationalization of the IPC, Mullah Mostafa promised the United States that if his Kurdish *peshmergas* prevailed against the Iraqi forces and succeeded in establishing a foothold in Kirkuk, he would turn over the Kirkuk oil fields to the United States, and it could depend on a reliable ally in OPEC.[35] In an interview with the *Washington Post* in June 1973, Mullah Mostafa again sought to commit the United States to his cause by stating that if US support were substantial, the Kurds could take over Kirkuk and give the oil fields to US companies to operate, hence negating the recent nationalization of the IPC.[36]

Although the United States did not take Mullah Mostafa's claims seriously, the Iraqi government used his statements to justify the Ba'th Party's paranoia about an alleged Iranian-Israeli-US masterplan to dismember Iraq and establish a puppet state in Iraqi Kurdistan. Iraq's fear of dismemberment was heightened by periodic reports about the direct involvement of "large numbers" of Iranian army soldiers fighting on the side of Kurds. According to one Iraqi analyst, by 1975, Iran had deployed two army regiments inside Iraq.[37] However, as the Pike Report indicated, and as the downfall of the Kurdish insurgency clearly showed, neither the Shah nor the United States wanted Mullah Mostafa to prevail militarily over the Iraqi forces. Their aim was to sap Iraqi resources without causing the demise of the Iraqi state. However, this cardinal objective was not "imparted to our clients [the Kurds], who were encouraged to continue fighting."[38]

US support for Mullah Mostafa was crucial from a psychological perspective. As he later confessed, he never trusted the Shah and could not count on his "goodwill" to continue to provide weapons and other types of support to the Iraqi Kurds. For Mullah Mostafa, US participation would function as insurance against a sudden shift of policy by the Shah's government; he thought that the United States would not allow the Shah to suddenly drop his support for the Kurdish movement.[39] As subsequent events demonstrated, Mullah Mostafa gravely miscalculated the intentions of the United States and failed to comprehend the broader goals of Iranian foreign policy in the region.

Why didn't Mullah Mostafa pursue a more peaceful avenue to gain autonomy for Iraqi Kurdistan, as contained in the 1970 March Manifesto? Why did he mortgage the future of Kurdish autonomy to US, Israeli, and Iranian interests when it appeared that the Ba'thi government was going to give concessions to Kurdish demands? According to Iraqi accounts, his refusal to negotiate in good faith with Baghdad simply reflected his desire to prevent the return of normalcy to Kurdistan, which would have affected his leadership of the Kurdish movement and his domination of the KDP. Furthermore,

Mullah Mostafa's intransigence was explained by the Iraqis in terms of "traps" set by the Israeli Mossad, the Shah's SAVAK, and the US CIA to use the Kurds to prevent the development of a strong, independent, and economically thriving Iraq.[40] Although, as we have seen, there was an element of truth in the Ba'thi explanation of his "hawkish" posture toward Baghdad, a number of other factors contributed to the widening chasm between Mullah Mostafa and the Iraqi government.

After the announcement of the March Manifesto and before unilateral implementation by the government, two nearly successful assassination attempts were made against Mullah Mostafa. Although the government condemned both attempts, there was strong suspicion that Ba'thi elements were behind them.[41] In fact, the KDP's security elements submitted evidence that indicated the possibility of government involvement in these assassination attempts. A further cause of tension between Mullah Mostafa and the Ba'thi regime in the early 1970s was the deportation of fifty thousand Iraqi citizens of Iranian origin to Iran. It was not the first, nor the last, time that the Iraqi regime expelled thousands of its citizens and forced them into neighboring Iran. Many of these Iraqis had lived there for generations, and their Iranian ancestry had no significance for them. They neither spoke Persian nor had any affinity for Iranian culture or politics, and their Iraqization was thorough and complete. But the Ba'thi regime used them as scapegoats for the Shah's policies and its own failure. What distinguished the 1971–1972 deportation of these "Iranians" from other waves of deportations was that a large number of them had come from areas between Khaneqain and Amara, which had a sizable number of Shi'a Kurds. Mullah Mostafa interpreted the expulsion of these Kurds as yet another attempt by the Iraqi government to decimate the Kurdish population while promising them greater autonomy.[42]

A more serious source of conflict between the Ba'thi government and Mullah Mostafa was the sustained policy of Arabization that the government pursued during the so-called transition period of 1970–1974. As discussed in Chapter 3, Arabization took many forms, including large transfers of the Arab population to Kurdish regions and resettlement of Kurds in the southwestern desert regions of the country. Added to this was the government's refusal to include Kirkuk and its oil fields as part of the Kurdish autonomous region.

Considering everything, Mullah Mostafa's alliance of convenience with Iran, Israel, and the United States was a rational move on his part to maximize his gains and minimize his losses. From the Kurdish perspective, however, it was unfortunate that as he was becoming more alienated from the Ba'thists, the Shah was searching to lessen Iranian-Arab tensions and establish a modus vivendi with his Arab neighbors. The impending British withdrawal from the Gulf contributed to the lessening of tension and led to a series of confidence-building measures by both the Arabs and the Shah.

Nevertheless, the Shah continued to view Ba'thi Iraq as a destabilizing threat to Gulf security. Egyptian-Iranian relations, however, showed signs of improvement. President Nasser, while maintaining that "Arabism" in the Gulf remained one of his administration's paramount concerns, expressed a desire to allow the littoral Arab states to emerge as the guardians of Arab interests in the region.[43]

In October 1968, the Shah tried to forge closer ties with the conservative Arab regimes of the Gulf by making a goodwill trip to Saudi Arabia. During his visit, the Shah reiterated the necessity of closer cooperation between Iran and the Arab world in order to prevent the spread of Arab radicalism and Soviet influence. This was followed by the Shah's January 1969 announcement in New Delhi that he would not forcefully reincorporate Bahrain into Iran, but would allow the wishes of the local population, which by now was overwhelmingly Arab, to prevail. In other words, the Shah renounced Iran's long-standing claims to the Gulf shaikhdom of Bahrain, thus allaying Saudi Arabia's fear of Iranian expansionism and removing a major sore point between Iran and the Arab states, in general, and Gulf countries, in particular.[44] When the Ba'thi authorities launched a vitriolic criticism of Nasser's handling of the Arab-Israeli conflict, Tehran and Cairo ironically found themselves "on the same side in opposition to an Arab state."[45]

With the death of Gamal Abdul Nasser in 1970 and the coming to power of Anwar Sadat, closer links between Egypt and Iran were established. As Sadat's regime gradually moved away from its reliance on the Soviet Union and sought to adopt a pro-Western posture, a marked change occurred in Cairo's foreign policy regarding the Gulf states. While Sadat sought to maintain Egypt's leading role in Arab politics, he nevertheless adopted a less activist posture toward pan-Arab causes and an increasingly accommodationist stance toward the pro-Western countries in the Gulf, including Iran. As a consequence of shifts in Egypt's foreign policy and the Shah's wooing of Saudi Arabia, a Tehran-Cairo-Riyadh axis began to counter the Moscow-Baghdad-Damascus axis in the region.

As the Iranian-Egyptian links became stronger, Iraq found itself increasingly isolated. This isolation increased when the Shah succeeded in improving Iran's relations with Syria. By mid-1974, Saddam Hussein had grudgingly concluded that in order to break down Iraq's isolation and defeat the Kurdish uprising on the political front, he needed to reach an accommodation with the Shah's government. King Hussein of Jordan, who had maintained good relations with both the Shah and Saddam Hussein, played an important role in paving the way for an eventual Iranian-Iraqi rapprochement. During the 1974 Arab Summit in Rabat, King Hussein arranged a meeting between Iraqi representatives and an Iranian delegation that had traveled to Morocco to meet with the Iraqis.[46] Other Arab intermediaries, such as the Algerians, continued to arrange intermittent meetings between the two sides throughout the remainder of 1974 and until March 1975.

The urgency of reaching an agreement with the Shah became more pronounced when the Soviet Union decided to curtail weapons shipments to Iraq in early 1975. As Saddam Hussein later acknowledged, by the time he had decided to make an agreement with the Shah, the Iraqi military possessed only three heavy missiles and very few artillery shells.[47] If the Shah and the United States wanted to destroy Iraq, they were in a position to do so by early 1975. It is not clear what prompted Moscow to withhold critically needed weapons from Iraq. The Soviets may have been disenchanted with the isolation of the Iraqi regime in the Arab world and were hoping to bring about changes in the Iraqi regime by withholding weaponry. More importantly, the Soviets did not want to damage their chances to improve relations with Iran, a country with which they had hoped to develop extensive economic links and a country that was more important to the Soviet geostrategic design in the Middle East than Iraq was.

The negotiations between Iraq and the Shah's government had disturbed the Kurds. Mullah Mostafa was well aware of the efforts of various Arab parties, such as Jordan, Algeria, and Egypt, to end the conflict between Ba'thi Iraq and monarchical Iran. In late February 1975, the KDP dispatched a high-level delegation to Cairo to express concerns about a possible deal between a weakened Iraq and Iran that would be detrimental to the Kurdish cause. The KDP delegation asked Sadat to use his influence to preserve Kurdish interests in the event of an Iranian-Iraqi rapprochement. President Sadat reportedly assured the Kurds that there were no negotiations between the two sides.[48] As it turned out, President Sadat did not want to derail the impending negotiations between Iran and Iraq by publicly admitting their existence to the Kurds.

Multilateral efforts to bring about a settlement of the Iran-Iraq crisis bore fruit in March 1975 when Algerian president Boumedienne arranged a historic meeting between the Shah and Saddam Hussein, vice-president of Iraq's Revolutionary Command Council and de facto power wielder in Iraq. This meeting, which took place during a summit meeting of the Organization of Petroleum Exporting Countries (OPEC) in Algiers, resulted in the signing of the Algiers Agreement on March 6, 1975. Because Iraq's diplomatic and military positions vis-à-vis Iran had been weakened by the time the Algiers Agreement was signed, the best Iraq could hope for was a commitment by the Shah to terminate his support for the Kurdish uprising. In return, Iraq had to concede to a number of territorial adjustments, including acceptance of the Thalweg Line, or mid-channel of the Shatt al-Arab, as the boundary between the two countries. Since the Shatt al-Arab waterway was Iraq's only outlet to the Gulf, the Ba'thi regime had always insisted on total control of this river, claiming that Iraq's economic survival depended on complete sovereignty over the Shatt al-Arab. Iran, on the other hand, had insisted that the waterway was crucial for its economic and navigational purposes, and that, according to the principles of international law governing a shared body of water like the Shatt al-Arab, the Thalweg Line was the boundary between the two countries.[49] Saddam Hussein's concession on this point was a bitter blow to the prestige of the Ba'thi regime.

The Algiers Agreement was augmented by the Protocol Concerning the Delimitation of the River Frontier Between Iran and Iraq and the Treaty of International Boundaries and Good Neighborliness, both of which were signed in Baghdad on June 13, 1975, by Iran's foreign minister, Abbas Ali Khalatbary, and his Iraqi counterpart, Sa'dun Hamadi.[50] In addition, the Algiers Agreement called for establishment of a joint Iranian-Iraqi commission to implement its provisions. All violations of the agreement were to be reported to this commission, which would then seek to resolve any conflict. Both countries also agreed to invite Algeria to all meetings of the Iranian-Iraqi commission.

Some analysts have argued that a major factor in Saddam Hussein's willingness to grant major concessions to Iran on territorial and boundary issues stemmed largely from the pressure placed on Iraq by other Arab countries to extricate itself from its debilitating crisis so that it could concentrate its energies against the common enemy—the state of Israel. In fact, Saddam Hussein claimed that the Algiers Agreement was signed for the higher good of the Arab people.[51] Arab pressure did play a role in bringing the two sides to the negotiating table, but Iraq's inability to defeat the Kurdish uprising and increasing Iranian military pressure were equally important, if not more important, in compelling Saddam Hussein to offer major concessions. In the end, there was "little doubt who in the Algiers Agreement made the most concessions. Whereas Saddam went out of his way to placate the Shah by acknowledging Iran's sovereignty over half of the Shatt-al-Arab, the Shah made no practical concessions unless non-interference in the domestic affairs of another sovereign state can be considered one. In the Algiers Agreement, Hussein 'bought' the inviolability of Iraq's frontier, a fundamental and self-evident attribute of statehood, by paying the high price of territorial concessions."[52]

If one analyzes the Algiers Agreement strictly according to the territorial concessions made by Baghdad, one would have to concur with this judgment. On the other hand, what mattered most for Saddam Hussein in 1975 was the survival of the Ba'thi regime and the settlement of the Kurdish problem on his terms. Looked at from this limited perspective, there is no question that without the Algiers Agreement, the Ba'thi regime would have suffered a coup de grace. Instead, the Kurdish cause and Mullah Mostafa's leadership suffered a major blow. Within hours of the issuance of the Algiers Agreement, Baghdad launched a major offensive against the demoralized Kurdish *peshmergas* and eliminated any noticeable Kurdish resistance within two weeks.[53]

Thousands of Kurds took refuge in Iran following the announcement of the Algiers Agreement and Mullah Mostafa's orders to give up the fight. The Iraqi army was then free to carry out the government's policy of depopulating Kurdish villages and deporting their residents to the southwestern desert region of the country. In the words of Samir al-Khalil:

> Families of Kurds were bundled up in army trucks and transported to large hastily improvised camps or to Arab villages west of the Euphrates where they were settled in small groups. . . . Troops placed the [Kurdish] villagers on trucks to be carried off at night in long caravans along sealed routes. Having reached their destinations families were supplied with a tent, and grouped in fives in so-called villages. Movement was prohibited except for official business. The men were assigned jobs at fixed pay.[54]

Of those Kurds who decided to return to their villages from their refuge in Iran and take advantage of the general amnesty offered by the Iraqi government, some 85 percent were rounded up and deported to the southwest desert.

The estimated number of Kurds affected by the Ba'thi policy of deportation in the aftermath of Mullah Mostafa's defeat has ranged from 50,000 to 350,000, depending on the source.[55] The Iraqi government obliquely acknowledged the population transfers by stating that the government's policy was to establish a ten-kilometer security belt along the Iranian border, and that villagers in the security belt had to be transferred elsewhere in the country.[56] On the political front, the impact of the Algiers Agreement was the fragmentation of the Kurdish front into competing movements and political parties, which led to the debilitation of Kurdish unity in Iraq.

THE IRAN-IRAQ WAR AND THE KURDS

The Iranian Revolution of 1978–1979 brought about profound transformations in Iran's domestic and international politics. The new Islamic regime in Iran, which espoused pan-Islamic views, was perceived by Iraq as a threat to its secularist ideology. Ayatollah Khomeini's triumphant return to Iran in February 1979 coincided with an upsurge of Shi'a political activism in Iraq. Numerous anti-Ba'thi demonstrations in the southern holy cities of Najaf and Karbala were reported in early 1979. Antiregime demonstrations had even spread to Saddam City, the poor Shi'a neighborhood in Baghdad. The genesis of these demonstrations was purely local as they were organized under the aegis of the Iraqi Shi'a opposition group *al-Da'wa* (The Call). However, there is no denying that Ayatollah Khomeini's message of Islamic revivalism had a profound impact on the new-found activism of the Iraqi Shi'as. Many demonstrators carried pictures of Khomeini, along with banners containing slogans such as "Yes to Islam, no to Aflaq [an original founder of Ba'thism] and Saddam."[57] Moreover, an eminent Shi'a scholar, and the spiritual guide of *al-Da'wa*, Ayatollah Mohammad Baqer al-Sadr, began to publicly support the goals of the Iranian Revolution and hoped that similar ideas would take root in Iraq.

Public and popular protests against Ba'thi secularism worried Iraqi authorities that the ideals of the Iranian Revolution would spill over to their country and incite the Shi'as, who constitute over 55 percent of Iraq's population, to overthrow Saddam Hussein's minority regime. In fact, Iraqi officials on numerous occasions expressed fear that the Shah's policies of "hegemonic expansionism" and "chauvinistic nationalism" toward Iraq were being replaced by Khomeini's exhortations to "export" the Islamic revolution to their country.[58] Indeed, high-ranking clerics in Iran had labeled Iraqi Ba'thi socialism as "atheistic" and anti-Islamic and intensified their moral and material support for the *al-Da'wa* movement.

Iraq's response to the Shi'a movement was swift and brutal. The regime wanted to put an abrupt end to the uprising before it grew and spread north to the Kurdish regions. With massive arrests and executions of Shi'a activists, the Ba'thi regime began to put pressure on Ayatollah Sadr to leave Najaf and desist from issuing *fatwas* (religious edicts) against the government. Instead, Sadr intensified his exhortations to the Iraqis to overthrow Saddam Hussein's government. On June 12, 1979, Ayatollah Sadr sent a message strongly condemning the government and asking the people to eschew pan-Arabism and Ba'thism as political creeds and follow the example of Iran's Islamic path. Shortly thereafter, Sadr issued a *fatwa* forbidding Iraqi Muslims from being members of the Ba'th Party. Sadr's edicts provoked major demonstrations throughout Iraq, including Kurdish regions where sympathy demonstrations were held for Shi'a victims of the government's repression. On July 6, Ayatollah Sadr recorded a message in which he referred to the rulers of Iraq as "bloody murderers" and "despots," and called upon all Iraqis to do their utmost to get rid of Saddam Hussein and his Ba'thi regime.[59]

In another powerful message, which may have been recorded in early 1980, Ayatollah Sadr stressed the importance of Sunni-Shi'a and Arab-Kurdish cooperation in a united effort to overthrow the Ba'thi regime, in a popular uprising, and rebuild a "noble, free Iraq, where Islamic justice will abound and human dignity will reign."[60] Determined to prevent an uprising, the Ba'thi authorities put Ayatollah Sadr under house arrest in Najaf and later brought him to Baghdad and executed him in April 1980. The Iraqi government portrayed the Shi'a demonstrations as examples of Iranian "interference" in Iraq's domestic affairs, and used them as justification for launching a full-scale invasion of Iran on September 22, 1980. Notwithstanding this claim, there is now good reason to believe that Saddam Hussein attacked Iran to establish Iraqi hegemony in the Gulf and to revive his irredentist ambitions in the oil-rich Iranian province of Khuzistan. As

Fred Halliday noted, the Ba'thists were "quite happy to see Khomeini call for a revolt and carefully nurtured the conflict along the Iran-Iraq border so as to heighten tensions."[61]

Purported violations of the Algiers Agreement by Iran were also cited as justification for the Iraqi invasion of Iran. These alleged violations involved "Iranian interference in the domestic affairs of Iraq" and the supposed violation of Iraqi air and ground space by Iranian forces between April and September 1980.[62] The accuracy of Iraqi charges was never affirmed by independent sources. In fact, as Gary Sick noted, available evidence "suggests that Iraq conducted a systematic buildup of its military forces between April and September 1980 in preparation for a lightning offensive [against Iran]."[63] The subsequent invasion of Iran, which involved bombing targets throughout the country and capturing four thousand square miles of Iranian territory, was disproportionate to the alleged Iranian provocation. The Ba'thi government never alleged that Iran was intending to invade Iraq, nor did it claim that Iran was massing forces along its border regions with Iraq. The "total absence of any Iranian military preparation was unmistakably obvious in the first few weeks of the war."[64]

Preceding the Iraqi invasion of Iran, both sides routinely charged each other with border violations. According to one study, between April 11 and September 11, 1980, Iraq announced 352 alleged Iranian attacks across the border, while Iran accused Iraq of 172 military incursions inside its territory.[65] Such incidents had been common along the Iran-Iraq border regions even before the advent of the Islamic Republic in Iran, and certainly had never been considered as a casus belli. On September 17, 1980, Saddam Hussein gave a clear signal of what was to come in five days by denouncing the Algiers Agreement which he had negotiated with the Shah, and tearing up a copy of it on television. Saddam Hussein then stated that Iraq had made the decision to recover its territory by force, and to bring the Shatt al-Arab waterway under total Iraqi control and sovereignty.[66] In a special session of the Iraqi National Assembly, Saddam Hussein interjected a Kurdish dimension to his justification for abrogating the Algiers Agreement by stating that the Islamic Republic, like the Shah's regime before it, had embarked upon a policy of supporting Kurdish "mutiny" inside Iraq.[67]

Contrary to Saddam Hussein's assertion, it seems unlikely that the Islamic Republic had the necessary resources or the organizational support to continue the Shah's Kurdish policy toward Iraq, especially in view of the fact that the Islamic Republic was already in the throes of combat with its own Kurds. In fact, Iraq had turned the tables and was fomenting a Kurdish revolt inside Iran. According to Eric Rouleau, a correspondent for the influential Paris daily, *Le Monde*, who interviewed the KDPI's Ghassemlou, Iraq was a major source of foreign assistance to the KDPI. In his book, *My Turn to Speak*, exiled Iranian president Bani-Sadr referred to documents captured from the Kurds that implicated Iraq as being heavily involved in all facets of

Kurdish turmoil in Iran after the victory of the Iranian Revolution.[68]

Although it is difficult to ascertain the extent of Iranian and Iraqi involvement in inciting Kurdish uprisings in each other's country before the onset of the Iran-Iraq War, after the war started both sides took specific measures to involve their Kurdish populations in the war effort. Iraq was the first to play its Kurdish card as a strategic tool to weaken Iran. Infighting among various Kurdish groups also made it easier for Baghdad to use its Kurdish card. For example, Talabani's PUK was fighting the KDP-Provisional Leadership led by the Barzani brothers. Ghassemlou's KDPI "hated Barzani's Iraqi KDP because it had accepted arms from the Shah."[69] In general, the effectiveness of the Kurdish resistance against Iraq was weakened by the absence of a unified Kurdish front in the first two years of the Iran-Iraq War.

In January 1981, the first effective Iraqi attempt to play its Kurdish card occurred when the Ba'thi government established a supply route to *peshmergas* of Ghassemlou's KDPI near the cities of Qasr-e Shirin and Nowdesheh. The control of Nowdesheh was Iraq's prime objective, as the city's strategic location would deny Iran the use of the Baghdad-Tehran highway. The Iraqis were successful in overwhelming the relatively small and lightly armed *pasdaran* and regular Iranian military units stationed in the area. With Baghdad's assistance, the KDPI established a major operational headquarters in Nowdesheh and launched a three-month guerrilla offensive against Iranian forces with some success.[70]

Beginning in April 1981, the KDPI—aided by Talabani's PUK, Iranian opposition guerrilla groups *Mujahidin-e Khlaq* and *Fadaiyan-e Khalq*, and Iraqi weapons and ammunition—forced the *pasdaran* units to retreat from major cities in Iranian Kurdistan, including Sanandaj, the capital of Kurdistan and an important military outpost. The KDPI and its supporters then contemplated a frontal attack on the city of Mahabad and the establishment of a "liberated Kurdish zone" in the same fashion as the Kurds who set up the ill-fated Kurdish Republic of Mahabad forty-five years earlier.

Iranian forces succeeded in regrouping and launched a series of counteroffensives against the KDPI. Moreover, by April 1982, an Iranian offensive in the north had inflicted heavy casualties on Iraqi forces, forcing them to retreat from Iranian territory. Consequently, the fortunes of the KDPI changed in May 1982 when Iranian ground forces under the command of Colonel Sayyad Shirazi launched a series of highly successful attacks against the KDPI's forces and bases. Colonel Shirazi's strategy was simple, yet effective. He coaxed Ghassemlou's forces into spreading themselves too thin, then encircled the overstretched forces and dealt them a devastating blow from which they never recovered. Ghassemlou's hopes of creating a "liberated Kurdish zone" all but vanished, and the KDPI was reduced to a marginal Iraqi instrument in the Iran-Iraq War.[71] In order to salvage his floundering fortunes, Ghassemlou contacted former Iranian president Bani-Sadr and invited him to join him in setting up a parallel government and unseating the ruling clerics in Tehran. Ghassemlou reassured Bani-Sadr that the goal of his movement was "autonomy for Kurdistan, democracy for Iran." Fearing that Ghassemlou was harboring separatist motives, Bani-Sadr refused to accept his invitation.

After bringing its own Kurdish uprising under control and expelling Iraqi forces from Iranian Kurdistan, the Islamic Republic began to play its own Kurdish card. On balance, the Iranians were more successful than the Iraqis in exploiting their Kurdish assets during the Iran-Iraq War. Not only had the Islamic Republic acquired the support of Massoud and Idris Barzani's KDP by 1983, it had also succeeded in attracting the support of one-time Marxist-Leninist Jalal Talabani's PUK in a united Kurdish front against the Iraqi regime. Surprisingly, by 1987 Talabani was echoing Tehran's call for the overthrow of the Ba'thi regime in Baghdad and its replacement with an Islamic republic.[72]

As the Iraqi regime began to fear the prospect of a potentially destabilizing Iranian-Kurdish front in the north, Saddam Hussein reportedly sought to open secret negotiations with the Kurds.[73] While seeking to reach a modus vivendi with its Kurdish groups, however, Iraq came under heavy pressure from Ankara to clamp down on Kurdish activities along the border regions with Turkey. Turkey claimed that the border areas under the control of Massoud and Idris Barzani's KDP were being used as staging grounds for anti-Turkish Kurdish incursions. Furthermore, the Turkish government was blaming Iraqi Kurds for major disturbances that were taking place throughout southeastern Turkey. In the period 1981–1982, eighty thousand Kurds were reportedly arrested in Turkey, and two thousand more were detained in 1983.[74] Because Iraqi oil was transported through a pipeline that connected the Kirkuk oil fields to the Turkish Mediterranean coast, the Ba'thi government could ill afford to alienate Turkey and jeopardize its own lifeline. Consequently, the Iraqis succumbed to Turkish pressure and, in April 1983, signed an agreement on joint security measures allowing Turkish troops to enter Iraqi territory in "hot pursuit" of Kurdish guerrillas.

In May 1983, Kurdish guerrillas operating from Iraqi bases crossed into Turkey and killed several Turkish soldiers. The Turks invoked their April hot pursuit agreement, and thousands of their troops entered Iraqi Kurdistan in a search-and-destroy mission that resulted in the capture of hundreds of Kurdish *peshmergas* and their leaders. Many of the captured Kurds were handed over to Baghdad, where they were executed or received lengthy prison sentences.[75] By the summer of 1983, a combined Iraqi-Turkish war against the Kurds had begun. The Kurds, particularly the Barzanis' KDP, needed to form an alliance with Iran to counteract this new threat.

In July 1983, Iran launched a new offensive against Iraqi forces under the code name *Wal Fajr-2*. This marked the first time that Iraqi Kurds and Iranian troops had coordinated their military activities during the Iran-Iraq War. As a result of *Wal Fajr-2* operations, the Barzanis' KDP, in cooperation with Iranian forces, recaptured Haj Omran. The recapture of Haj Omran and its environs had both strategic and psychological significance. It was an area where Ghassemlou's KDPI had set up a major operational base, and had been used by Iraqi forces as a supply route through which assistance to the KDPI and their own forces was funneled. Haj Omran was also a mountain stronghold of Mullah Mostafa Barzani prior to the signing of the Algiers Agreement. The recapture of Haj Omran was a "poignant reassertion by Barzani's sons of the family's decades-long struggle against a central government in Iraq."[76] Throughout the summer, Iranian forces continued to outmaneuver the Iraqis along the Kurdish border regions. On September 16, a division of the Iranian army assisted by KDP *peshmergas*, whom the Iranian government described as a group of Iraqi Muslim combatants, penetrated deep inside Iraqi Kurdistan and captured large quantities of weapons and equipment, which they gave to the anti-Iraqi Kurds. Three days later, Iraq retaliated by bombing the cities of Baneh and Marivan in Iranian Kurdistan.

Iran launched *Wal Fajr-4* on October 19, 1983, against Iraqi targets throughout the northern front. The immediate objectives of *Wal Fajr-4* were to push Iraqi troops far enough back so the Iranian cities of Marivan and Baneh would be out of Iraqi shelling range, to gain control of the strategic heights in the Penjwin valley, and to force the remnants of the KDPI out of their bases. The supporting group in *Wal Fajr-4* included not only the KDP *peshmergas,* but also Shi'a elements from the south and other anti-Saddam groups. The success of *Wal Fajr-4* was not only a cause of concern for the Iraqi regime, but also for Jalal Talabani, whose PUK was being outmaneuvered by its adversary, the KDP.

In order to reverse their fortunes, Saddam Hussein and Jalal Talabani began to negotiate in November 1983. By early December, the PUK had apparently reached an understanding with the Ba'thi government, and a cease-fire was declared. The immediate benefit of this cease-fire was that the Iraqis could concentrate on fighting the Iranian-KDP elements in the north and the PUK could count on Iraqi support in its struggle against its adversaries.[77] As part of an overall agreement on the resolution of the Kurdish problem that was to follow, Talabani demanded the extension of the Kurdish autonomous region to include parts of Kirkuk, the allocation of 20 to 30 percent of Kirkuk oil revenues for the economic development of Kurdistan, a halt to Arabization and deportation of Kurds, the formation of a forty-thousand-man Kurdish defense force, and release of all "political and military prisoners" by both sides.[78] Baghdad was apparently willing to meet most of these demands. Even on the thorny issue of the status of Kirkuk, a compromise was reportedly made whereby a joint Arab-Kurdish-Turkoman administration would govern the city of Kirkuk, including the oil fields, while the rest of the Kirkuk province would become part of the Kurdish autonomous region.[79] The Iraq-PUK agreement was never publicly reported, as obstacles began to develop before implementation.

In March 1984, Iraq arrested twenty-four Kurds and charged them with desertion and draft dodging. They were subsequently executed, despite the PUK's intervention on their behalf. At the same time, government forces clashed with Kurdish students at Irbil University, where an unspecified number of students were killed by Iraqi soldiers. Concurrently, the Talabani–Saddam Hussein relations became tense when progovernment troops killed Talabani's brother and his two daughters. More important, the demise of the agreement between the PUK and the Iraqi government was attributed to Turkish pressure put on Saddam Hussein not to grant any significant concessions to the Kurds. In mid-October 1984, a Turkish delegation led by Foreign Minister Vahit Helefoglu visited Iraq. According to the PUK, Helefoglu warned Iraq that Turkey would shut down the vital Kirkuk oil line, hence paralyzing Iraq economically, if Baghdad granted major concessions to the Kurds. Obviously, Turkey was worried about the spill-over effects that concessions would have on its own restive Kurdish population.[80] On October 18, Talabani terminated negotiations with Iraqi authorities, and the brief political honeymoon between the two sides came to an abrupt end. In the same month, another Iraqi-Turkish security agreement was signed, allowing each side to go beyond the hot pursuit provisions of the earlier agreement. Both countries could now penetrate each other's territory in pursuit of Kurdish *peshmergas* and remain there for up to three days to accomplish their mission.[81]

Between late 1984 and the beginning of 1986, the Iran-Iraq War entered a relatively quiet phase in which which both sides launched only limited ground offensives. However, Iranian support for the KDP during this period allowed the KDP to increase the number of raids against Iraqi and PUK targets. On September 8, 1985, Iran and its Kurdish allies launched an attack against Iraqi forces and captured over 240 square kilometers of territory in Iraqi Kurdistan. Although the new territory, which was located west of the Iranian city of Piranshahr, had little strategic value for the conduct of the war, it clearly showed that Iran "now dominated the battle for the Kurds and could exploit its alliances to achieve limited gains of Iraqi territory."[82]

As the Kurdish cards stacked up higher against Saddam Hussein, Turkey increased its cross-border raids into Iraq. Turkey also threatened to cut off trade with Iran if Tehran continued aiding anti-Iraq Kurdish groups. After a rapprochement between Talabani's PUK and Iran, Turkish fears of Iraqi disintegration reached a new plateau. The right-wing Turkish press even speculated about an alleged Iranian objective of seizing Kirkuk and its oilfields.[83] Some Turks also speculated that the United States was encouraging Turkey to capture Kirkuk before Iraq was dismembered as a means to deny Iran a decisive victory in its war with Iraq.[84] Speculations aside, the Turkish government did make a concerted effort to warn Iran that its support of Kurdish groups would have adverse consequences.

Turkish foreign minister Vahit Helefoglu stressed the importance of Kurdish issues to visiting high-level Iranian foreign ministry officials in October 1986. He told the Iranian delegation that Turkey would like to stay neutral in the Iran-Iraq War. At the same time, Helefoglu stated that his country wanted the Kirkuk-Iskenderun oil pipeline to remain immune from either direct Iranian attacks or those conducted by Iranian-supported Kurds. Although the Iranian deputy foreign minister indicated his appreciation of the importance of the pipeline for the Turkish economy, he nevertheless stated: "We are at war with Iraq and we cannot give assurances to any country."[85] Although Iran did not attack the pipeline during the course of the Iran-Iraq War, the issue remained a point of contention between Ankara and Tehran.

In late 1986, the Turkish air force bombed a number of Kurdish villages in northern Iraq on the pretext of destroying PKK camps. The Iranian government filed a bitter protest with Turkish authorities over the bombings of the Iraqi Kurds, which were particularly ill-timed from the Iranian perspective as the Islamic Republic was preparing to launch another offensive, in cooperation with the Iraqi Kurds, through Haj Omran against the enemy's northern forces.[86] In response to the rising tensions between Iran and Turkey over the Kurdish issue, and to alleviate fears of Iranian territorial ambitions in Iraq, the Islamic Republic in December 1986 organized a gathering in Tehran called the Conference on the Cooperation of the Iraqi People. This conference brought together representatives of anti–Saddam Hussein elements, including Kurds. While President Ali Khamenei reaffirmed Iran's commitment to the territorial integrity of Iraq, he stated that Iran would not hesitate to challenge another country's intervention in Iraqi affairs. In the same vein, Prime Minister Hussein Mussavi warned other countries not to take advantage of Iraq's weakness to revive old territorial claims against that country.[87] Although Turkey was never named in these warnings, it was clear that Iranian authorities were addressing Turkish officials and their lingering claims for Mosul and Kirkuk.

In early 1987, Iran launched a two-pronged offensive against Iraq. On January 9, Iran launched a major offensive against Basra in the south in an operation code-named *Karbala-5*. A few days later, Iranian forces attacked in the north in *Karbala-6*. These two operations were designed to force Iraq to defend itself simultaneously on two fronts. *Karbala-6*, however, seemed to have been launched as a diversionary tactic, with *Karbala-5* the main thrust of Iran's offensive. In *Karbala-6*, Iranian forces did not seek to penetrate Iraqi defensive lines.[88] They simply seized hills overlooking Iraqi positions and allowed their Kurdish allies to occupy them before they withdrew.

On February 12, 1987, Iran carried out a two-day offensive near Haj Omran and claimed that it was aiming toward Irbil. The nature of the attack and its brief duration indicated that it was a diversionary move on the part of Iran. Shortly thereafter, however, Iran carried out another major offensive in the north, *Karbala-7*. This offensive, which was launched on March 4, 1987, took place near Gerdmand Heights, located within the vicinity of Haj Omran and east of the Iraqi Kurdish town of Rowandiz. *Karbala-7* operations included Iranian regular army units and *pasdaran,* as well as a combined Kurdish force that now included *peshmergas* from both the KDP and PUK. Within twenty-four hours of the commencement of *Karbala-7*, the combined Iranian-Kurdish units had captured the Gerdmand Heights and seized other positions above the Iraqi Kurdish town of Shoma Mostafa.[89] Despite these gains, Iraqi forces were in no danger of being overrun in major cities in the north, such as Kirkuk, and their oil pipelines and major highways in the north were heavily defended against Kurdish or Iranian attacks. Furthermore, the Iraqi government's "ruthlessness and considerable tenacity," along with Turkish-Iraqi collaboration, had thwarted Kurdish actions in major Kurdish areas in Iraq.[90] Nonetheless, Iranian officials insisted in May that anti-Iraqi Kurds were indeed conducting successful sabotage operations against military and economic targets deep inside Iraqi Kurdistan, and that joint Iranian-Kurdish attacks against Iraqi forces had succeeded in demoralizing Saddam Hussein's forces in Kurdistan.[91]

The apparent success of Iranian-Kurdish cooperation compelled Saddam Hussein to order the destruction of hundreds of "hostile" Kurdish villages. The destruction of these villages continued throughout 1988 and into 1989, even after a cease-fire had been arranged in the Iran-Iraq War. The Iraqi Kurds have claimed that much of the destruction was done through a combination of chemical weapons and simple bulldozing techniques.[92] By July 1987, the Iraqis had committed over thirty-five thousand combat troops to the "pacification" of Kurdish villages, causing the ranks of the *peshmergas* to increase to nearly ten thousand fighters.[93] This was an indication of the seriousness with which Iraq viewed the Kurdish threat in the north. As fighting continued on the northern front, Iraqi forces accelerated the depopulation of Kurdish villages and escalated the bombing of villages. These policies redounded to the detriment of the Iraqi objective of the "pacification" of Kurdistan; they created "at least two new guerrillas for every one that was killed or imprisoned. For the first time, the KDP and similar groups began to threaten control of the countryside and to give Iran's slow advances in the north strategic meaning."[94]

In March 1988, a new Iranian-Kurdish offensive was launched on the northern front. By this time, the United States had tilted heavily toward the Iraqis by reflagging Kuwaiti oil tankers and confronting the Islamic Republic in the Gulf. Furthermore, the West and its Arab allies in the Gulf had concluded that an Iranian victory had to be averted at all costs, and they increased their financial, political, and military assistance to Saddam Hussein's regime. By attracting direct and indirect US support, Saddam Hussein managed to internationalize the war, thus making it costlier for Iran and its Kurdish allies to pursue the conflict. Although US support for

Saddam Hussein began to show positive results on the southern front, and enabled the Iraqis to gradually reverse battlefield setbacks in the southern marshes and adjacent regions of Iraq, Saddam Hussein's forces could not score any noticeable victories on the northern front.

Tactical mistakes in the Kurdish areas were instrumental in preventing Saddam's forces from exploiting their advantage in manpower and weaponry against the Iranian-Kurdish forces. As Anthony Cordesman and Abraham Wagner observed:

> [Iraqi] units withdrew from many of the heights and ridges in the area but then deployed forward to defend the towns at the border. Giving up the rough mountain terrain allowed the Iraqi forces to be outflanked, and several towns could not be held without defending the surrounding heights. . . . Iraqi forces had further problems in dealing with Kurdish infiltration behind their lines of communication and, according to some reports, Iran even managed to use its speed boats to move its troops through part of the reservoir.[95]

As a result of tactical mistakes in the north, up to four thousand soldiers from Iraq's Forty-third Division were killed, and the country lost large amounts of light weapons, munitions, artillery pieces, armored vehicles, and tanks. However, Iran could not turn its victories in the Kurdish north into victories in the south, which had become the main battlefield of the Iran-Iraq War. By using its best troops in the north, Iran could not muster enough forces to defend its southern flank against increasingly emboldened Iraqi counterattacks.

By June 1988, Iranian fortunes in the south were deteriorating rapidly, and Iranian forces were abandoning captured Iraqi territory. Reports in the Iranian media portrayed these defeats as tactical battlefield retreats, but it was clear to most people, including the country's leadership, that Iran could not achieve a victory against the militarily superior Iraqi forces and their US and Arab allies.[96] To make matters worse for Tehran, the Iraqis had resorted to the widespread use of chemical weapons against Iranian targets. It was within this context that Iran formally announced its acceptance of UN Security Council Resolution 598 on July 18, 1988, leading to a cease-fire between the two belligerents.

Shortly after the announcement of Iran's acceptance of the UN resolution, Baghdad launched a major operation throughout Iraqi Kurdistan. Initially, fifteen thousand troops were deployed for this operation, but by mid-August 1988, their numbers had reached sixty thousand.[97] A few days after the cease-fire went into effect on August 20, Saddam Hussein ordered a "clean up" operation against Kurdish villages that had opposed his government during the war. The Iraqi army occupied all major roads linking Kurdish villages to each other and to the outside, and on August 25, the Iraqi air force launched air attacks using conventional and chemical weapons against Kurdish villages.[98] The severity of these attacks was such that between August 25 and September 1, more than fifty thousand Kurdish refugees fled to Turkey from their villages in Iraq.[99]

A group of health care professionals was sent to Turkish Kurdistan by the Massachusetts-based Physicians for Human Rights to examine the condition of Iraqi Kurdish refugees, and to investigate the use of chemical and poison gas against the Kurds. The following general conclusions were published in their report on February 1989:

1. *Iraqi aircraft attacked Kurdish villages in northern Iraq with bombs containing lethal poison gas on August 25, 1988.* This conclusion is based on responses to a systematically administered questionnaire, videotaped eyewitness accounts, and findings on physical examination of those residing in refugee camps in southeastern Turkey at the time of the mission.

2. *Poison gas bombs killed humans and animals nearby, and caused severe suffering among survivors.* Refugees consistently reported that attacks were carried out by low-flying jets early in the morning of August 25, 1988. Bombing runs were followed by the appearance of yellowish clouds at the site of bomb bursts. . . . No survivor reported being closer than 50 meters to a bomb blast.

3. *Survivors told consistent stories about the August 25 attacks, even when residing in separate camps with no opportunity to communicate.* Statistical analysis of responses to the questionnaire demonstrated that refugees originating from the same village gave mutually consistent answers regarding the time of the attack, weather conditions, number of attacking jets, and number of casualties in their village.

4. *Survivors showed medical findings consistent with exposure to poison gas.* We examined a middle-aged man who was a casualty of poison gas attacks. He had several extensive lesions on his back and flank, consistent with chemical burns by a blistering poison gas such as mustard gas (yperite). . . . Two children were also casualties, but had a different pattern of injury. . . . More than a dozen other refugees showed us skin lesions that had almost completely healed. Their pattern of distribution on face, hands, neck and other exposed skin surfaces was consistent with patients' histories of exposure to blistering chemical agents.

5. *Eyewitness accounts, the pattern of symptoms reported, and physical evidence obtained by others point to the use of lethal poison gases including, but not restricted to, sulfur mustard (yperite).* . . . The pattern of injury and time-course of symptoms are consistent with observations on [Iranian] victims of Iraqi chemical weapons made by UN investigatory teams from 1984 through 1988. . . . Eyewitness accounts of deaths beginning within minutes of exposure, however, cannot be explained by mustard gas alone. The sum of the evidence is most consistent with use of at least one agent in addition to sulfur mustard.[100]

These conclusions were corroborated by independent human rights sources and Western journalists who visited the Kurdish regions and interviewed victims of Iraqi attacks.[101]

The poison gas attacks in August 1988 were not the first time the Ba'thi government had used chemical weapons against its adversaries. During the Iran-Iraq War, Baghdad routinely used such weapons against Iranian targets, and later admitted to using chemical weapons against Iranians. The human rights organization Middle East Watch, quoting one expert, suggested that Iraq may have even resorted to the small-scale use of poison gas against the Kurds at the height of Mullah Mostafa's rebellion in 1974–1975.[102] However, the first major Iraqi chemical attack against Kurdish civilians that received worldwide attention occurred in March 1988. On March 16 and 17, Iraqi forces, using a combination of mustard gas and other internationally outlawed chemicals, attacked the Iraqi Kurdish city of Halabja, killing five thousand inhabitants.[103] The indiscriminate use of chemical weapons by the Ba'thi regime was not only a clear violation of the Geneva Protocol of 1925, which bans the use of poison gas in war, it was also a war crime against defenseless Kurdish civilians, the magnitude of which was initially supressed by Iraq's denial of Kurdish massacre.[104]

During the Iran-Iraq War, the city of Halabja was a center for anti–Saddam Hussein Kurdish movements, and it was the scene of several Iranian-Kurdish victories against Iraqi forces. Thus, the people of Halabja were apparently chosen to be made an example of what happened to those who sided with Iran. Rather than confronting Iranian-Kurdish forces with con-ventional weapons, Iraq apparently decided to use poison gas as a terror weapon to force the Kurds to desist from challenging Ba'thi forces in the north. Once the news of massive civilian casualties at Halabja reached the outside world, some reports speculated that the civilian population was caught in the middle of a major battle and victimized by poison gas used by both Iraq and Iran. The United States, among others, refrained from criticizing Iraq, partly because of the confusion surrounding the events at Halabja. How-ever, testimonies of survivors of the attack clarified that the battle for Halabja had already been won by Iranian forces and their Kurdish allies, and the city was in the control of anti-Iraqi elements when chemical weapons were dropped.

Although the international community remained surprisingly silent about the massacre at Halabja, Iran protested vigorously to the United Nations and demanded that the UN secretary general send an investigating team to the area. UN investigators, led by Dr. Manuel Dominguez, traveled to Iran and Iraq and examined survivors of the gas attack. In Iran, the patients Dr. Dominguez examined were "for the most part civilians who were listed as having been gassed at Halabja on dates between March 16 and 18 . . . [while the Iraqis] produced no victims or evidence to sustain allegations that the gas attack at Halabja in mid-March was the work of Iran."[105]

Iraq's use of chemical weapons against its Kurdish population caused a flood of Kurdish refugees. By October 1988, sixty thousand Kurds had fled to Turkey. Of these, seventeen thousand requested voluntary transfers to Iran, where they could join Massoud Barzani's KDP.[106] Some Kurdish leaders lobbied the United States to intercede on behalf of the Kurds. The PUK's secretary general, Jalal Talabani, arrived in Washington in June 1988 and held talks with middle-ranking State Department officials. As a protest, Iraq canceled a scheduled meeting between Secretary of State George Shultz and his Iraqi counterpart, Tariq Aziz. Baghdad viewed the cancellation of the Shultz-Aziz meeting as only a minor setback to Iraqi-US relations because, at the time, the United States was trying to bolster its alliance with Baghdad and to downplay the importance of Saddam Hussein's use of chemical weapons against the Kurdish uprising.[107] Iraq's relations with the United States suffered another setback, however, in November 1988 when the Iraqi government ordered Haywood Rankin, head of the Political Section of the US Embassy in Baghdad, to leave the country. Ba'thi authorities were incensed that Rankin had taken an unauthorized trip to the Kurdish region in the north.[108] The Iraqi government remained apprehensive about any outside contact with the Kurds.

During the summer of 1988, US legislators were showing signs of uneasiness over US-Iraqi relations as mounting evidence of the use of poison gas against the Kurds was putting the Ba'thi regime on the defensive. In September, when the US Senate voted to impose economic sanctions against Iraq in retaliation for using chemical weapons, Ba'thi authorities strongly protested to the United States for what they viewed as unwarranted and unjustified interference in Iraq's domestic affairs generated by "baseless rumors" and "unsubstantiated" evidence. Kuwait, a close ally of Saddam Hussein at the time, came to Iraq's defense by accusing the foreign media of "fabricating" the poison gas attacks against the Kurds in order to derail the growing friendship between the United States and the Gulf's dominant Arab state.[109] According to Iraqi sources, tens of thousands of Iraqis marched past the US Embassy in Baghdad denouncing the Senate's vote. Saddam Hussein issued a statement charging that the real purpose of the anti-Iraq vote was to divert world attention from the Palestinian uprising in the occupied territories in Israel.[110]

In October 1988, the US Senate took a tougher line when it voted to impose both economic and military sanctions against Iraq. The Senate's proposal called for a ban on the shipment of arms, military support equipment, and military-related technology to Iraq; and it called for US vetoes of loans from international lending agencies to Baghdad. The bill also called for the severance of diplomatic relations with Iraq if the government did not stop its chemical attacks on Kurdish targets. By late 1988, it seemed that Iraqi-US relations were reaching a breaking point over Iraq's use of chemical weapons. However, in November the Reagan administration intervened to smooth Iraqi-US relations by approving over $1 billion in credit guarantees to Baghdad for the purchase of agricultural commodities from the United States.

Throughout the second half of 1988 and the first half of 1989, Iraq focused on deflecting international condemnation of its use of poison gas against the Kurds, while announcing a major amnesty program for Kurds wishing to return from refugee camps in Turkey and Iran. The Ba'thi regime continued to deny that it had used chemical weapons against the Kurds. At times, Turkey issued supportive statements denying Iraq's use of chemical weapons. Ankara was concerned mostly with repatriating Iraqi Kurdish refugees and did not want any more. Furthermore, Turkey did not want to jeopardize its lucrative trade arrangements with Iraq, nor did it want to give Baghdad any excuse to renege on its $2 billion debt to Ankara. Therefore, it seemed that Turkey's corroboration of Iraqi denials had less to do with real evidence and more to do with commercial considerations.[111] It also appeared that the Turkish government had reached a tacit understanding with Saddam Hussein to deny the UN teams full access to refugee camps in southeastern Turkey to interview victims of poison gas attacks.

In early September 1988, officials representing the UN High Commissioner for Refugees (UNHCR) and the International Committee of the Red Cross visited Iraqi Kurdish refugees in shelters in the Iranian province of West Azerbaijan. They stated that despite the refugees' reports of Iraqi use of chemical weapons, the members of the team did not see evidence of this. At the same time, a two-person UNHCR team toured Kurdish refugee camps in southeastern Turkey. This group said that they had not received reports from Turkish medical authorities, nor had they seen evidence, to substantiate the refugees' claim of Iraqi use of chemical weapons against the Kurds. Based on these reports, the Turkish Foreign Ministry announced on September 14 that it would not allow any more UN experts into Turkey for the purpose of determining if Iraq had used chemical weapons against the Kurds.[112]

Many eyewitness accounts and investigations by independent human rights organizations and medical teams, however, had already uncovered evidence of Iraqi use of chemical weapons. On September 8, 1988, Amnesty International, in a strong appeal to the UN Security Council, condemned the continuing systematic attacks on Kurdish villages by Iraqi troops "using overwhelming force, including chemical weapons. . . . The mass killings are part of a systematic and deliberate policy by the Iraqi government to eliminate large numbers of Kurds."[113] Amnesty International later issued a detailed report on the victimization of children and documented a number of incidents of deliberate killings of children in the Iraqi attacks on Kurdish towns and villages.[114]

Unfazed by condemnation of its Kurdish policy, the Ba'thi government launched a public relations campaign to woo Kurdish refugees back to Iraq. In early September 1988, President Saddam Hussein issued a general amnesty to the Kurds, and by the end of the month, Iraqi authorities claimed that more than sixty-one thousand Kurdish refugees had returned home and were being provided for by the Iraqi government. One month later, with much fanfare, the government announced that a new town of Halabja would be built in Sulaymanieh governorate, and the government would allocate plots of land to as many people from the now-destroyed Halabja as possible.[115]

Despite the Iraqi government's optimistic estimations, the number of Kurdish refugees returning to Iraq remained low. As a result, Saddam Hussein announced on March 2, 1989, a second amnesty for all Kurds, except for the leadership of the Kurdish resistance movement and "agents of Iran." The Kurds were given until the end of April to take advantage of this second amnesty offer or forfeit their right of return.[116] However, the amnesty offer was undermined in April with the initiation of a sustained program of depopulating Kurdish villages along the Iranian and Turkish borders in order to establish a 30-kilometer buffer zone. This was justified as necessary to enhance Iraq's national security.[117] The establishment of the buffer zone and the population transfers helped convince Kurdish refugees not to return from Turkey and Iran. Thus, Saddam Hussein issued a third amnesty offer in March 1990. This time, he extended his amnesty offer to all Iraqi Kurds, including leaders of the opposition guerrilla groups supported by Iran.[118] The Kurds still remained wary of accepting Saddam's overture.

The September 1989 parliamentary elections in the Kurdish autonomous region were billed by the Ba'thi authorities as the dawn of a new era in Iraqi-Kurdish relations, and the government called upon its Kurdish population to turn out in full force. The government later announced that the elections were evidence of the success of its Kurdish policies; it reported almost 100 percent participation by the people of the three Kurdish provinces of Sulaymanieh, Irbil, and Dahuk. The elections resulted in the Ba'th Party winning thirty seats in the fifty-member legislative council for the autonomous region. The other seats were won either by independent candidates or members of pro-government Kurdish parties.[119] Neither Jalal Talabani's PUK nor Massoud Barzani's KDP contested the elections.

Perhaps no single exogenous factor was more important in boosting Saddam Hussein's confidence in dealing with his domestic agenda, including the Kurdish problem, than Iraq's developing relations with the United States in the 1980s. The Reagan administration's concern with preventing the "export" of Iran's Islamic revolution was no doubt a principal variable in developing the "mindset" in Washington, as the relationship became known among policymakers in the United States.[120] The beginning of the so-called honeymoon between Washington and Baghdad dated back to late 1981 and early 1982 when Saddam Hussein's invading army was chased back into Iraqi territory by Iranian forces. As his military position began to deteriorate, Saddam Hussein sent feelers to the United States, hoping to improve relations and gain US support for his war against the Islamic Republic.

The United States, still indignant at the "loss" of Iran, and hounded by the memory of the Iran hostage crisis of 1979–1980, was eager to help Iraq. The Reagan administration's ploy to "demonize" Iran and portray it as a "crazed wasteland of fanatics and their victims, a country governed by madmen and peopled by their unquestioning followers,"[121] justified their new-found friendship for the Ba'thi government in Iraq. Apparently, the Reagan administration was cognizant of the potential pitfalls in forging an anti-Iran alliance with Baghdad. According to Geoffrey Kemp, the top Middle East expert in President Reagan's National Security Council: "It wasn't that we wanted Iraq to win the war, we did not want Iraq to lose. We really weren't naive. We knew he [Saddam Hussein] was an S.O.B., but he was our S.O.B."[122]

The first concrete sign of Washington's tilt toward Baghdad came in March 1982 when the State Department removed Iraq from the list of countries supporting "international terrorism." As Noel Koch, the Defense Department's top counterterrorism official, divulged, the United States still considered Iraq a prime sponsor of terrorism. However, the Reagan administration wanted to help Saddam Hussein's regime succeed in the Iran-Iraq War; thus removing Iraq from the list of countries sponsoring terrorism was viewed within the broader context of Reagan's Gulf policy. This move allowed the United States to extend $2 billion in credits to Iraq, including $300 million for the purchase of US rice and wheat, thereby alleviating the severe economic strains under which the Iraqi regime was operating.[123] Despite the growing coincidence of interest between Washington and Baghdad, the two sides still had not reestablished diplomatic relations, which were severed after the June 1967 Arab-Israeli War.

Formal diplomatic relations between the United States and Iraq were restored on November 26, 1984. Iraqi foreign minister Tariq Aziz described the restoration of US-Iraqi diplomatic ties as a reflection of Iraq's growing importance in the world and its political maturity.[124] As US-Iraqi ties were strengthening, the Reagan administration made overtures to Iran, leading to what became known as the Iran-Contra affair. In the United States, the secret sales of weapons to Iran were interpreted as futile and embarrassing attempts by the Reagan administration either to exploit a geopolitical opening to Iran by currying favor with "moderate" factions in the Islamic Republic, or to influence Iran to help bring about the release of US hostages believed to be held in Lebanon by pro-Iranian groups. Although these factors may have influenced the United States in its "strategic opening" to Iran in the mid-1980s, there were other equally important variables that influenced the Reagan administration to sell arms to the Islamic Republic.

During the summer of 1985, analysts in Reagan's National Security Council and the CIA prepared a report predicting the imminent downfall of Ayatollah Khomeini and the Iranian government.[125] The CIA's Iran analyst, Graham Fuller, predicted a fierce struggle for power as a result of the demise of the Iranian government,[126] and based on intelligence information, the National Security Council predicted that long-term US interests would be threatened if Iran disintegrated.[127] In hindsight, the analyses contained in these reports were faulty, but they nevertheless contributed to the decision leading to the Reagan administration's arms sales to the Islamic Republic.[128]

Another explanation for US arms sales to Iran is based on the theory that the principal objective of the Reagan administration's geopolitical opening to the Islamic Republic was to encourage a military coup that would bring to power "some person or group less hostile to the US and Israel."[129] It was hoped that the arms would be funneled to the coup leaders. The arms sales were also supposed to serve Israel's geopolitical objectives by preoccupying Iraq with war with Iran, thus weakening the eastern flank of Arab opposition to Israel. As became evident later, Israel did play an active role in the arms shipments to Iran and in promoting US policies toward Iran.[130] Irrespective of the causes of the Iran-Contra affair, the revelations of the Reagan administration's secret deals with the Islamic Republic created a political whirlwind that led to another major US tilt toward Iraq.

The Reagan administration distanced itself from the implications of the Iran-Contra affair by taking a more passive posture toward Iraq and its suppression of the Kurds. In addition to reports made by independent human rights organizations about Iraq's destruction of Kurdish villages, the United States had firsthand reports from its own investigating officials that confirmed allegations made against the Ba'thi regime by independent organizations. For example, Peter Galbraith, a professional staff member of the Senate Foreign Relations Committee, who visited Iraqi Kurdistan in 1987, prepared an extensive report documenting Iraq's destruction of Kurdish villages. In Galbraith's words: "The place [Iraqi Kurdistan] had a kind of eerie silence and beauty, but what had once been an area filled with villages and life and some 2 million people was suddenly empty. The Kurdish villages that had been there almost since the beginning of time were gone. Their inhabitants had been moved to concentration camps erected hastily around a few major towns."[131] Although the US Senate passed resolutions aimed at punishing Iraq, particularly after reports of the use of chemical weapons against the Kurds became public, neither President Reagan nor President Bush took any meaningful actions. It was only after Iraq's invasion of Kuwait on August 2, 1990, that the Bush administration shifted its benign policy toward Saddam Hussein's Iraq.

Of course, it was not just the power brokers in Washington who remained silent in the face of Iraqi atrocities. As Christopher Hitchens poignantly observed:

> How many lobbyists and arms peddlers spent how many evenings during the eighties at the Washington dinner table of Iraq's U.S. ambassador, Nizar Hamdoon? And how often, do you imagine, was Hamdoon asked even the most delicately phrased question about his government's

continued killing of the Kurds, including unarmed women and children?[132]

Even some policy-oriented intellectuals, who had become prisoners of their own anti-Iranian rhetoric, encouraged the administration to pursue a pro-Ba'thi foreign policy. Again, Christopher Hitchens's remarks are worth repeating:

> It can be amusing to look up some of Saddam's former fans. Allow me to open for you the April 27, 1987, issue of *The New Republic*, where we find an essay engagingly entitled "Back Iraq," by Daniel Pipes and Laurie Mylroie. These two distinguished Establishment interpreters, under the unavoidable subtitle "It's time for a U.S. 'tilt,'" managed to anticipate the recent crisis [Iraq's invasion of Kuwait] by more than three years. Sadly they got the name of the enemy wrong.[133]

In the same vein, a report prepared by three military analysts at the US Army War College, and released just before Iraq's invasion of Kuwait, supported Saddam Hussein by claiming that he enjoyed significant popular support. The report concluded: "Thus today in Iraq we have a regime that views its rule as legitimate, and an army that is confident and supportive of the regime's policy; on top of which, all opposition inside Iraq has collapsed. The Kurdish movement has been crushed. . . . The Iraq of today is not the same entity that existed when the [Iran-Iraq] war broke out in 1980. . . . We must do everything in our power to gain appreciation of the scope of these changes."[134] On the issue of Iraq's chemical weapons use, the report sought to exonerate the Ba'thi government by stating that there was no conclusive evidence that Baghdad used poison gas against its Kurdish population. The authors of this Pentagon report reiterated Saddam Hussein's oft-mentioned justification for possession of chemical weapons:

> In the specific case of Iraq's possession of chemicals, Baghdad cited national security as a justification, arguing that chemical weapons are the answer to Iranian zealotry. The chemicals inspire panic in the fanatical Iranians, and are thus effective in breaking up their human wave attacks. Viewed in this light, gas can be seen as the Iraqis' most significant deterrent.[135]

In view of these analyses, it was not surprising that Saddam Hussein resorted to the use of chemical weapons with relative impunity.

THE INVASION OF KUWAIT,
THE GULF WAR, AND THE KURDISH REVOLT

On August 2, 1990, Iraqi forces invaded Kuwait after several weeks of acrimonious charges by Saddam Hussein against the rulers of Kuwait for overproducing oil, lowering prices, and thus "impoverishing" Iraq, which needed higher oil revenues to finance reconstruction projects after eight years of war with neighboring Iran. After occupying Kuwait, Saddam Hussein revived the old Iraqi claim to Kuwait and declared it to be the nineteenth province of Iraq.[136] President Bush ordered the deployment of a large number of US air, naval, and ground troops in and around Saudi Arabia under Operation Desert Shield. When Operation Desert Shield was transformed into Operation Desert Storm with the start of the Allied war against Iraq in January 1991, the United States had deployed over 500,000 troops in the Arabian peninsula.

With the largest deployment of US troops overseas since the heyday of the Vietnam War, President Bush identified four goals: (1) the unconditional withdrawal of Iraqi troops from Kuwait, (2) the protection of the lives of US citizens living in Kuwait and Iraq, (3) the defense of Saudi Arabia and a commitment to the security and stability of the Gulf, and (4) the restoration of the al-Sabah family as the legitimate government of Kuwait.[137] Perhaps the fifth, but unstated, goal in confronting Iraqi aggression against Kuwait was the overthrow of Saddam Hussein. Sadly, nowhere in the US agenda was mention made of helping popular democratic institutions and forces, or aiding in the Middle Eastern people's struggle for self-determination. Well aware of the abysmal human rights records and undemocratic natures of Saudi Arabia and Kuwait, perhaps the United States felt inhibited in this regard.

The Iraqi regime, which had been courted and supported by the United States throughout the 1980s, was turned overnight into a demonic entity with superpower ambitions. Reports of Iraq using chemical weapons against the Kurds and Iranians, which had been ignored, were publicized in US print and electronic media as if they were novel revelations. The Iraqi dictator was described as another Hitler by the Bush administration and transformed into "a worldwide metaphysical threat. . . . [Iraq] was verbally obliterated except for its by now isolated leader."[138] A host of analysts joined in a chorus of condemnations of Iraq. A host of individuals in academic, journalistic, and policymaking circles, who had in one way or another supported Saddam Hussein's foreign policy in the 1980s, joined the bandwagon with no compunction.

On the morning of the Iraqi invasion of Kuwait, Jalal Talabani, who was at his home in Damascus, was informed by a friend of Saddam Hussein's latest move. The Iraqi Kurdish leader reportedly expressed satisfaction at hearing this news, thought that Saddam Hussein had committed a monumental blunder, and predicted that it would lead to his downfall.[139] On August 12, 1990, Talabani made his second trip to the United States in two years, hoping he would succeed in attracting US support for his PUK. According to one account, Talabani met with middle-ranking State Department officials and offered to raise a thirty-thousand-man army in northern Iraq within weeks in order to reduce pressure on US forces stationed

in Saudi Arabia. Talabani also offered to launch guerrilla attacks in cities
throughout Iraq and to try to assassinate Saddam Hussein on behalf of the
United States. US officials were not receptive to Talabani's offers, causing a
Talabani aide to threaten to make a deal with Saddam instead because "in this
world, there are no permanent enemies."[140] While in the United States,
Talabani reportedly also met with Senator Claiborne Pell, chairman of the
Senate Foreign Relations Committee, and Senator John Kerry, chairman of
the subcommittee on terrorism. Neither senator endorsed US involvement in
Kurdish armed rebellion against Saddam Hussein, nor did they promise to
arrange US funding for Iraqi opposition movements.[141]

With the start of Allied attacks against Iraq, the Kurds feared that they
might become the victims of a war they did not support. Specifically, the
Kurds were apprehensive about the consequences of US bombing runs
originating from the Incirlik air base in Turkey against targets in Kurdish-
inhabited northern and western Iraq. They also feared an Iraqi backlash against
Turkey that would result in Turkish counterattacks. As one Kurdish civil
rights lawyer stated, "We see the war as a disaster. . . . If Turkey fights Iraq,
it will be mainly the Kurdish population that gets hurt."[142] Massoud Barzani
sought to keep Iraq's Kurdish areas out of the war zone by rejecting outside
pressure to open a second front against Saddam's forces. Barzani's main
concern was that if a second front were established, Saddam Hussein might
retaliate by using chemical weapons against Kurdish villages as he did in
1988.[143]

Notwithstanding Massoud Barzani's initial hesitation to open a second
front against Saddam Hussein, Iraqi Kurds revolted in March 1991 after the
defeat of Saddam's military by the US-led forces in the southern theater. A
CIA-run radio station (The Voice of Free Iraq) operating from Jedda, Saudi
Arabia, had been encouraging a Kurdish revolt for several weeks, and the
Kurds were led to believe that they would receive outside assistance if they
led an uprising against the Iraqi government.[144] Initially, the Kurds gained
control of a few cities, but they were driven back by Iraqi forces attacking
them from the air and land. As a consequence, Kurdish villages were
devastated once more, and another mass exodus of Kurdish refugees started.
An estimated 500,000 Kurds fled to Turkey and 1.5 million to Iran when
they realized they were defenseless. Thus, the number of Kurdish casualties
was reduced compared to the devastated Shi'a south, which had suffered the
brunt of the Allied bombings.[145] Once again, fear of reprisal appeared to have
been a major factor in the Kurdish flight in March and April 1991. Saddam
Hussein's cousin, Ali Hassan Majid, who led the 1988 poison gas attacks
against the Kurds, was appointed interior minister after the Kurdish uprising
started. According to eyewitness reports, the new interior minister traveled to
Kirkuk, rounded up a large number of young men, and warned them of severe
consequences if they did not cease their revolt.[146] According to Kurdish
eyewitnesses, people had been fleeing Kirkuk and other Kurdish cities in

large numbers since early March when the revolt broke out. In Sulaymanieh, many people fled on April 3, just before the Iraqis arrived and began bombing the city. International eyewitness accounts reported that people were afraid that what happened in Kirkuk would take place in Sulaymanieh, and they fled the city before the Iraqi army could descend upon them.[147]

In addition to terrorizing the civilian population, Saddam Hussein's crackdown on the Kurdish uprising left deep rifts in the opposition. Some members of the Kurdish opposition made matters worse when they began to harass and threaten Kurds who worked for the government as civil servants or who worked in the oil refineries. In any case, the effectiveness of the Iraqi forces in putting down the Kurdish rebellion and the plight of the refugees compelled the two leading groups within the Iraq Kurdistan Front, the PUK and KDP, to seek peace with the Iraqi regime.

Many Kurds felt that with a defeated Saddam Hussein, the time was right to sign an agreement that would maximize their prospects of gaining autonomy within a federated Iraqi state. Furthermore, the Kurds reasoned that if another person or group came to power in Baghdad, there would be no guarantee that they would not behave the same way toward the Kurds as Saddam Hussein. Without a peaceful settlement, some Kurdish leaders also thought that there would be a permanent refugee problem, creating fertile ground for outside powers to exploit the Kurdish situation and "for all sorts of negative tendencies" to develop within the refugee population.[148] Another impetus for an Iraqi-Kurdish rapprochement was the high price Kurdish soldiers had paid by serving in the Iraqi army during the Gulf War. According to one estimate, two hundred thousand Kurds were members of the Iraqi occupation army in Kuwait. Although no casualty figures are available, it is safe to assume that they were among the several thousand Iraqi soldiers who died during the saturation bombing runs of Iraqi targets during the war.

Many reported Iraqi army deserters who escaped with their weapons to Iran were Kurdish soldiers.[149] Kurdish soldiers were strongly criticized by Shaikh Saud al-Sabah, the Kuwaiti ambassador to the United States, for alleged brutality against Kuwaitis. In an interview given to *USA Today*, Ambassador al-Sabah claimed that eighty percent of the Iraqi occupation soldiers who were "raping Kuwait, pillaging Kuwait were Kurds. . . . I don't personally have much sympathy as you have for the Kurds. . . . They are more brutal, they are more violent than the rest of the Iraqis. . . . There are Kurds who stole everything and pillaged everything."[150] Surprisingly, such sentiments were similar to the Iraqi government's principle of collective responsibility, utilized when punishing the Kurdish population. This principle, according to Samir al-Khalil, had been "legislatively recognized and systematically practiced inside Iraq" against the Kurds. It transferred blame to entire families or communities for the transgressions of one or more members of that community.[151]

The first round of Iraqi-Kurdish negotiations was held in late April 1991 in Baghdad between Ba'thi authorities and a team of Kurdish negotiators representing the Iraq Kurdistan Front headed by Jalal Talabani. The other members of the Kurdish team included Rasoul Mamand, secretary general of the Kurdish Socialist Party, Sami Abdul Rahman, secretary general of the People's Party of Kurdistan, and Nashirwan Barzani, a nephew of Massoud Barzani, representing the KDP. The inclusion of representatives of various Kurdish groups as members of the negotiating team was intended to demonstrate that the Kurds were a united front.

Talabani was careful not to raise high expectations. He insisted that he was simply negotiating with the Iraqis and was not intent on signing a final agreement with the government. Nonetheless, he described a new mood of "realism" in Baghdad with regard to recognition of Kurdish autonomy. As the talks progressed, Talabani stated that he had "never seen such a positive attitude before. We could not overthrow them [the Ba'thi forces], and they could not crush us. So we are both looking for another solution, which is a peaceful solution."[152] Responding to criticism of his overtures toward Saddam Hussein, especially from the Shi'a opposition in the south, Talabani and his colleagues retorted that anyone in their position would have done the same thing to avert a calamitous tragedy. "We cannot accept another Armenia and the depopulation of Kurdistan. I would have been against negotiations otherwise. But we cannot just act as a political party, we have three million refugees to think about. We need them to go home and rebuild. . . . We have no friends to help us. . . . If we were supported by others, we could fight for a long time, but without the Kurdish people at home, we can't do anything."[153]

Despite the start of negotiations, most Kurds doubted they would succeed and continued to oppose the regime. To some observers, negotiating with Saddam Hussein was an acknowledgment of the failure of Kurdish fighters to wage a sustained, unified, full-scale war against the regime. Even when the Kurds occupied a town, they were unable to govern it and establish order. In the words of a Kurdish elder, there was "no recognized form of cooperation among the clans. They did not know how to operate the tanks, planes, and helicopters they seized from the Iraqis."[154] These sentiments were echoed by Jalal Talabani as he lamented the Kurdish lack of unity and organizational cohesiveness.[155]

The Talabani-led team of Kurdish negotiators did not sign an agreement with the Iraqi government. However, another round of Iraqi-Kurdish talks began in June 1991. This time, the negotiations were led by the KDP's Massoud Barzani, whose talks with Saddam generated optimism that peace was at hand when the KDP announced the impending signing of an agreement on Kurdish autonomy. The status of Kirkuk, which had derailed many previous negotiations, remained an unresolved issue, causing opposition to the impending deal with Saddam Hussein. At the same time, Iran announced the formation of the Kurdish Islamic Movement to oppose any concessions to the Iraqi regime.[156] The new movement, to be led by Ahmad Barzani, encompassed "all Islamic elements" who rejected compromise with the Ba'thi regime.

A major reason for Iran's opposition was the provision in the agreement that committed the Kurds to joining Saddam's forces in fighting Iraqi Shi'as in the south. Iran was also intent on exploiting the close collaboration between the Iraqi regime and the Iranian opposition mujahidin guerrillas by enticing the Kurds to attack the mujahidin forces inside Iraq. Eyewitness reports that publicized mujahidin participation on the side of the Iraqi army against the Kurdish uprising helped the Iranian cause. British journalist David Hirst reported on one incident in which the Kurdish *peshmergas* trapped fifty-seven pro-Iraqi mujahidin fighters (including seventeen women) in a school and shot them all to death.[157]

Although the details of Barzani's agreement with the Iraqi government were not publicly divulged, Kurdish negotiators revealed the outline of the agreement:

1. The Kurdistan Front would be obligated to support the 1968 revolution that brought the Ba'th Party to power. (Barzani said his agreement with Saddam called for separating the Ba'th Party from the government.)
2. The Kurdish Front would need the Ba'th's permission to contact foreign governments and organizations.
3. The [Kurdish] Front would be obliged to back the Ba'th Party against any of its enemies. First, that would mean Iran. Second, [it would require] the Kurds to help suppress the Shi'as in the south.
4. All Kurdish political prisoners would be freed immediately.
5. The Kurds' clandestine radio stations would be shut down and they [the Kurdish groups] would get time on the government radio and television stations in the [Kurdish] region.
6. Once the oil sales resume, Baghdad and the Kurds will negotiate a formula for turning over a "significant" share of the revenues to the regional government.
7. Baghdad will compensate those Kurds whose homes have been destroyed or who suffered torture at the central government's hands.
8. Kurdish elders will rule the region for three months at which point elections will be held in the [Kurdish] autonomous region. National elections will be held within six to twelve months.[158]

For a while, it seemed that all partners in the Iraq Kurdistan Front were going to agree with Massoud Barzani and sign a peace agreement with Baghdad. However, Jalal Talabani's PUK rejected Barzani's plan. Instead, Talabani, in a surprise announcement from Turkey, proposed that Turkey take a more active role in solving the Iraqi Kurdish problem and denounced Abdullah

Ocalan and his PKK for continuing the Kurdish struggle against the Turkish state.[159] Once again, the Kurds became victims of their own personal and group rivalries.

In July 1991, talks on Kurdish autonomy were moved from Baghdad to the Kurdish city of Irbil, where Kurdish leaders met with Izzat Ibrahim, Saddam Hussein's second in command in the ruling Revolutionary Command Council. In addition to the autonomy demands made in prior talks, the Kurds put forward a new proposal for establishing democracy in Iraq that would involve the oppressed Shi'a majority.[160] Although no agreement was reached, the Iraqis, perhaps by default, allowed more Kurdish armed presence in the region, including the major cities of Irbil and Sulaymanieh. The close proximity of armed *peshmergas* to Iraqi troops caused a number of skirmishes between the two sides. On July 21, after three days of fighting, the *peshmergas*, mostly from the KDP, ousted Iraqi troops from Sulaymanieh.[161] This marked the first time since the March uprisings that a major Kurdish city was reclaimed by Kurdish forces. Iraqi authorities accused Iran of inciting the Kurdish attacks on the Iraqis by sending money, infiltrators, and weapons to the Kurds. This charge of interference in Iraq's domestic affairs was vehemently denied by Iran, and it accused Iraq of blaming exogenous factors for its own inability to solve its Kurdish problem peacefully.[162] Ironically, after their capture of Sulaymanieh, the *peshmergas* found themselves providing police protection to officials who had been appointed by the Iraqi government, including Sulaymanieh's governor.

The Kurdish uprisings in Iraq and the subsequent refugee problems in the aftermath of the Gulf War presented major challenges to the United States and its allies in the war, including Turkey. The Turks were not pleased with the flood of over 500,000 Kurdish refugees into their country. In fact, they opposed the mass entry of Kurds into Turkey and closed their borders for a few days immediately after the first surge of refugees entered southeastern Turkey. At the same time, the Turkish government continued a secret dialogue with Iraqi Kurdish leaders, mindful of the fact that promoting autonomy for Iraqi Kurds would have unpredictable repercussions for Turkey's restive Kurdish population. President Ozal's decision to hold talks with the Iraqi Kurds was apparently predicated on the assumption that they were about to gain autonomy and might even declare independence from Iraq, which the Turkish government opposes.[163]

Furthermore, the Turks wanted to prevent the creation of permanent or semipermanent refugee camps and their "Palestinianization," in which the camps would become breeding grounds for Kurdish guerrillas who would fight alongside PKK *peshmergas* against Turkey. Also, Ankara feared that refugee camps would become "a new source of discord between Turkey and the West, if the West supported Kurdish nationalist aspirations."[164] An additional factor that prompted Turkey to oppose the mass entry of Kurdish refugees was that it viewed the refugee exodus as a deliberate plot by Saddam

Hussein to destabilize Turkey. One high-ranking Turkish army officer contended that if Saddam Hussein wanted to prevent a mass exodus of Kurds from Iraq, he could have easily ordered Iraqi soldiers to encircle the Kurds, rather than "pushing" them toward the Turkish border.[165]

To the surprise of some outsiders, pressure to prevent a large influx of Iraqi Kurds into Turkey after the Gulf War also came from within Kurdish circles in Turkey. This marked one of the few instances in which the interests of the Turkish Kurds and the state coincided. As a member of Van's Kurdish committee stated: "If the Turkish government opens the border, . . . then the world will forget the problem. It will be a matter of refugees, of money, and we Kurds will have to forget our land."[166] When Allied forces established a "safe haven" zone inside Iraq, deploying seventeen thousand troops, Turkey welcomed the move. However, friction and misunderstanding caused by the presence of Western troops near the Iraqi-Turkish border led to uneasiness among Kurds about the wisdom of such a force. Opposition leaders and the Turkish press complained that "US and British commanders are acting as colonial masters."[167] The Western allies were sensitive about this issue as well. When a British marine unit manhandled a high-level Turkish official and prevented him from inspecting the Kurdish camps, the unit was ordered out immediately, and British defense secretary Tom King was sent to Ankara to deliver a formal apology to the Turkish government.

PKK guerrillas exploited the presence of Western troops by accusing the Turkish government of mortgaging the Kurdish future to "international imperialism and neocolonialism" and betraying Turkish national interests and sovereignty rights. As a result, the PKK launched a series of attacks on Turkish targets, culminating in the murder of three high-ranking provincial officials in Sohal on April 28, 1991, and the winning of local support for its stance against the Western military presence in Kurdistan.[168] The PKK's resurgence was reflected in the volume of threats issued by its operatives against Allied installations in northern Iraq and Turkey, and against "traitors" Massoud Barzani and Jalal Talabani, who engaged in dialogues with the Turkish and Iraqi governments.

Finally, the stationing of five thousand US, British and French troops on Turkish soil beginning in July 1991 under the media-bestowed code name Operation Poised Hammer generated pitfalls for Turkey. This force, which was intended to act as a deterrence to further Iraqi military moves against the Kurds and, if deterrence failed, to function as a "rapid reaction force" to intervene in Iraq, prompted domestic opposition within Turkey. The Turkish press and opposition leaders reacted negatively to the stationing of the force on Turkish soil. Many Turks not only feared that their country's sovereignty might be jeopardized by the presence of a Western rapid reaction force in their country, but also thought it imprudent for Turkey to alienate its neighbors by collaborating with Western countries in interfering in their domestic affairs. Erdal Inonu, the Social Democratic opposition leader, has also complained bitterly that Turkey had no duty to act as protector of ethnic groups in other countries. If such protection was to be provided, it should have been under the auspices of the United Nations. All in all, the broad spectrum of Turks who expressed displeasure at their country's involvement in the Allied military venture feared that in the end the Western rapid reaction force would be the "hammer" and Turkey the "anvil" of Operation Poised Hammer.[169]

When the Gulf War ended in February 1991 with Iraq's military defeat and what amounted to an unconditional surrender by Saddam Hussein's government, the Bush administration was confident that the Iraqi military would stage a coup and overthrow Saddam Hussein. The CIA estimated that Saddam's regime would be overthrown within six months to a year after the disorderly and humiliating Iraqi surrender and capitulation to US-imposed conditions.[170] When the predicted overthrow of Saddam Hussein did not materialize, Washington, in concert with British and Saudi Arabian officials, began to court a variety of Iraqi opposition groups, including the largely discredited exiled groups in London and Syria.

The US-led search for a suitable (i.e., pro-Western and/or pro-Saudi) replacement for Saddam Hussein was disrupted by spontaneous, grassroots uprisings by the Shi'a majority in the south in early March 1991 and the Kurdish minority in the north immediately thereafter. Fearing the breakup of the Iraqi state, the United States initially ruled out intervention in defense of the anti–Saddam Hussein uprisings. The Bush administration explained its refusal to help in terms of its desire not to interfere in other countries' internal affairs. As a result, on March 5, four days after President Bush had publicly exhorted the Iraqi people to "get rid of Saddam," the White House issued a statement saying: "We don't intend to get involved in Iraq's internal affairs."[171] This assertion was astonishing, given the fact that the United States had just massively involved itself in Iraq's affairs and was not only encouraging the overthrow of the Iraqi government (a call that became more strident in tone and repetitiveness throughout the summer of 1991), but was also taking active steps to further destabilize Iraq.

The lack of US assistance for the Kurdish and Shi'a rebels had little to do with observing the internationally recognized principle of noninterference in other countries' domestic affairs. The fear of an Iraqi breakup, and the regional instability that such a breakup would engender, was the primary factor in dissuading the Bush administration from assisting the rebels. Furthermore, the Bush administration had concluded that the insurgencies would fail to dislodge Saddam Hussein. Both Washington and Riyadh still felt that a coup, staged by officers controlled by or sympathetic to US and Saudi interests, was the preferred option.[172] The US phobia about Iran also contributed to the Bush administration's hesitance to provide immediate help to the Shi'as. As a State Department official explained, the United States "shared with the Saudis a concern about Iranian-backed radical Shi'a coming to power in Iraq."[173] When the Kurdish uprising followed, the United States feared the total collapse of Baghdad's military and the "Lebanonization" of Iraq. In addition, concerns about the spill-over effects of the success of the Kurdish uprising in Iraq, and its implications for Turkish stability, prompted the Bush administration to take a neutral stand.

Even if the United States had decided to intervene, some argued, there would have been no guarantee that the suffering of the Kurds would be alleviated. As Professor Shibley Telhami of Cornell University argued in an op-ed article in the *New York Times*, US intervention would have misled the Kurds because the United States "cannot shape Iraq's political system. U.S. involvement would only excite the Kurds enough to make the fight bloodier, and they would be let down later—their lot for decades."[174] Daniel Pipes, of the Foreign Policy Research Institute in Philadelphia, also warned the Bush administration about overzealous involvement in Iraq's civil war with the hope of US forces in control and General Schwarzkopf ruling the country. As Pipes cautioned: "It sounds romantic, but watch out. Like the Israelis in southern Lebanon nine years ago, American troops would find themselves quickly hated. . . . Staying in place would become too painful, leaving too humiliating."[175] Debates about the wisdom of US military involvement in Iraqi Kurdish affairs became academic as events inside Iraq compelled the Bush administration to extend its involvement beyond providing food and shelter to the growing number of Kurdish refugees; steps needed to be taken to ensure their physical safety.

With the specter of thousands of hungry and dying Kurds trapped in the mountainous region of Kurdistan looming larger, pressure on the international community to intervene grew stronger. The European Community (EC), in its April 8, 1991, emergency summit meeting in Luxembourg, endorsed a proposal by British prime minister John Major to establish a "safe haven" for the Kurds in northern Iraq. A similar proposal had been made earlier by President Ozal of Turkey. The safe haven would operate under the auspices of the United Nations, with troops from the Allied forces, and involve a two-stage process. The first stage would involve bringing the Kurds down from the mountains, and the second stage would require the safe return of the Kurds to their homes.[176] Prime Minister Major contended that his proposal was within the framework of the UN Security Council's resolution authorizing humanitarian assistance to the people of Iraq. Britain also cited the 1948 Genocide Convention as legal justification for the implementation of his proposal to prevent the "genocide" of the Kurds. The United States supported the legality of establishing a UN-controlled safe haven in northern Iraq by referring to a recent precedent in which the UN established safe areas for Indochinese refugees on the Cambodian-Thai border.

The Bush administration warned Iraq not to interfere with the humanitarian efforts to aid the Kurdish refugees. The United States prevented the Iraqi military from flying north of the thirty-sixth parallel, located just south of Irbil. Then, on April 17, the United States moved troops into northern Iraq to secure sites for establishing safety zones for the Kurds under the direction of US, British, and French soldiers. From the start, the legality of establishing an extraterritorial unit inside a sovereign country was challenged. Ahmad Hussein Khudayer, the new Iraqi foreign minister, rejected the US move by stating that his country and the United Nations had already reached an agreement to ameliorate the Kurdish crisis by allowing the UN to run "humanitarian centers" for the refugees in northern and southern Iraq. Prime Minister Hamadi reiterated his country's intention to resist "with its means" Western military encroachments in Iraqi Kurdistan.[177] The Soviet Foreign Ministry issued a statement casting doubt on the legality of the US move. Vitaly Churkin, spokesman for the Soviet Foreign Ministry, indicated that establishing a safe haven without Iraq's consent would violate the UN charter and set "an undesirable precedent." Furthermore, Churkin noted the serious problem such a safe haven would create for the UN Security Council "in connection with the need to define borders, the international legal status of the zone, and the ethnic makeup of its population."[178] The Soviets, however, were pressured by the United States and its Western allies to drop their opposition, and by late April, they gave a guarded endorsement of the idea of a safety zone inside Iraq.

By May 1991, Western forces had established a seventy-five-by-thirty-mile safety zone. Although United Nations observers were present in the zone and one hundred to five hundred UN security guards moved into the area, it was clear that it was a US-run zone, and not a UN-run zone. However, US officials indicated that US and other Western troops would move out of the area soon and that they would like the United Nations to run the safety zone in Iraq. On May 22, the United States appeared to extend the zone to Dahuk, located just outside the declared safety zone for the Kurds. Although some feared that the United States was unilaterally expanding its military presence in northern Iraq, US officials insisted that this move was a temporary measure designed to allow doctors, engineers, and other specialists to provide the needed services to convince 100,000 Kurdish refugees to return home. By agreement, Iraqi soldiers evacuated Dahuk, but were allowed to stay within four miles of the city limits.[179]

By mid-July 1991, Western troops had completed their withdrawal from the safety zone in northern Iraq. As previously mentioned, after evacuating from Iraq, Western forces set up a rapid reaction force based in Silopi in Turkey, five miles from the Iraqi border. Although the size, structure, and term of existence of this force was to be finalized in consultation with Turkey, the force's stated mission was to prevent another Iraqi attack on the Kurds, and hence obviate the need for a mass Kurdish exodus to Turkey. The location of the rapid reaction force close to the Cudi mountain range could create problems; the area has long been an important hideout for the PKK guerrillas. Periodic clashes have taken place between the PKK forces and

Turkish soldiers near the Silopi base, and in early July 1991, Silopi was the scene of a skirmish between the two sides.[180] In early August, Turkish troops, backed by fighter planes and helicopters, launched a massive five-day operation against Kurdish strongholds and carried their military attacks into Iraq. Kurdish villagers accused the Allied troops stationed in Turkey of acquiescing to this operation. Given the PKK's stated opposition to the Western military presence in Turkey, it is conceivable that troops of the rapid reaction force might be dragged into the long-standing Kurdish-Turkish conflict with incalculable consequences.

Notwithstanding US involvement on behalf of the Kurds, in the long run, the contours of US foreign policy in the Middle East are determined by macro concerns such as maintaining the stability of friendly regimes and enhancing strategic, political, and economic interests in the region. Within this context, the United States will not promote Kurdish nationalism, and few in Washington, or in Baghdad, believe the sincerity of the oft-repeated Kurdish political slogan "autonomy for Kurdistan, democracy for Iraq." As a senior Bush administration Middle East analyst put it: "It's autonomy today, but a separate state tomorrow. We all know that." Another Bush administration official put it more bluntly, saying: "It probably sounds callous, but we did the best thing not to get near [the Kurdish revolt]. They're nice people, and they're cute, but they're really just bandits. They spend as much time fighting each other as central authority. They're losers."[181] Such cynical views undoubtedly contributed to the formulation of Washington's policies toward the Kurdish uprising in Iraq in 1991.

Finally, Iran's response to the Kurdish refugee problem needs to be examined. Unlike Turkey, which closed its border to the Iraqi Kurds and reopened it only because of international pressure and the massive humanitarian aid given to it by international agencies and the West, Iran opened its border to fleeing Kurds from the beginning. The number of Kurdish refugees in Iran eventually reached 1.5 million, triple the number in Turkey. Given the fact that Iran already housed one of the largest refugee populations in the world, mostly Afghans and Iraqi Shi'as, the influx of Iraqi Kurds gave the Islamic Republic the largest refugee population in the world.

The response of the international community to the Kurdish refugee problem in Iran was slow. When some Western countries finally did contribute to the humanitarian efforts of the Iranian government, the response was minimal compared to Turkey. The disproportionate response of the West to the plight of the Kurdish refugees in Iran suggests that Iran's isolation from the West, particularly the United States, created a blind spot in the eyes of the international donor agencies, which are dominated by Western donors. By mid-May 1991, the United States had contributed more than $200 million for Kurdish refugee relief operations, less than $20 million of which was earmarked to assist the Kurdish refugees in Iran. For every dollar spent by international relief agencies on a Kurdish refugee in Iran, $7.60 was spent on a Kurdish refugee in Turkey. At the same time, according to international relief agencies, Iran was spending $10 million per day from its strained budget to care for the Kurdish refugees in Iran.[182] As an analysis made by the US Committee for Refugees indicated, the net result of this disproportionality was that the "refugees for whom Iran was the nearest border were penalized for their host government's poor relations with the United States. The foreign policy bias that drives US refugee policy not only resulted in less food and dirtier water for refugees in Iran, but perhaps accounts for the inability of 'the best minds of the refugee world' to see the approach of the most monumental refugee wave in memory."[183]

For the magnitude of its response to the Kurdish plight and the enormity of the economic burden it shouldered to accommodate the refugees' needs, Iran received praise from the Kurds. As one Iraqi Kurd stated: "The point is not whether our refugees are well fed. We must first thank the Islamic Republic which opened its borders and did not let our people die in the snow."[184] Likewise, several international relief agencies praised Iran's efforts on behalf of the Kurdish refugees. As an international relief officer asked: "Which European country would have admitted such a flow of refugees? . . . [I am] impressed by the efficiency of the Iranian administration and the rapidity with which they settled these refugees."[185]

From the beginning of the first refugee influx, Iranian officials and religious figures issued edicts asking all Iranians to assist the Kurds as a national, moral, and religious duty. As a consequence, the Kurds were not simply quartered in refugee camps, many were welcomed into Iranian homes throughout Kurdistan and Western Azerbaijan. By mid-April, the population of the city of Piranshahr had reached 125,000, up from its pre-refugee size of 25,000. Schools, mosques, and other public centers in many Iranian cities were turned into shelters for the Iraqi Kurds.[186] However, as the number of refugees soared, Iranian resources reached a breaking point. Health conditions began to deteriorate in some refugee camps. Dysentery and the lack of adequate medical care caused deaths in overcrowded camps. Typhoid fever broke out in a camp in Salmas, which housed 25,000 refugees, raising concern among the medical staff that without outside assistance, death tolls in some camps would increase rapidly.[187] This and similar incidents compelled the Iranian authorities to ask for immediate outside assistance.

Political obstacles hampered relief efforts from the West. First, Iran remained suspicious of US aid. Officials in the Islamic Republic suspected that the United States wanted to destabilize the region by stationing troops in the area on the pretext of establishing a "safe haven" for the Kurds. As some "radical" Iranian officials saw it, the main objective of creating a safety zone in northern Iraq was the de facto partitioning of Iraq and the establishment of "a second Israel" in the region.[188] Second, the Bush administration did not want to signal a diplomatic opening to Iran by being overanxious to send relief for the refugees in Iranian territory. However, in late April 1991, a US

Air Force C-141 transport plane received authorization to deliver a 145,000-pound load of privately donated blankets to Iran, marking the first time since 1979 that a US military plane landed in Tehran's Mehrabad airport on an officially divulged mission.

Shortly after receiving the first US shipment, Iran complained bitterly about the poor quality of the items sent for the refugees. The Iranians criticized the shipment for being "soiled and unusable," and indicated that it would be returned. Secondhand clothing, quite common in Western donations and acceptable by recipients of aid in many countries, is frowned upon in Iran. Within Islamic Iran's cultural framework, donations of secondhand clothing are equated with the perception that the recipients are unworthy. US officials rejected Iranian claims and declared that all items shipped to Iran were usable.[189]

European aid to Iran had a more auspicious beginning than that of the United States. Iran accepted financial and other types of aid from the EC, and even allowed German troops to enter Iran and transport relief supplies to, and build refugee camps for, the Kurds. This marked the first time that the Islamic Republic had allowed foreign military forces to set up a base for any kind of mission inside the country. However, political problems soon surfaced between Iranian governmental authorities and European aid workers. Some aid workers and medical staff complained about red tape and interference in their routine functions. Others complained about the exorbitant landing fees that some relief agencies were allegedly charged. In May, a Norwegian plane carrying relief supplies was reportedly forced to abort its mission when it was informed of the landing fees, which it could not afford to pay.[190]

Another major complaint by European donors was that their contributions did not receive adequate recognition from Iranian officials. As a result, an EC representative in Tehran in May 1991 asked the Iranian government to issue an official statement in the Iranian press detailing the amount of aid given by the EC for the Kurdish refugees. This aid, which amounted to $250 million, included tents, blankets, and food. In addition, some $150 million of relief was brought in by groups associated with member countries of the EC.[191] These and similar problems not only reflect the enormous sociocultural and economic strains under which humanitarian relief agencies must operate, they also demonstrate the politicization of international humanitarian aid by both donor and recipient countries.

6

WHITHER KURDISTAN?

The emergence of the modern nation-state system and the concomitant rise of secular nationalism in the Middle East have profoundly affected interethnic relations in the region. In general, the rise of centrally controlled and highly stratified states in the twentieth-century Middle East has not accommodated the demands of ethnic nationalism. In other words, the state bureaucracy that emerged in the individual nations tended to ignore ethnic diversity and structured the political system to the benefit of the dominant ethnic group.[1] As a result, a number of nonassimilating minorities, to use Crawford Young's terminology, have emerged to challenge the hegemony of the dominant group(s) in the society.[2] The Kurds, particularly in Iraq and Turkey, have been prime examples of nonassimilating minorities.

The extension of the European-designed nation-state system to the Middle East followed a period of either European colonization or indirect domination. As Charles Tilly noted, this meant that European-drawn boundaries, which in most cases had been imposed "without regard to the distribution of peoples, became defended frontiers of post-colonial states; only rarely did the new states accommodate to their cultural heterogeneity by partition or by reordering of administrative subdivisions."[3] As state power increased, and as the primacy of the state as the dominant actor on the international scene solidified, the world became "more tolerant of a state's massacre or displacement of its own residents on the ground of their disloyalty to the regime in power, with the result that civilian deaths from state action came to rival deaths in combat, and refugees mounted to millions."[4]

The onset of the Cold War between the United States and its Western allies and the Soviet Union further contributed to the militarization of states in the Middle East, increasing the ability of the power wielders to forcefully impose their hegemony on largely heterogeneous Middle Eastern societies. Whereas pluralism and cultural accommodation had been a recognized feature of many Middle Eastern societies for several centuries, militarism and great power interventionism made it easier for the ruling groups to marginalize other groups on the basis of ethnic, cultural, linguistic, and religious peculiarities. The upsurge of ethnonationalism is a clear reaction to the inability of territorial states in the modern Middle East to respond to marginalization.[5] In response to the challenge of ethnonationalism, governments have adopted policies to destroy cultural identities and values. Such policies have been implemented with regard to the Kurds in Iran, Iraq, and Turkey.

The challenge of Kurdish nationalism to the central governments in Turkey, Iran, and Iraq has been affected by the geographic location of Kurdistan. In his study of ethnic collective movements, Hooshang Amirahmadi noted that territories located in "mountainous or forest areas, or provinces bordering other states with similar ethnic populations, have engaged in ethnic collective movements more frequently and effectively than ethnic provinces in central locations and with flat bare plains."[6] The vitality of Kurdish movements is undoubtedly due to Kurdistan's mountainous territory and geography, which allows for a degree of insulation from outside intrusion. However, as the Kurdish case has demonstrated, geography can also be a detrimental factor for collective ethnic movements operating in a zone of interregional conflicts and great power rivalry.

The duration, intensity, and strength of ethnic movements are positively correlated with the rise of irredentist and secessionist tendencies in those movements. When, or whether, ethnonationalist movements develop secessionist tendencies is also affected by domestic and international politics.[7] As we have seen with the Kurds, when domestic and international conditions were ripe, separatist tendencies were manifested in the establishment of a "republic," as in the case of the establishment of the Kurdish Republic of Mahabad. When such conditions were not appropriate, overt separatist tendencies were not present. For example, the major Kurdish groups in recent decades, with the exception of the PKK in Turkey, have called for autonomy within the state in which they live and have not advocated separatism.

In his typology of secessionist movements, Donald Horowitz contends that the largest number of secessionist movements are found among "backward groups" in economically "backward regions." A backward group is defined as one whose members have not benefited from opportunities in education and advanced nonagrarian jobs, and have not been integrated into the mainstream of society.[8] Horowitz places the Iraqi Kurds in the category of groups with the highest potential for secessionism. However, as I have argued elsewhere, the recent history of the Kurds has clearly demonstrated that a myriad of internal and external obstacles will continue to thwart Kurdish secessionism. Factionalism, ideological incompatibility, and linguistic and cultural barriers have severely hampered Kurdish chances for successful secessionist drives.[9] Iranian Kurds are culturally closer to other Iranian nationalities than to Kurds in Iraq or Turkey. This does not imply that they have forsaken their Kurdishness. It simply means that cultural factors favoring secessionism are not operative among the majority of Iranian Kurds. On the other hand, secessionist tendencies are more prevalent among both

Turkish and Iraqi Kurds. This is partly because Turkish and Arab culture is more alien to the Kurds than the Iranian culture.

KURDISH SELF-DETERMINATION
AND INTERNATIONAL LEGAL PRINCIPLES

The right of self-determination has been recognized by various international covenants in the twentieth century. The exact nature of this principle, and how it applies to different entities, has been a matter of juridical contention and differing interpretations. Ethnic minorities such as the Kurds have invoked the principle of self-determination to justify demands for autonomy or independence. There are as many as five thousand ethnic communities in today's world but only some 175 independent nation-states. Does the principle of self-determination give each of these ethnic groups a legal right to a sovereign nation-state of its own? If so, international order would become chaotic with five thousand states vying for influence, power, and prestige. As will be discussed, the right of self-determination has not been defined in international legal principles as sanctioning secession by ethnic minorities. Furthermore, under the prevailing practice, many multiethnic states have viewed the definition of minorities and the extent of their rights as purely domestic issues, outside the purview of international law.[10] Some states have simply disregarded their heterogeneity and have declared themselves to be ethnically homogeneous, thus obviating the need to consider the rights of minority groups.[11] In the case of Turkey, the rejection of heterogeneity has resulted in the denial of Kurdish identity at great cost to the Kurds.

The denial or severe curtailment of the rights of ethnic minorities led Gurr and Scarritt to develop a typology of 261 minority groups who are accorded "separate and unequal treatment" by the dominant cultural or political groups in their countries. In other words, these groups have been "at risk" because of the systematic denial of their political, cultural, economic, and civil rights by the agents of the territorial state.[12] Gurr and Scarritt classified the Kurds among minority groups with latent separatist tendencies who have demonstrated greater political assertiveness in recent years. They further contended that since the Kurds live in relatively closed societies, ethnic conflict is more likely to manifest in the form of rebellions or civil wars.[13] This will make more possible the internationalization of ethnic conflict and intervention by outside forces in the guise of protecting the minority at risk.

If the Kurds are classified as a sizable minority at risk, what can they expect from the community of nations, in terms of recognition of their rights of self-determination and protection? Can international law and organizations promote these rights under the current state-centric approach to international relations? The primacy of domestic jurisdiction in the internal affairs of states and the concomitant principle of state sovereignty have been clearly stated in Article 2, Paragraph 7 of the Charter of the United Nations. At the same time, Article 1 of the UN Charter gives prominence to the concept of self-determination.

The apparent conflict between these two concepts stems from different interpretations of the term "self-determination." Gudmundur Alfredsson has identified five different meanings for the concept:

1. the right of a people to determine its international status, including the right to independence, sometimes referred to as external self-determination;
2. the right of a state population to determine the form of government and to participate in government, sometimes extended to include democratization or majority rule and sometimes called internal self-determination;
3. the right of a state to territorial integrity and non-violation of its boundaries, and to govern its internal affairs without external interference;
4. the right of a minority within or even across state boundaries to special rights—not only protection and non-discrimination, but possibly the right to cultural, educational, social and economic autonomy for the preservation of group identities; [and]
5. the right of a state, especially claimed by the developing countries, to cultural, social and economic development.[14]

Of these meanings of self-determination, two have been dominant in the application of international law. These are definitions one and three, external self-determination, expressed in the form of decolonization efforts, and the territorial integrity and nonviolability of state boundaries. In other words, secession has not been recognized as a supportable element of the right of self-determination.[15] Yet the moral and psychological appeal of this principle has propelled many ethnic groups, including some Kurds, to seek support for their secessionist tendencies by invoking the doctrine of self-determination.

With the beginning of a major decolonization era after the end of World War II, self-determination became closely identified with the anticolonial rights of peoples. The United Nations became a major vehicle for sanctioning decolonization efforts and dismantling colonial empires. Some people have sought, albeit unsuccessfully, to include the right of secession or regional autonomy as part of decolonization. However, the overwhelming majority within the community of nations has rejected the notion of linking decolonization and secessionist rights.

Colonialism has been seen by most members of the international community as a palpable evil. . . . Colonialism could also be denounced by most world leaders with righteous impunity because most were not themselves leaders of colonial Powers. Finally, and most importantly, there were a finite number of colonies on the globe in 1945. As long as it had no colonial possessions, a State embracing colonial self-determination in an ostentatious manner could squeeze a good deal of propaganda mileage out of a relatively harmless principle. Under these conditions, there was no danger that one's rhetoric could come hauntingly back on the lips of a disaffected rebel within one's own country.[16]

In addition, there are a number of practical arguments against the international promotion of secessionism, or of autonomy demands that might lead to secessionist impulses.

The fear of Balkanization is used as a major argument against secessionism. In other words, secessionism in areas where tribal or clan divisions are operative could lead to the creation of small states that lack political cohesion and economic viability. Hence, their establishment would lead to international disorder and internal decay. Given the history of Kurdish movements, Balkanization is a distinct possibility should secessionism succeed in Kurdistan. A second argument against secessionism is that it could lead to indefinite divisibility among multiethnic societies. That is, no nation, particularly those in the Middle East with large Kurdish populations, "has a population so homogeneous that it cannot be subdivided into smaller groups of greater homogeneity. . . . Once a right to secession is admitted, there are no clear limits to this process; it could conceivably be carried out until each clan or atomic family within a society constituted an entity entitled to self-determination."[17]

Another argument against international recognition of secessionist rights is that secession, or the threat of secession, by a disaffected minority could lead to the destabilization of democratic systems, or it could impede the emergence of consensual politics and democratic frameworks in states striving to establish a popularly mandated democracy. Many Turks have argued that the secessionist activities of the PKK have had a debilitating impact on the development of democratic institutions in their country, particularly during the 1970s and 1980s. Finally, the secession of an ethnic group could lead to a situation in which other minorities feel trapped in the seceding province and placed at the mercy of the laws of the new state.[18] This would be particularly true in an independent Kurdistan, in which large antagonistic minorities, such as the Azeris, Turkomans, and Lors, would inevitably find themselves under the yoke of their historical rivals.

For these and similar reasons, the United Nations has not equated the right of self-determination with the right of secession. The response of former UN secretary general U Thant in January 1970 to a reporter's question regarding the harsh reaction of the Nigerian federal government to the secessionist drive by the country's ethnic Biafrans epitomizes the international community's attitude toward secessionism.

> You will recall that the United Nations spent over $500 million in the Congo primarily to prevent the secession of Katanga from the Congo. So, as far as the question of secession of a particular section of a Member State is concerned, the United Nations' attitude is unequivocable [sic]. As an international organization, the United Nations has never accepted and does not accept and I do not believe it will ever accept the principle of secession of a part of its Member States.[19]

This discussion was not meant to imply that the rights of individuals and groups have been ignored by the United Nations, or by the principles of public international law, only that the oft-mentioned principle of self-determination does not provide legal justification for the type of secessionism and/or autonomy that some Kurdish groups, particularly in Turkey, have been striving for. However, there has developed a large body of international doctrines and principles with near universal acceptability that are applicable to the Kurdish dilemma in the Middle East.

INTERNATIONAL HUMANITARIAN PRINCIPLES AND THE KURDS

Before the twentieth century, nation-states were the only proper subject of international law. The rights of individuals and groups were the exclusive domain of the states where they resided. However, a number of developments began to challenge the excessively state-oriented focus of international law. For example, diplomatic efforts to protect the rights of minorities, particularly religious minorities, and military interventions to protect their rights were incorporated into state interactions. This practice became particularly pronounced in treaties signed between Christian Europe and the Muslim Middle East. In the waning years of the Ottoman Empire, European countries imposed a number of treaties on the Ottoman Sultan through which they demanded protection and special treatment for Christian minorities, such as the Armenians, the Assyrians, and the Maronites, living under his jurisdiction. For example, the Treaty of Berlin (1878) obligated the Ottoman authorities to "carry out without further delay the improvements and reforms demanded by local requirements in the provinces inhabited by the Armenians . . . [and] to guarantee their security" against other groups, such as the Muslim Kurds.[20] These treaties also provided the pretext for military intervention against the Ottoman Turks by European powers harboring colonial pretensions.

Other changes showed the emergence of concern for the protection of the rights of the individual in the nineteenth century. Efforts were undertaken to abolish slavery and devise measures for the prosecution of people involved in the slave trade. Humanitarian concern for the welfare of the victims of armed conflict led to the establishment of the International Committee of the Red Cross, a nonpartisan organization involved in promoting individual rights and relief on a global scale. However, it was not until after World War I and the formation of the League of Nations that individual and minority rights were catapulted to the forefront of international law. In fact, the first formalized multilateral machinery for the protection of minorities was established by the League of Nations. The Council of the League of Nations was granted authority to examine alleged violations of minority rights, while the Permanent Court of International Justice (the precursor to the International Court of Justice) had "compulsory jurisdiction over disputes between members of the Council and states concerning the protection of minorities."[21] However, compulsory jurisdiction was not always exercised equitably; the more powerful states in the West resorted to the League's mandate to further their political goals in colonized and semicolonized countries. Moreover, the final version of the League's Covenant omitted all references to the rights of national minorities and gave those groups no standing before the League.[22]

After World War II and the establishment of the United Nations, multilateral protection of human rights and ethnic rights received major attention, and the codification of these rights began to challenge the state-centric focus of international law. In December 1948, the General Assembly of the United Nations adopted the Universal Declaration of Human Rights, which has been accepted as "the main pillar of the International Bill of Rights, and is usually considered to be part and parcel of international customary law."[23] In its preamble, the Universal Declaration claims to provide a "common standard of achievement for all peoples and all nations, to the end that every individual and every organ of society, keeping this Declaration in mind, shall strive by teaching and education to promote respect for these rights and freedoms and by progressive measures, national and international, to secure their universal and effective recognition and observance."[24]

Since adoption of the Universal Declaration of Human Rights, a number of other resolutions have been approved by the UN General Assembly that, together with the Universal Declaration, have become the corpus of the International Bill of Human Rights. These additional components of the International Bill of Human Rights are: the International Covenant on Civil and Political Rights, the Optional Protocol to the International Covenant on Civil and Political Rights, and the International Covenant on Economic, Social, and Cultural Rights. These turn the provisions of the Universal Declaration of Human Rights "into binding treaties, provide greater detail about the rights protected, and supply implementation procedures the states parties must follow."[25] Notwithstanding the efforts to codify internationally desirable human rights principles and to develop universal human rights standards, neither the UN Charter nor the Declaration of Human Rights addresses the issue of ethnic and minority rights in specific terms. In fact, there are no references to the term "minority" in these documents. However, many ethnic minorities, such as the Kurds, have invoked the principles of nondiscrimination contained in these documents to advance their political causes.

This omission was remedied when the United Nations General Assembly passed other human rights resolutions. For example, Article 27 of the International Covenant on Civil and Political Rights states: "In those states in which ethnic, religious or linguistic minorities exist, persons belonging to such minorities shall not be denied the right, in community with the other members of their group, to enjoy their own culture, to profess and practice their own religion, or to use their own language."[26] It is this article that the Kurds could invoke in defense of their cultural and linguistic rights in the Middle East. The United Nations Human Rights Commission's Subcommission on the Prevention of Discrimination and the Protection of Minorities, which was established in 1946 by the Economic and Social Council, provides the machinery for minorities to pursue their rights within the UN framework. However, critics have correctly pointed out that the Subcommission occupies "a very low place in the UN hierarchy and that it spends too much time discussing procedural rather than substantive issues. . . . It seems to lack a clear idea of its role and . . . sense of direction."[27]

Some noteworthy attempts by the United Nations to tackle ethnic and minority abuses have been made, including the adoption of landmark treaties such as the Genocide Convention of 1948, the International Convention on the Elimination of All Forms of Racial Discrimination (adopted by the UN General Assembly in 1965), and the International Convention on the Suppression and the Punishment of the Crimes of Apartheid (passed by the General Assembly in 1973).[28] Of these, the Genocide Convention has the most direct applicability to Kurdish conditions during periods of extreme, overt suppression—for example, in Iraq during the 1991 suppression of the Kurdish uprising.

Genocide, which means "any act committed with the intent to destroy, in whole or in part, a national, ethnical, racial, or religious group,"[29] has been applied to the victims of the Holocaust in Nazi Germany. Article 2 of the Genocide Convention defines this offense as incorporating any of the following acts:

- killing members of the group;
- causing serious bodily or mental harm to members of the group;
- deliberately inflicting on the group conditions of life calculated to bring about its physical destruction in whole or in part;

- imposing measures intended to prevent births within the group; [or]
- forcibly transferring children of the group to another group.[30]

Parties to the Genocide Convention agreed to enact domestic legislation to provide penalties for individuals guilty of committing genocide. In addition, Article 8 of the Convention stipulates that a party to the Convention may call upon the United Nations to take appropriate measures to prevent or suppress acts of genocide.

Based on the analyses of the Kurdish situation, one can argue that the first three acts listed above have, at times, applied to the treatment of the Kurds in Iraq and Turkey, and to some extent in Iran, in the recent past. It would be exceedingly difficult, however, to charge the governments of those countries with genocide against their Kurdish population because similar suppressions of ethnic minorities occur regularly in many other member states of the United Nations.

Harff and Gurr have identified forty-five instances of genocides and "politicides" committed by states against their populations since World War II.[31] Although there is no universally accepted definition of politicide, Harff and Gurr have defined the term to mean the promotion and execution of state policies that result in the deaths of a substantial number of members of groups whose political opposition or hierarchical position places them in direct confrontation with the regime in power. Suppression and large-scale killings of members of such groups are labeled as "geno/politicide" committed by the state.[32] In their typology of geno/politicide, Harff and Gurr have identified Iraqi Kurds as victims of "repressive/hegemonic politicide," and Iranian Kurds as victims of "revolutionary politicide."[33] The operational utility of these terms, however, remains questionable and may lead to the vague and problematic extension of genocide to all types of violent suppression of dissent.

CONSTITUTIONAL/LEGAL
TECHNIQUES AND KURDISH INTEGRATION

The foregoing discussion clearly demonstrates the limitations of international legal remedies in enhancing minority rights in an international order dominated by state-centric views and institutions. However, laws can be effectively used to promote constitutional and legal arrangements that can lead to the accommodation of minority rights and the lessening of ethnic tensions in multiethnic societies.[34] For example, constitutional and statutory reforms can be implemented to protect the status of minorities. These reforms can be aimed at specific institutional arrangements to ensure equal treatment for members of ethnic minorities not only by the state apparatus, but also by private institutions and individuals.[35] Nondiscrimination statutes, which have been enacted in the United States since the 1960s, are examples of these reforms. Of course, such statutes should not be duplicated in countries whose legal systems and institutions are vastly different from the Anglo-Saxon model. Nonetheless, legislation already exists to implement indigenously designed "equal rights" in Iran, Iraq, and Turkey. Electoral laws, systems of proportional representation, and the like are useful beginnings in seriously dealing with the integration of the Kurds into the mainstream of sociopolitical life.

A carefully crafted constitutional scheme leading to the establishment of a genuine pluralistic polity is the best means to promote Kurdish integration in Iran, Iraq, and Turkey. Assimilation, which has characterized Turkey's Kurdish policy, may succeed in the short run in stemming the tide of ethnonationalism. In the long run, however, the human and material costs to the state of forced assimilation are likely to be quite high, resulting in, among other things, the rise of armed resistance movements by the affected minority. In addition, assimilation carries a negative connotation because it implies the superiority of the dominant group's culture.[36]

Pluralism, on the other hand, creates a condition of diversity with unity, in which ethnic groups coexist in a territorial state in a relationship of interdependence. In many ways, the multiethnic empires of the Middle East, such as the Persian and Ottoman empires, were characterized by ethnic pluralism. It was only after the creation of the European-style nation-state system that ethnic chauvinism replaced old loyalties and patterns of interaction that had developed over the centuries among various ethnic groups in Iranian and Turkish domains. Furthermore, for pluralism to succeed in multiethnic societies, there must be a "large measure of freedom within the state for minorities in the interest of real rather than formal equality."[37] Various autonomy agreements signed between the Iraqi governments and the Kurds failed because of the absence of real equality for the Kurds. Even if the autonomy schemes of the 1960s and 1970s had been implemented, the likelihood of Kurdish separatism would have increased in the absence of genuine democratic institutions in Iraq. The challenge for a state is how to approach the issue of devolution without engendering secessionism on the part of the ethnic groups that are the intended beneficiaries of the state's devolutionary programs. As Donald Horowitz observed:

> Most such [devolution] agreements are concluded against a background of secessionist warfare or terrorist violence. Where central authority is secure, as in India, the appropriate decision can be made and implemented by the center [the government authorities]. But, where the very question is how far the writ of the center will run [as in Iraq], devolution is a matter of bilateral agreement, and an enduring agreement is an elusive thing.[38]

In a democratic and pluralistic setting, the multiplicity of ethnic groups can act as a hedge against authoritarianism and domination of the state apparatus by one group. Ahmad Chalabi, an anti–Saddam Hussein Iraqi opposition member, contended that the demands for political representation have remained strong, as evidenced by the March 1991 Kurdish and Shi'a uprisings, and that promoting ethnic autonomy would not result in the disintegration of Iraq, as many have argued. The Kurds are cognizant of the geopolitical realities of the Middle East, and their leadership would not risk intervention by outside forces by dismembering Iraq.[39] However, Chalabi's model is not devolutionary pluralism, but the reestablishment of the "democratic experience under the [Hashemite] monarchy."[40] However, the Iraqi monarchy was neither democratic nor responsive to the rights of the Kurdish minority.

All in all, two desirable techniques, both of which require constitutional restructuring, can be mentioned as desirable ways to reduce conflict between the Kurds and the central authorities in Iran, Iraq, and Turkey. First, the establishment of genuine federal structures and a move away from the strong centralism that characterizes all three countries can help bring about democratic, participatory systems. Nigeria, with its myriad of ethnic and religious groups, has succeeded for the most part in reducing ethnic violence through its functioning federalism.[41] This process must be implemented in stages and not imposed in a short time frame. Imposed federalism would likely fail in the long run, as it did in Yugoslavia in 1991. Each country will have to develop its federal structure within its own unique political milieu and with respect to its own unique Kurdish problem.

Second, changes in electoral laws, which can be implemented without a federal system, can help establish a system of proportional representation.[42] Although this system of representation could lead to the proliferation of political parties and unstable coalition governments, it would provide equitable avenues for ethnic minorities to develop a stake in the viability of the larger state. In other words, if ethnic minorities were not underrepresented in the decisionmaking institutions of the national government, as is the case with the Kurds, they would develop greater loyalty to the broader interests of the state. This, in turn, could lead to the development of political alignments that are based on broader interests than the parochial interests of ethnic groups. Ethnic identification, and demands for the recognition of ethnic rights, most likely would persist, even with successful constitutional restructuring. However, such ethnic demands would be less likely to lead to violent conflict if avenues for genuine political participation were open to all groups.

NOTES

CHAPTER ONE

1. Francis Fukuyama, "The End of History?" *The National Interest*, no. 16 (Summer 1989): 4.
2. Ibid., 14–15.
3. For a collection of excellent essays on the politicization of ethnicity in different settings, see Gerard Chaliand, ed., *Minority Peoples in the Age of Nation-States*, translated by Tony Berrett (London: Pluto Press, 1989).
4. Joseph Rothschild, *Ethnopolitics: A Conceptual Framework* (New York: Columbia University Press, 1981): 6.
5. David Brown, "Ethnic Revival: Perspectives on State and Society," *Third World Quarterly* 11, no. 4 (October 1989): 8.
6. For an excellent analysis of the role of the state as an independent and increasingly important variable, see Theda Skocpol, "Bringing the State Back In: Strategies of Analysis in Current Research," in Peter B. Evans, Dietrich Rueschemeyer, and Theda Skocpol, eds., *Bringing the State Back In* (New York: Cambridge University Press, 1985): 3–37. See also Theda Skocpol, *State and Social Revolutions: A Comparative Study of France, Russia, and China* (New York: Cambridge University Press, 1979); Mansoor Moaddel, "State-Centered vs. Class-Centered Perspectives on International Politics: The Case of U.S. and British Participation in the 1953 Coup Against Premier Mossadeq in Iran," *Studies in Comparative International Development* 24, no. 2 (Summer 1989): 3–23; James A. Caporaso, ed., *The Elusive State: International and Comparative Perspectives* (Newbury Park, CA: Sage Publications, 1989); and Edward S. Greenberg and Thomas F. Mayer, eds., *Changes in the State: Causes and Consequences* (Newbury Park, CA: Sage Publications, 1990).
7. One of the best and certainly the most comprehensive book on the history of the Kurds until the end of the sixteenth century is Sharaf-ed-din Khan Bitlisi, *Sharafnameh* (Tehran: Elmi Publications, n.d.). This book, written in 1596 in Persian by a prominent Kurd, remains an invaluable source of historical data on the Kurds. Also, consult Morad Owrang, *Kurd Shenasi* (Kurdology) (Tehran: Rangin Publications, 1967): 75–78 and 103–111; Mozaffar Zangeneh, *Doodeman-e Aryai: Kurd va Kurdistan* (The Aryan Lineage: Kurd and Kurdistan) (Tehran: Chehr Publications, 1968): 35–62 and 75–94; Nasser Mohseni, *Joghrafiya-e Kurdistan* (The Geography of Kurdistan) (Boroojerd, Iran: Lavian Publications, 1948): 79–91; Thomas Bois, *The Kurds*, translated by M.W.M. Welland (Beirut: Khayats, 1966): 7–18; Abdul Rahman Ghassemlou, *Kurdistan and the Kurds* (Prague: Publishing House of the Czechoslovak Academy of Sciences, 1965): 33–45; Gerard Chaliand, "Introduction," in Gerard Chaliand, ed., *People Without a Country: The Kurds and Kurdistan*, translated by Michael Pallis (London: Zed Press, 1980): 8–18; and Hassan Arfa, *The Kurds: An Historical and*

Political Study (London: Oxford University Press, 1966): 1–32.

For a succinct review of recent Kurdish history and politics, see Laura Donnadieu Aguado, "The Kurds in the Middle East: Struggle for National Liberation," *Ethnic Studies Report* 5, no. 2 (July 1987): 9–17; Andrew Whitley, "The Kurds: Pressures and Prospects," *The Round Table*, no. 279 (July 1980): 245–248; William E. Hazen, "Minorities in Revolt: The Kurds of Iran, Iraq, Syria, and Turkey," in R. D. McLaurin, ed., *The Political Role of Minority Groups in the Middle East* (New York: Praeger Publishers, 1979): 49–75; Eden Naby, "Rebellion in Kurdistan," *Harvard International Review* 2, no. 3 (November 1979): 1, 5–7, and 29; and Eden Naby, "The Iranian Frontier Nationalities: The Kurds, the Assyrians, the Baluchis, and the Turkmens," in William O. McCagg, Jr., and Brian D. Silver, eds., *Soviet Asian Ethnic Frontiers* (New York: Pergamon Press, 1979): 85–96.

8. C. J. Edmonds, "Kurdish Nationalism," *Journal of Contemporary History* 6, no. 1 (1971): 87.

9. Ibid., 87–88.

10. Nader Entessar, "The Kurdish Mosaic of Discord," *Third World Quarterly* 11, no. 4 (October 1989): 86.

11. Mehrdad Izady, "A Kurdish Lingua Franca?" *Kurdish Times* 2, no. 2 (Summer 1988): 13.

12. See George S. Harris, "Ethnic Conflict and the Kurds," *The Annals of the American Academy of Political and Social Science* 433 (September 1977): 113.

13. Izadi, "A Kurdish Lingua Franca?" 15.

14. Harris, "Ethnic Conflict," 113.

15. For a succinct analysis of the condition of the Jewish Kurds in Iran, see Paul J. Magnarella, "A Note on Aspects of Social Life Among the Jewish Kurds of Sanandaj," *Jewish Journal of Sociology* 11, no. 1 (June 1969): 51–57.

16. See Martin Short and Anthony McDermott, *The Kurds*, 3d ed. (London, Minority Rights Group, March 1977): 6.

17. Whitley, "The Kurds," 248, and Shaikh Ezzedin Hussein's interview in *MERIP Reports*, no. 113 (March–April 1983): 9–10.

18. Joane Nagel, "The Conditions of Ethnic Separatism: The Kurds in Turkey, Iran, and Iraq," *Ethnicity* 7, no. 3 (September 1980): 280–281.

19. For a detailed study of the concept of internal colonialism in multiethnic societies, see Michael Hechter, *Internal Colonialism* (Berkeley, CA: University of California Press, 1975). See also Frank W. Young, "Reactive Subsystems," *American Sociological Review* 35, no. 2 (April 1970): 297–307.

20. Nagel, "The Conditions of Ethnic Separatism," 281.

21. Crawford Young, *The Politics of Cultural Pluralism* (Madison, WI: University of Wisconsin Press, 1976): 522–523.

22. For an excellent discussion of this issue, see Leonard M. Helfgott, "The Structural Foundations of the National Minority Problem in Revolutionary Iran," *Iranian Studies* 13, nos. 1–4 (1980): 195–212.

23. Ibid., 211.

24. Akbar Aghajanian, "Ethnic Inequality in Iran: An Overview," *International Journal of Middle East Studies* 15, no. 2 (May 1983): 216, table 2.

25. Ibid., 217, table 3.

26. Ibid., 218, table 4. For a useful source on the subject of poverty among urban poor in Iran, consult Farhad Kazemi, *Poverty and Revolution in Iran: The Migrant Poor, Urban Marginality and Politics* (New York: New York University Press, 1980).

27. For details, see *Kurdistan* (the annual publication of the Kurdish Student Society in Europe) 17 (1974): n.p.

28. *Pesh Merga* (a publication of the Kurdish Democratic Party), nos. 10–11 (March and June 1978): 5.

29. Ibid., 6.

30. Abdul A. al-Rubaiy, "The Failure of Political Integration in Iraq: The Education of the Kurdish Minority," *Intellect* 102, no. 2357 (April 1974): 444.

31. Ibid.

32. *Pesh Merga*, nos. 12–13 (September and December 1978): 14.

33. *Pesh Merga*, no. 5 (April 1976): 7–8, and nos. 6–7 (August and December 1976): 28–29; and *Kurdistan* 17 (1974): n.p.

34. Charles G. MacDonald, "The Kurds," *Journal of Political Science* 19 (1991): 133.

35. Milton J. Esman, "Ethnic Pluralism and International Relations," *Canadian Review of Studies in Nationalism* 17, nos. 1–2 (1990): 88.

36. Nader Entessar, "Kurdish Identity in the Middle East," *Current World Leaders* 34, no. 2 (April 1991): 281.

CHAPTER TWO

1. For details, see Rashid Yassemi, *Kurd va Payvastegi-e Nejadi va Tarikhi-e Uo* (The Kurd and His Racial and Historical Bonds) (Tehran: Amir Kabir Publications, 1984): 203–209.

2. Ibid., 204.

3. See, for example, John R. Perry, *Karim Khan Zand: A History of Iran, 1747–1779* (Chicago: University of Chicago Press, 1979): 184–194.

4. A. R. Ghassemlou, "Kurdistan in Iran," in Chaliand, *People Without a Country*, 117.

5. Arfa, *The Kurds*, p. 48.

6. Ibid., 63. For a succinct description of Simko's rebellion, see Martin van Bruinessen, "Kurdish Tribes and the State of Iran: The Case of Simko's Revolt," in Richard Tapper, ed., *The Conflict of Tribe and State in Iran and Afghanistan* (London: Croom Helm, 1983): 364–400.

7. See, for example, Ghassemlou, "Kurdistan in Iran," 117, and Derk Kinnane, *The Kurds and Kurdistan* (London: Oxford University Press, 1964): 47.

8. Arfa, *The Kurds*, 63–64.

9. Joseph S. Szyliowicz, *Education and Modernization in the Middle East* (Ithaca, NY: Cornell University Press, 1973): 243–244.

10. Kinnane, *The Kurds*, 47, and M. Reza Ghods, *Iran in the Twentieth Century: A Political History* (Boulder, CO: Lynne Rienner Publishers, 1989): 108.

11. Ghods, *Iran*, 108.

12. Amin Banani, *The Modernization of Iran, 1921–1941* (Stanford, CA: Stanford University Press, 1961): 120–125.

13. For a detailed analysis of the traditional patterns of land ownership in Kurdistan, see Ghassemlou, *Kurdistan and the Kurds*, 124–129.

14. Ghods, *Iran*, 110.

15. Ervand Abrahamian, *Iran Between Two Revolutions* (Princeton, NJ: Princeton University Press, 1982): 170–171.

16. William Eagleton, Jr., *The Kurdish Republic of 1946* (London: Oxford University Press, 1963): 23. For a brief analysis of the Soviet dimension of the Kurdish independence struggle, see William Linn Westermann, "Kurdish

Independence and Russian Expansion," *Foreign Affairs* 70, no. 3 (Summer 1991): 50–54.

17. Rouhollah K. Ramazani, "The Autonomous Republic of Azerbaijan and the Kurdish People's Republic: Their Rise and Fall," in Thomas T. Hammond, ed., *The Anatomy of Communist Takeovers* (New Haven, CT: Yale University Press, 1975): 458.

18. Ervand Abrahamian, "Communism and Communalism in Iran: The Tudah and the Firqah-i Dimukrat," *International Journal of Middle East Studies* 1, no. 4 (October 1970): 315.

19. Ibid., 311.

20. Abrahamian, *Iran*, 413–414.

21. Ibid., 414–415.

22. Arfa, *The Kurds*, 71–72.

23. For details, see Eagleton, *The Kurdish Republic*, 33–35, and Archie Roosevelt, Jr., "The Kurdish Republic of Mahabad," in Chaliand, *People Without a Country*, 136–138.

24. Arfa, *The Kurds*, 73.

25. See Kinnane, *The Kurds*, 49.

26. Eagleton, *The Kurdish Republic*, 36.

27. Ibid., 38.

28. Roosevelt, "The Kurdish Republic," 138–139.

29. Eagleton, *The Kurdish Republic*, 44.

30. Ibid., 58, and Ramazani, "The Autonomous Republic," 461.

31. Ghassemlou, *Kurdistan and the Kurds*, 77. For a succinct analysis of Kurdish nationalism in monarchical Iran, see Richard W. Cottam, *Nationalism in Iran*, rev. ed. (Pittsburgh: University of Pittsburgh Press, 1979): 67–74.

32. Roosevelt, "The Kurdish Republic," 140–141.

33. For details, see Ghods, *Iran*, 159–178, and Abrahamian, *Iran*, 388–415.

34. Eagleton, *The Kurdish Republic*, 63.

35. See Roosevelt, "The Kurdish Republic," 143.

36. Ibid.

37. Ghods, *Iran*, 148–149.

38. Ibid., 149.

39. Ghassemlou, "Kurdistan in Iran," 120.

40. Arfa, *The Kurds*, 102–103.

41. For details, see Richard W. Cottam, *Iran and the United States: A Cold War Case Study* (Pittsburgh: University of Pittsburgh Press, 1988): 86–89.

42. Ghods, *Iran*, 181.

43. For a detailed description of the National Front's platform, see *Bakhtar-e Emrooz*, July 7, 1950.

44. For an excellent collection of articles on the politics of oil nationalization in Iran, see James A. Bill and W. Roger Louis, eds., *Mussadiq, Iranian Nationalism, and Oil* (Austin, TX: University of Texas Press, 1988).

45. Ghassemlou, "Kurdistan in Iran," 122.

46. The literature on this subject is extensive. For example, see Cottam, *Iran*, 95–109; Kermit Roosevelt, *Countercoup: The Struggle for the Control of Iran* (New York: McGraw-Hill, 1979); James A. Bill, *The Eagle and the Lion: The Tragedy of American-Iranian Relations* (New Haven, CT: Yale University Press, 1988): 51–97; Mark J. Gasiorowski, *U.S. Foreign Policy and the Shah: Building a Client State in Iran* (Ithaca, NY: Cornell University Press, 1991): 57–84; Hussein Fardoost, *Zohoor va Soqoot-e Saltanat-e Pahlavi* (The Rise and Fall of the Pahlavi Dynasty), vol. 1 (Tehran: Ettela'at Publications, 1991): 176–184; and Marvin Zonis, *Majestic Failure: The Fall of the Shah*

(Chicago: University of Chicago Press, 1991): 100–105.

47. See Nader Entessar, "The Kurds in Post-Revolutionary Iran and Iraq," *Third World Quarterly* 6, no. 4 (October 1984): 923.

48. Ibid., 924.

49. See Nariman Yalda, "Federalism and Self-Rule for Minorities: A Case Study of Iran and Kurdistan" (Ph.D. diss., Claremont Graduate School, 1980): 127.

50. Ghassemlou, "Kurdistan in Iran," 124.

51. Ibid., 125.

52. Yosef Gotlieb, *Self-Determination in the Middle East* (New York: Praeger Publishers, 1982): 100.

53. Entessar, "The Kurds," 923.

54. Quoted in David Menashri, "Khomeini's Policy Toward Ethnic and Religious Minorities," in Milton J. Esman and Itamar Rabinovich, eds., *Ethnicity, Pluralism, and the State in the Middle East* (Ithaca, NY: Cornell University Press, 1988): 217.

55. *Matn-e Kamel-e Qanoon-e Assassi-e Jomhoori-e Islami-e Iran* (The Complete Text of the Constitution of the Islamic Republic of Iran) (Tehran: Hamid Publications, 1983): 28.

56. David McDowall, *The Kurds*, new ed., (London: Minority Rights Group, March 1989): 17.

57. Shaul Bakhash, *The Reign of the Ayatollahs: Iran and the Islamic Revolution* (New York: Basic Books, 1984): 73.

58. *Ayandegan*, June 20, 1979.

59. *Kayhan*, July 7, 1979.

60. Quoted in Bakhash, *The Reign*, 78.

61. Nikki R. Keddie, "The Minorities Question in Iran," in Shirin Tahir-Kheli and Shaheen Ayubi, eds., *The Iran-Iraq War: New Weapons, Old Conflicts* (New York: Praeger Publishers, 1983): 99.

62. See Franjo Butorac, "Iran's Revolution and the Kurds," *Review of International Affairs* (Belgrade) 31 (April 20, 1980), and Charles MacDonald, "The Kurdish Challenge and Revolutionary Iran," *Journal of South Asian and Middle Eastern Studies* 13, nos. 1 and 2 (Fall–Winter 1989): 57.

63. Patricia J. Higgins, "Minority-State Relations in Contemporary Iran," in Ali Banuazizi and Myron Weiner, eds., *The State, Religion and Ethnic Politics: Afghanistan, Iran, and Pakistan* (Syracuse, NY: Syracuse University Press, 1986): 186.

64. Ibid., 186–187.

65. For a thorough description of the concept of *velayat-e faqih*, see Ayatollah Khomeini, *Hokoomat-e Islami* (Islamic Government) (Tehran: n.p., 1971).

66. See Shaikh Ezzedin Hussein's interview in *MERIP Reports*, no. 113 (March–April 1983): 9–10.

67. Ibid., 9.

68. For an excellent analytical study of the *Mujahidin-e Khalq*, see Ervand Abrahamian, *The Iranian Mojahedin* (New Haven, CT: Yale University Press, 1989). See also, Sepehr Zabih, *The Left in Contemporary Iran* (London and Stanford, CA: Croom Helm/Hoover Institution Press, 1986).

69. Abdul Rahman Ghassemlou's interview in *MERIP Reports*, no. 98 (July–August 1981): 17. See also "Barnameh va Assasnameh-e Hezb-e Demokrat-e Kurdistan-e Iran" (The Platform and Constitution of the Kurdish Democratic Party of Iran), Third Congress of the KDPI, 1973.

70. Mostafa Chamran, *Kurdistan* (in Persian) (Tehran: Foundation of Martyr

Chamran, 1985): 153, and *Kurdistan: Imperialism va Groohaye Vabaste* (Kurdistan: Imperialism and the Dependent Groups) (Tehran: Political Bureau of the Islamic Revolutionary Guards Corps, 1980).

71. Chamran, *Kurdistan*, 156.

72. Entessar, "The Kurds," 925–926.

73. For a brief analysis of inter- and intra-Kurdish skirmishes, see "What Is Happening in Kurdistan?" *Review of Iranian Political Economy and History* (RIPEH) 3, no. 2 (Fall 1979): 55–59.

74. For details, see Chamran, *Kurdistan*, 43–106.

75. *Ayandegan*, August 6, 1979.

76. McDowall, *The Kurds*, 17. See also Chamran, *Kurdistan*, 74–83.

77. Richard Sim, "Kurdistan: The Search for Recognition," *Conflict Studies*, no. 124 (November 1980): 7.

78. Ibid., 8. See also Entessar, "The Kurds," 927–928.

79. For details, see "Barnameh va Assasnameh-e Hezb-e Demokrat-e Kurdistan-e Iran" (The Platform and Constitution of the Kurdish Democratic Party of Iran), Fourth Congress of the KDPI, February 19–23, 1980.

80. Sepehr Zabih, *Iran Since the Revolution* (Baltimore: Johns Hopkins University Press, 1982): 89.

81. Ibid., 90, and Abrahamian, *The Iranian Mojahedin*, 243–244.

82. Abrahamian, *The Iranian Mojahedin*, 248.

83. *Iran Times*, March 8 and 29, 1985.

84. Nozar Alaolmolki, "The New Iranian Left," *Middle East Journal* 41, no. 2 (Spring 1987): 230.

85. Nasser Mohajer, "Ensheab dar Hezb-e Demokrat-e Kurdistan-e Iran" (A Division Within the Kurdish Democratic Party of Iran), *Aghazi No*, no. 7 (Summer 1988): 25–29.

86. Ibid., 27.

87. *Kayhan*, July 28, 1989.

88. *Kayhan*, July 15, 1989.

89. *Iran Times*, July 28, 1989.

90. Ibid.

91. Steve Sherman and Safa Haeri, "The Slaying of Abd al-Rahman Qassemlou," *Middle East International*, no. 355 (July 21, 1989): 12.

92. *Iran Times*, July 21, 1989.

93. "Ma Terror-e Vahshianeh-e Doctor Ghassemlou ra Mahkoom Mikonim" (We Condemn the Barbaric Terror Killing of Dr. Ghassemlou), *Aghazi No,* special bulletin (July 18, 1989).

94. See "Jonbesh-e Moqavemat-e Kalq-e Kurd va Komala" (The Resistance Movement of the Kurdish Masses and Komala), document series no. 2, 1980, 1–9.

95. Entessar, "The Kurdish Mosaic," 90.

96. *Iran Times*, October 28, 1983.

97. Alaolmolki, "The New Iranian Left," 231.

98. Ibid.

99. *Pishrow* (organ of Komala), June 23, 1981, 1.

100. See Koorosh Moddaressi, "Kurdistan va Ayandeh-e Mobarezeh-e An" (Kurdistan and the Future of its Struggle), *Besooye Socialism* (theoretical journal of the Communist Party of Iran) 2, no. 5 (March 1990): 1–53.

101. Ibid., 10–12.

102. Ibid., 14–16.

103. *Iran Times*, September 1, 1989.

104. *Komonist* (central organ of the Communist Party of Iran), July 1987, p. 8, and "A Year of Mass Armed Struggle in Kurdistan," *Bolshevik Message* (a

publication of the Communist Party of Iran—the Committee Abroad), July 1987, 1–3.

105. "Interview with Comrade Ibrahim Alizadeh," *Pishrow*, no. 23 (September 1990): 6–7.

106. For details, see "Dar Bareh-e Fa'aliyat-e Hezb dar Kurdistan: Assnadi az Mabahes-e Darooni-e Hezb-e Komonist-e Iran" (About the Activities of the Party in Kurdistan: Documents from Internal Discussions of the Communist Party of Iran), August 1990, 77–93.

107. Ibid., 34–58.

108. "E'lamiy-e Hoqooq-e Payi-e Mardom-e Zahmatkesh dar Kurdistan" (Announcement of the Basic Rights of the Toiling People in Kurdistan), *Besooye Socialism* 2, no. 5 (March 1990): 63–69.

109. MacDonald, "The Kurdish Challenge," 68.

CHAPTER THREE

1. Edmonds, "Kurdish Nationalism," 89.

2. Ibid. For a good analysis of the late-nineteenth- and early-twentieth-century Kurdish revolts, see Chris Kutschera, *Le Mouvement National Kurde* (Paris: Flammarion, 1979).

3. See Peter Sluglett, *Britain in Iraq 1914–1932* (London: Ithaca Press, 1976): 14, and Ismet Sheriff Vanly, "Kurdistan in Iraq," in Chaliand, *People Without a Country*, pp. 158–159.

4. Sluglett, *Britain in Iraq*, 116–117, and Arfa, *The Kurds*, 111.

5. Arfa, *The Kurds*, 113, and McDowall, *The Kurds*, 18.

6. McDowall, *The Kurds*, 18, and Kinnane, *The Kurds*, 36.

7. Arfa, *The Kurds*, 113.

8. C. J. Edmonds, *Kurds, Turks and Arabs: Politics, Travel, and Research in North-Eastern Iraq, 1919–1925* (London: Oxford University Press, 1957): 28–75.

9. Kinnane, *The Kurds*, 36.

10. For a brief description of the implications of the Treaty of Sèvres, see Gotlieb, *Self-Determination*, 74–77, and Gerald A. Honigman, "British Petroleum Politics, Arab Nationalism and the Kurds," *Middle East Review* 15, nos. 1 and 2 (Fall 1982–Winter 1982/83): 34–36.

11. For the text of Articles 62–64 of the Treaty of Sèvres, see Sheri Laizer, *Into Kurdistan: Frontiers Under Fire* (London: Zed Books, 1991): 129.

12. Ibid.

13. Honigman, "British Petroleum Politics," 33–38, and Stephen C. Pelletiere, *The Kurds: An Unstable Element in the Gulf* (Boulder, CO: Westview Press, 1984): 58.

14. Pelletiere, *The Kurds*, 58, and Edmonds, *Kurds, Turks and Arabs*, 398.

15. Bois, *The Kurds*, 151.

16. Edmonds, *Kurds, Turks and Arabs*, 116–124, and Sluglett, *Britain in Iraq*, 116–123.

17. Vanly, "Kurdistan in Iraq," 161.

18. Arfa, *The Kurds*, 117–118.

19. McDowall, *The Kurds*, 19.

20. Bois, *The Kurds*, 152, and Kinnane, *The Kurds*, 41.

21. Arfa, *The Kurds*, 122.

22. Ibid., 123. See also Uriel Dann, "The Kurdish National Movement in

Iraq," *Jerusalem Quarterly,* no. 9 (Fall 1978): 135–136.

23. See the text of the letter in F. David Andrews, ed., *The Lost Peoples of the Middle East: Documents of the Struggle for Survival and Independence of the Kurds, Assyrians, and Other Minority Races in the Middle East* (Salisbury, NC: Documentary Publications, 1982): 90.

24. Ibid., 83–84.

25. Peter Sluglett, "The Kurds," in Committee Against Repression and for Democratic Rights in Iraq, ed., *Saddam's Iraq: Revolution or Reaction?* rev. ed. (London: Zed Books, 1989): 187.

26. Ibid., 187–188.

27. Andrews, *The Lost Peoples,* 128–130.

28. Ibid., 131.

29. For the ouline of the KDP's program, see ibid., 134–137.

30. Sluglett, "The Kurds," 188.

31. Richard F. Nyrop, ed., *Iraq: A Country Study* (Washington, DC: U.S. Government Printing Office, 1979): 61.

32. See Mustafa Nazdar, "The Kurds in Syria," in Chaliand, *People Without a Country,* 215–217.

33. Marion Farouk-Sluglett and Peter Sluglett, *Iraq Since 1958: From Revolution to Dictatorship* (London: I. B. Tauris, 1990): 79–80.

34. For details, see Hanna Batatu, *The Old Social Classes and the Revolutionary Movements of Iraq: A Study of Iraq's Old Landed and Commercial Classes and of its Communists, Ba'thists, and Free Officers* (Princeton, NJ: Princeton University Press, 1978): 659–662.

35. Ibid., 662.

36. Sluglett, "The Kurds," 189.

37. For details, see Batatu, *The Old Social Classes,* 866–889.

38. Ibid., 919, and Farouk-Sluglett and Sluglett, *Iraq Since 1958,* 70–72.

39. Batatu, *The Old Social Classes,* 920.

40. Sa'ad Jawad, *Iraq & the Kurdish Question 1958–1970* (London: Ithaca Press, 1981): 46–50.

41. Ibid., 47.

42. McDowall, *The Kurds,* 19.

43. Edmund Ghareeb, *The Kurdish Question in Iraq* (Syracuse, NY: Syracuse University Press, 1981): 38–39.

44. Martin van Bruinessen, "The Kurds Between Iran and Iraq," *MERIP Middle East Report* 16, no. 4 (July–August 1986): 16.

45. Farouk-Sluglett and Sluglett, *Iraq Since 1958,* 81.

46. See Jawad, *Iraq,* 63–105, and Ghareeb, *The Kurdish Question,* 39–40.

47. Jawad, *Iraq,* 108–112, and Farouk-Sluglett and Sluglett, *Iraq Since 1958,* 81.

48. Batatu, *The Old Social Classes,* 971–972.

49. Ibid., 972–973.

50. For a detailed description of the different rounds of fighting between the Kurds and the Ghassem regime between 1961 and 1963, see Edgar O'Ballance, *The Kurdish Revolt: 1961–1970* (Hamden, CT: Archon Books, 1973): 74–98, and David Adamson, *The Kurdish War* (London: George Allen & Unwin, 1964).

51. Adamson, *The Kurdish War,* 108–110.

52. Jawad, *Iraq,* 63–105.

53. Batatu, *The Old Social Classes,* 985, and Sim, "Kurdistan," 10.

54. Farouk-Sluglett and Sluglett, *Iraq Since 1958,* 85–87.

55. *Al-Ahram,* September 27, 1963.

56. Batatu, *The Old Social Classes,* 986. For revelations about King

Hussein's CIA connections, see *International Herald Tribune*, February 19–20, 1977.

57. O'Ballance, *The Kurdish Revolt*, 99.
58. Ibid., 100.
59. Ibid.
60. Ibid., 101–102.
61. Arfa, *The Kurds*, 145.
62. Ibid., 148, and Ghareeb, *The Kurdish Question*, 40.
63. Entessar, "The Kurds," 917–918.
64. Ghareeb, *The Kurdish Question*, 41.
65. Edith Penrose and E. F. Penrose, *Iraq: International Relations and National Development* (London: Benn, 1978): 338–340, and Majid Khadduri, *Republican Iraq: A Study in Iraqi Politics Since the Revolution of 1958* (London: Oxford University Press, 1969): 198–200.
66. Khadduri, *Republican Iraq*, 274, and Pelletiere, *The Kurds*, 189–192.
67. For details, see Batatu, *The Old Social Classes*, 1073–1110.
68. O'Ballance, *The Kurdish Revolt*, 150.
69. Ibid., 151.
70. Quoted in ibid., 152.
71. Pelletiere, *The Kurds*, 162, and *New York Times*, January 19, 1969.
72. A copy of the Pike Report was leaked to the *Village Voice* and published in its February 23, 1976, issue.
73. Dann, "The Kurdish National Movement," 141; Sim, "Kurdistan," 11; McDowall, *The Kurds*, 20–21; and Majid Khadduri, *Socialist Iraq: A Study in Iraqi Politics Since 1968* (Washington, DC: Middle East Institute, 1978): 231–240.
74. For the complete text of the March Manifesto, see At-Thawra (central organ of the Iraqi Ba'th Party), *Settlement of the Kurdish Problem in Iraq* (Baghdad: At-Thawra Publications, n.d.): 111–122. An extended excerpt of this document can be found in Short and McDermott, *The Kurds*, appendix 1, 25–26.
75. Lee C. Buchheit, *Secession: The Legitimacy of Self-Determination* (New Haven, CT: Yale University Press, 1978): 160.
76. Adamson, *The Kurdish War*, 92.
77. McDowall, *The Kurds*, 21.
78. Quoted in Ghareeb, *The Kurdish Question*, 89.
79. Ibid., 105, and McDowall, *The Kurds*, 21.
80. Entessar, "The Kurds," 919.
81. At-Thawra, *Settlement of the Kurdish Problem*, 38–39.
82. Abbas Kelidar, "Iraq: The Search for Stability," *Conflict Studies*, no. 59 (July 1975): 10–11.
83. al-Rubaiy, "The Failure of Political Integration," 442, and Henry A. Foster, *The Making of Modern Iraq* (Norman, OK: University of Oklahoma Press, 1935): 254–258.
84. al-Rubaiy, "The Failure of Political Integration," 442.
85. Albert H. Hourani, *Minorities in the Arab World* (London: Oxford University Press, 1947): 115–116.
86. Watermann, "Kurdish Independence," 53.
87. For details, see "Arabization in Kurdistan-Iraq," *Pesh Merga* 17 (1974): 3–4; "The Situation of Kurds in Iraq," *Pesh Merga*, nos. 6–7 (August–December 1976): 27–29; and "Iraq," *Pesh Merga*, no. 5 (April 1976): 6–8.
88. *Pesh Merga*, nos. 10–11 (March–June 1978): 6.
89. "The Situation of the Kurds," 28.

90. Ibid., 29.

91. Entessar, "The Kurds," 920; Sim, "Kurdistan," 12; and Naby, "The Iranian Frontier Nationalities," 89.

92. For extracts of the Autonomy Law of 1974, see Short and McDermott, *The Kurds,* appendix 2, 27–29.

93. Dann, "The Kurdish National Movement," 142.

94. As quoted in Ghareeb, *The Kurdish Question,* 159. See also Omar Yahya Feili and Arlene R. Fromchuck, "The Kurdish Struggle for Independence," *Middle East Review* 9, no. 1 (Fall 1976): 56, and Hazen, "Minorities in Revolt," 64–65.

95. McDowall, *The Kurds,* 22.

96. Ibid., and Hazen, "Minorities in Revolt," 65.

97. Entessar, "The Kurdish Mosaic," 91–92, and Entessar, "Kurdish Identity," 278.

98. Van Bruinessen, "The Kurds Between," 24.

99. Quoted in *The Middle East,* no. 112 (February 1984): 10.

100. *Kayhan* (London), November 20, 1986.

101. *Iran Times,* December 27, 1987.

102. Van Bruinessen, "The Kurds Between," 25, and Mohammed H. Malek, "Kurdistan in the Middle East Conflict," *New Left Review,* no. 175 (May–June 1989): 86.

CHAPTER FOUR

1. Quoted in Kendal [Nezan], "Kurdistan in Turkey," in Chaliand, *People Without a Country,* 65.

2. Ibid., 65–66.

3. See Kinnane, *The Kurds,* 24.

4. The Kurdish Student Society in Europe revived this newspaper and resumed the publication of *Kurdistan* as its official organ shortly after World War II.

5. Bois, *The Kurds,* 142.

6. Kinnane, *The Kurds,* 25.

7. Ibid.

8. Bois, *The Kurds,* 143–144.

9. Robert Olson, *The Emergence of Kurdish Nationalism and the Sheikh Said Rebellion, 1880–1925* (Austin, TX: University of Texas Press, 1989): 107. Olson's book contains perhaps the most detailed analysis of this Kurdish revolt found in the English language.

10. Ibid., 41–51, and Martin van Bruinessen, *Agha, Shaikh and State: On the Social and Political Organization of Kurdistan* (Utrecht, The Netherlands: Ryksuniversiteit, 1978): 373 and 446–447.

11. Olson, *The Emergence of Kurdish Nationalism,* 45.

12. Ibid., 50.

13. Arfa, *The Kurds,* 34, and Kutschera, *Le Mouvement National Kurde,* 79–105.

14. Olson, *The Emergence of Kurdish Nationalism,* 154. See also van Bruinessen, *Agha, Shaikh and State,* p. 405.

15. Olson, *The Emergence of Kurdish Nationalism,* 155, and Arfa, *The Kurds,* 36–37.

16. Robert W. Olson, "The International Consequences of the Shaikh Sait

Rebellion," in Marc Gaborieau, Alexander Popovic, and Thierry Zarcone, eds., *Naqshbandis: Historical Developments and Present Situation of a Muslim Mystical Order* (Paris: Editions Isis, 1990): 404–406.

17. Kinnane, *The Kurds*, 30–31; Arfa, *The Kurds*, 40; and McDowall, *The Kurds*, 12.

18. Kendal [Nezan], "Kurdistan in Turkey," p. 65.

19. Quoted in ibid.

20. For details, see Robert Olson, "The Kocgiri Kurdish Rebellion in 1921 and the Draft Law for a Proposed Autonomy of Kurdistan," *Oriente Moderno*, new series, vol. 8, nos. 1–6, (January–June 1989): 41–56. Also, see van Bruinessen, *Agha, Shaikh and State*, 373–374.

21. Kendal [Nezan], "Kurdistan in Turkey," 67, and Arfa, *The Kurds*, 43–44.

22. Kendal [Nezan], "Kurdistan in Turkey," 68, and Bois, *The Kurds*, 147–148.

23. McDowall, *The Kurds*, 13, and Dankwart A. Rustow, *Turkey: America's Forgotten Ally* (New York: Council on Foreign Relations Press, 1987): 74.

24. Martin van Bruinessen, "The Kurds in Turkey," *MERIP Reports* 14, no. 2 (February 1984): 8.

25. Kendal [Nezan], "Kurdistan in Turkey," 74.

26. Ibid., 75.

27. Rustow, *Turkey*, 63.

28. Kendal [Nezan], "Kurdistan in Turkey," 76.

29. Ibid., 97.

30. Michael M. Gunter, "The Kurdish Problem in Turkey," *Middle East Journal* 42, no. 3 (Summer 1988): 393.

31. Van Bruinessen, "The Kurds in Turkey," 8.

32. Ibid.

33. Ibid., 9.

34. For details, see Majeed R. Jafar, *Under-Underdevelopment: A Regional Case Study of the Kurdish Area in Turkey* (Helsinki, Finland: Social Policy Association, 1976).

35. Ibid., 67–68.

36. Van Bruinessen, "The Kurds in Turkey," 9.

37. Michael M. Gunter, *The Kurds in Turkey: A Political Dilemma* (Boulder, CO: Westview Press, 1990): 64.

38. Ibid., 66.

39. Ibid., 67, and van Bruinessen, "The Kurds in Turkey," 8.

40. Gunter, *The Kurds in Turkey*, 66.

41. Ibid., 57–58.

42. *Melliyet*, May 21, 1988.

43. Entessar, "The Kurdish Mosaic," 94. See also Entessar, "Kurdish Identity," 279–280, and Suha Bolukbasi, "Ankara, Damascus, Baghdad, and the Regionalization of Turkey's Kurdish Secessionism," *Journal of South Asian and Middle Eastern Studies* 14, no. 4 (Summer 1991): 16–19.

44. Quoted in Gunter, *The Kurds in Turkey*, 60.

45. For a useful summary of the coup and its political aftermath, see Rustow, *Turkey*, 57–60.

46. Ibid., 57.

47. Ronnie Margulies and Ergin Yildizoglu, "Trade Unions and Turkey's Working Class," *MERIP Reports* 14, no. 2 (February 1984): 19. See also Fikret Ceyhun, "Development of Capitalism and Class Struggles in Turkey," in Berch Berberoglu, ed., *Power and Stability in the Middle East* (London: Zed Books, 1989): 64–67.

48. Gunter, *The Kurds in Turkey*, 67–68.

49. Gunter, "The Kurdish Problem," 399.

50. See Helsinki Watch, *News From Turkey*, February 1990, 1–12.

51. For details of this and other instances of Kurdish mistreatment by the junta, see "The Torture of Huseyin Yildirim," *MERIP Reports* 14, no. 2 (February 1984): 13–14, and Amnesty International, *Torture in the Eighties* (London: Amnesty International, 1984): 217.

52. Mehrdad R. Izady, "Persian Carrot and Turkish Stick: Contrasting Policies Targeted at Gaining State Loyalty From Azeris and Kurds," *Kurdish Times* 3, no. 2 (Fall 1990): 35.

53. *New York Times*, March 27, 1981.

54. Ibid.

55. *New York Times*, April 1, 1981.

56. Rustow, *Turkey*, 117–118.

57. Anthony Hyman, "Elusive Kurdistan: The Struggle for Recognition," *Conflict Studies*, no. 214 (1988): 10.

58. *Christian Science Monitor*, July 27, 1987.

59. Helsinki Watch, *Destroying Ethnic Identity: The Kurds of Turkey* (New York: Human Rights Watch, 1990). For a brief, and somewhat different, review of Kurdish insurgency in Turkey and the government's response to it, see Philip Robins, *Turkey and the Middle East* (London and New York: The Royal Institute of International Affairs/Council on Foreign Relations Press, 1991): 30–36.

60. See Gunter, *The Kurds in Turkey*, 76, and Martin van Bruinessen, "Between Guerrilla War and Political Murder: The Workers' Party of Kurdistan," *Middle East Report* 18, no. 4 (July–August 1988): 44.

61. Van Bruinessen, "Between Guerrilla War," 44.

62. *Kurdistan Report*, no. 15 (March 1985): 1–2.

63. Van Bruinessen, "Between Guerrilla War," 44.

64. *Tercuman*, December 4, 1988, and *Hurriyet*, December 21, 1988.

65. *Hurriyet*, September 8, 1988.

66. *Hurriyet*, January 23, 1989.

67. *Tercuman*, October 19, 1989.

68. *Tercuman*, November 7, 1989, and February 7, 1990.

69. *Iran Times*, November 24, 1989.

70. Ken Mackenzie, "Struggling With the Kurds," *Middle East International*, no. 373 (April 13, 1990): 13–14.

71. Aliza Marcus, "Hearts and Minds in Kurdistan," *Middle East Report* 20, no. 2 (March–April 1990): 41.

72. *Iran Times*, August 31, 1990.

73. Ibid.

74. *Manchester Guardian Weekly*, April 21, 1991.

75. Kurdish Institute (Paris), *Information and Liaison Bulletin*, no. 70 (January 1991): 2.

76. For example, see *Cumhuriyet*, January 27, 28, and 29, 1991, and *Milliyet*, January 31, 1991.

77. Kurdish Institute (Paris), *Information and Liaison Bulletin*, no. 70 (January 1991): 3.

78. Kurdish Institute (Paris), *Information and Liaison Bulletin*, no. 71 (February 1991): 4. See also *Le Monde*, February 7, 1991.

79. *Tercuman*, January 31, 1991.

80. *Christian Science Monitor*, February 7, 1991.

81. *New York Times*, March 12, 1991.

82. Ibid.

83. Helsinki Watch, *Destroying Ethnic Identity*, 5–6, and Helsinki Watch, *News From Turkey*, June 1990, 6.

84. *The Independent*, June 12, 1990.

85. *Hurriyet*, April 1, 1990.

86. ERKN-European Section, "'Serhildan': Uprising in Kurdistan," *Voice of Kurdistan*, no. 2 (August 1990): 1–6.

87. Quoted in Gunter, *The Kurds in Turkey*, 47.

88. For a useful synopsis of Ismail Besikci's book, *Kurdistan: An Interstate Colony*, see *Voice of Kurdistan*, no. 3 (January 1991): 11–13.

89. "Dr. Ismail Besikci Defies the Turkish State," *Kurdistan Liberation*, no. 2 (August–September 1990): 2.

90. Ibid., 2–3 and 6.

91. See, for example, Amnesty International, *Amnesty International Report 1989* (London: Amnesty International, 1989): 233–236; Helsinki Watch, *News From Turkey* (June 1990): 12–14; and The Initiative for Human Rights in Kurdistan, *A Report on State Terrorism in Turkish Kurdistan* (Bremen, Germany: Initiative for Human Rights in Kurdistan, 1990): 17–31.

92. Helsinki Watch, *News From Turkey*, June 1990, 13.

93. See, for example, *Tercuman*, February 11, 1986; *Milliyet*, October 17, 1987; *Cumhuriyet*, February 28, 1988, and January 10 and 17, 1990; *Hurriyet*, January 9, 29, and 30, 1990; *Gunes*, June 25, 1990; and The Initiative for Human Rights in Kurdistan, *A Report on State Terrorism*, 32–39.

94. *Hurriyet*, January 9, 1990.

95. The Initiative for Human Rights in Kurdistan, *A Report on State Terrorism*, 35–36.

96. Ibid., 38–39.

97. Helsinki Watch, *Destroying Ethnic Identity*, 19.

98. Quoted in ibid.

99. For details, see ibid., 19–26.

100. *Hurriyet*, October 23, 1989.

101. *Tempo*, May 27, 1990.

102. Helsinki Watch, *Destroying Ethnic Identity*, 13.

103. Ibid., 14.

104. *Milliyet*, September 8, 1988.

105. *Hurriyet*, September 28, 1988.

106. *2000'e Dogru*, October 30, 1988.

107. The Initiative for Human Rights in Kurdistan, *Silence Is Killing Them: A Report on the Situation of the Kurdish Refugees in Turkey* (Bremen, Germany: Initiative for Human Rights in Kurdistan, 1990): 16–17, and the U.S. Committee for Refugees, *World Refugee Survey 1991* (Washington, DC: U.S. Committee for Refugees, 1991): 78.

108. U.S. Committee for Refugees, *World Refugee Survey*, 78.

109. Ibid.

110. For details, see The Initiative for Human Rights in Kurdistan, *Silence Is Killing Them*, 13–15.

111. Amnesty International, *Iraqi Kurds: At Risk of Forcible Repatriation From Turkey and Human Rights Violations in Iraq* (New York: Amnesty International USA, June 1990): 1.

112. Ibid., 1–2.

113. Ibid., 7.

114. Ibid., 7–11.

115. The Initiative for Human Rights in Kurdistan, *Silence Is Killing Them*, 25.

CHAPTER FIVE

1. Shireen T. Hunter, *Iran and the World: Continuity in a Revolutionary Decade* (Bloomington, IN: Indiana University Press, 1990): 98.

2. Mark J. Gasiorowski, "Security Relations Between the United States and Iran, 1953–1978," in Nikki R. Keddie and Mark J. Gasiorowski, eds., *Neither East Nor West: Iran, the Soviet Union, and the United States* (New Haven, CT: Yale University Press, 1990): 157.

3. Amin Saikal, *The Rise and Fall of the Shah* (Princeton, NJ: Princeton University Press, 1980): 55.

4. John C. Campbell, *Defense of the Middle East* (New York: Praeger Publishers, 1960): 60–61.

5. Gasiorowski, "Security Relations," 157.

6. Nader Entessar, "Egypt and the Persian Gulf," *Conflict* 9, no. 2 (1989): 112.

7. Ibid., and Hunter, *Iran and the World*, 99.

8. Shahram Chubin and Sepehr Zabih, *The Foreign Relations of Iran: A Developing State in a Zone of Great Power Conflict* (Berkeley, CA: University of California Press, 1974): 148.

9. Saikal, *The Rise and Fall*, 57.

10. Entessar, "Egypt," 113.

11. Gasiorowski, "Security Relations," 158.

12. Ibid.

13. For details of Iranian-Israeli relations during the Shah's reign, see Robert B. Reppa, *Israel and Iran: Bilateral Relationships and Effects on the Indian Ocean Basin* (New York: Praeger Publishers, 1974); Marvin G. Weinbaum, "Iran and Israel: The Discreet Entente," *Orbis* 18, no. 4 (Winter 1975): 1070–1087; R. K. Ramazani, "Iran and the Arab-Israeli Conflict," *Middle East Journal* 32, no. 4 (Autumn 1978): 413–428; Uri Bialer, "The Iranian Connection in Israel's Foreign Policy—1948–1951," *Middle East Journal* 39, no. 2 (Spring 1985): 292–315; and Sohrab Sobhani, *The Pragmatic Entente: Israeli-Iranian Relations, 1948–1988* (New York: Praeger Publishers, 1989).

14. Nader Entessar, "Changing Patterns of Iranian-Arab Relations," *Journal of Social, Political and Economic Studies* 9, no. 3 (Fall 1984): 344, and Sobhani, *The Pragmatic Entente*, 53–57, 77–84, and 118–120.

15. *Manchester Guardian*, October 10, 1975.

16. *Assnad-e Laneh-e Jasoosi* (Documents of the Nest of Spies), vol. 11 (1979): 24–25.

17. Ibid., and Zonis, *Majestic Failure*, 70.

18. Sobhani, *The Pragmatic Entente*, 34. See also Michael Bar Zohar, "Ben Gurion and the Policy of the Periphery," in Itamar Rabinovich and Jehuda Reinharz, eds., *Israel in the Middle East* (London: Oxford University Press, 1984): 164–171, and Dan Raviv and Yossi Melman, *Every Spy a Prince: The Complete History of Israel's Intelligence Community* (Boston: Houghton Mifflin Company, 1990): 153–154.

19. Quoted in Michael Brecher, *Foreign Policy System of Israel* (New Haven, CT: Yale University Press, 1972): 278.

20. Sobhani, *The Pragmatic Entente*, 115.

21. Ibid., 46–47; Ghareeb, *The Kurdish Question*, pp. 142–145; Raviv and Melman, *Every Spy a Prince*, 82–83; and Gasiorowski, *U.S. Foreign Policy and the Shah*, 125.

22. Sobhani, *The Pragmatic Entente*, 47, and Benjamin Beit-Hallahmi, *The Israeli Connection: Who Israel Arms and Why* (New York: Pantheon Books,

1987): 19.

23. *Assnad-e Laneh-e Jasoosi* (Documents of the Nest of Spies), vol. 31 (1979): 15–17.

24. *Washington Post,* September 17, 1972.

25. Quoted in Ghareeb, *The Kurdish Question,* 143.

26. *Christian Science Monitor,* October 6, 1980.

27. *Washington Post,* December 13, 1970; Adamson, *The Kurdish War,* 94; and Fardoost, *Zohoor va Soqoot-e,* 500–504.

28. Ghareeb, *The Kurdish Question,* 138.

29. Quoted in ibid., 138–139.

30. Efraim Karsh and Inari Rautsi, *Saddam Hussein: A Political Biography* (New York: Free Press, 1991): 75.

31. *Village Voice,* February 23, 1976.

32. Karsh and Rautsi, *Saddam Hussein,* 75–76.

33. Ibid., 77, and Phebe Marr, *The Modern History of Iraq* (Boulder, CO: Westview Press, 1985): 223–224.

34. Farouk-Sluglett and Sluglett, *Iraq Since 1958,* 154.

35. Ghareeb, *The Kurdish Question,* 140, and *New York Times,* March 13, 1975.

36. *Washington Post,* June 22, 1973.

37. Jasim M. Abdulghani, *Iraq and Iran: The Years of Crisis* (Baltimore: Johns Hopkins University Press, 1984): 142.

38. *Village Voice,* February 23, 1976.

39. Ibid.; Pelletiere, *The Kurds,* 167–168; Ghareeb, *The Kurdish Question,* 140; and Karsh and Rautsi, *Saddam Hussein,* 75.

40. *Al-Thawra,* November 6 and 7, 1972.

41. Pelletiere, *The Kurds,* 168.

42. Farouk-Sluglett and Sluglett, *Iraq Since 1958,* 158.

43. Entessar, "Egypt," 113, and Chubin and Zabih, *The Foreign Relations of Iran,* 165.

44. Entessar, "Changing Patterns," 342.

45. Chubin and Zabih, *The Foreign Relations of Iran,* 166.

46. Kutschera, *Le Mouvement National Kurde,* 322–323.

47. Christine Moss Helms, *Iraq: Eastern Flank of the Arab World* (Washington, DC: Brookings Institution, 1984): 150.

48. Vanly, "Kurdistan in Iraq," 186.

49. For details and complete text of the Algiers Agreement, see Tareq Y. Ismael, *Iraq and Iran: Roots of Conflict* (Syracuse, NY: Syracuse University Press, 1982): 60–62. See also Helms, *Iraq,* 149.

50. For details, see Ismael, *Iraq and Iran,* 62–68.

51. *Al-Thawra,* March 8, 1975. See also Marr, *The Modern History of Iraq,* 233.

52. Karsh and Rautsi, *Saddam Hussein,* 83.

53. Helms, *Iraq,* 149. See also Feili and Fromchuck, "The Kurdish Struggle," 56–57, and Whitley, "The Kurds," 253–254.

54. Samir al-Khalil, *Republic of Fear: The Inside Story of Saddam's Iraq* (New York: Pantheon Books, 1990): 24.

55. Ibid.

56. *Manchester Guardian,* December 7, 1976.

57. Amazia Baram, "The Impact of Khomeini's Revolution on the Radical Shi'i Movement of Iraq," in David Menashri, ed., *The Iranian Revolution and the Muslim World* (Boulder, CO: Westview Press, 1990): 141.

58. Entessar, "Changing Patterns," 351, and Tariq Aziz, *On Arab-Iranian*

Relations (Baghdad: Ministry of Culture and Information, 1980): 40.
59. Baram, "The Impact of Khomeini's Revolution," 142–143.
60. Quoted in ibid., 143.
61. Fred Halliday, "A War of National Ambitions," *In These Times*, October 8–14, 1980, 3.
62. Gary Sick, "Trial by Error: Reflections on the Iran-Iraq War," in R. K. Ramazani, ed., *Iran's Revolution: The Search for Consensus* (Bloomington, IN: Indiana University Press, 1990): 108.
63. Ibid.
64. Ibid. See also R. K. Ramazani, *Revolutionary Iran: Challenge and Response in the Middle East* (Baltimore: Johns Hopkins University Press, 1988): 62–65.
65. Abdel-Magid Zemzemi, *La Guerre Irak-Iran: Islam et Nationalismes* (Paris: Albatross, 1985).
66. Liesl Graz, *The Turbulent Gulf* (London: I. B. Tauris, 1990): 34, and John Bulloch and Harvey Morris, *The Gulf War: Its Origins, History and Consequences* (London: Methuen, 1989): 38.
67. Ramazani, *Revolutionry Iran*, 60–61.
68. Abol Hassan Bani-Sadr, *My Turn to Speak: Iran, the Revolution & Secret Deals with the U.S.* (New York: Brassey's [US], 1991): 69.
69. Edgar O'Ballance, "The Kurdish Factor in the Gulf War," *Military Review* 61, no. 6 (June 1981): 18.
70. Entessar, "The Kurdish Mosaic," 95, and Edgar O'Ballance, *The Gulf War* (London: Brassey's Defence Publishers, 1988): 133–134.
71. O'Ballance, *The Gulf War*, 132–136.
72. Entessar, "The Kurdish Mosaic," 96, and *Christian Science Monitor*, May 26, 1987.
73. Frederick W. Axelgard, *A New Iraq?: The Gulf War and Implications for U.S. Policy*, Washington Papers 133 (New York: Praeger Publishers, 1988): 31.
74. *New York Times*, June 30, 1982, and Mordechai Nisan, *Minorities in the Middle East: A History of Struggle and Self-Expression* (Jefferson, NC: McFarland, 1991): 41.
75. O'Ballance, *The Gulf War*, 137. See also Nisan, *Minorities in the Middle East*, 43. For details of Iraqi-Turkish cooperation on the Kurdish problem during the Iran-Iraq War, see Robins, *Turkey*, 58–64, and Bolukbasi, "Ankara, Damascus, Baghdad," 23–28.
76. Axelgard, *A New Iraq?*, 31.
77. Ibid., 32, and McDowall, *The Kurds*, 24.
78. McDowall, *The Kurds*, 24; *Times* (London), January 4, 1984; and *Middle East Economic Digest*, January 6, 1984, 6.
79. Axelgard, *A New Iraq?* 33, and *Christian Science Monitor*, May 15, 1984.
80. McDowall, *The Kurds*, 25; *Christian Science Monitor*, May 15, 1984; and *Washington Post*, July 29, 1984.
81. O'Balance, *The Gulf War*, 141.
82. Anthony H. Cordesman and Abraham R. Wagner, *The Lessons of Modern War*, vol. 2, *The Iran-Iraq War* (Boulder, CO: Westview Press, 1990): 207.
83. See, for example, *Tercuman*, November 5, 1986.
84. *Milliyet*, November 17, 1986, and Ali-Fuat Borovali, "Kurdish Insurgencies, the Gulf War, and Turkey's Changing Role," *Conflict Quarterly* 7, no. 4 (Fall 1987): 37–38.
85. *Christian Science Monitor*, October 30, 1986.
86. Fuat Borovali, "Iran and Turkey: Permanent Revolution or Islamism in

One Country?" in Miron Rezun, ed., *Iran at the Crossroads: Global Relations in a Turbulent Decade* (Boulder, CO: Westview Press, 1990): 86.

87. Ibid.; Borovali, "Kurdish Insurgencies," 38; and *Ettela'at,* January 12, 1987.

88. Cordesman and Wagner, *The Lessons of Modern War,* 256–257.

89. Ibid., and *Washington Post,* March 15, 1987.

90. Shahram Chubin and Charles Tripp, *Iran and Iraq at War* (Boulder, CO: Westview Press, 1988): 106–107.

91. *Kayhan,* May 21, 1987; *Christian Science Monitor,* May 26, 1987; and *Iran Times,* May 29, 1987.

92. *Newsweek,* June 10, 1991.

93. *New York Times,* July 5, 1987.

94. Cordesman and Wagner, *The Lessons of Modern War,* 330.

95. Ibid., 369–370.

96. See *Kayhan,* June 3 and 5, 1988, and *Ettela'at,* June 3 and 4, 1988.

97. Malek, "Kurdistan," 92.

98. Ibid.; Graz, *The Turbulent Gulf,* 26-27; and Physicians for Human Rights, *Winds of Death: Iraq's Use of Poison Gas Against its Kurdish Population* (Somerville, MA: Physicians for Human Rights, 1989): 1–3.

99. Graz, *The Turbulent Gulf,* p. 27.

100. Physicians for Human Rights, *Winds of Death,* pp. 1–2.

101. For example, see Middle East Watch, *Human Rights in Iraq* (New Haven, CT: Yale University Press, 1990): 75–78.

102. Ibid., 148, fn. 62.

103. See ibid., 83–85; The Kurdish Program, "The Destruction of Iraqi Kurdistan," *Kurdish Times* 2, no. 2 (Summer 1988): 3–5; Bulloch and Morris, *The Gulf War,* 212; Karsh and Rautsi, *Saddam Hussein,* 169; and Simon Henderson, *Instant Empire: Saddam Hussein's Ambition for Iraq* (San Francisco: Mercury House, 1991): 114.

104. *New York Times,* September 10, 1988.

105. Middle East Watch, *Human Rights in Iraq,* 84.

106. Entessar, "The Kurdish Mosaic," 97, and *Iran Times,* October 21, 1988.

107. *Al-Khaleej,* June 16, 1988.

108. *Al-Nahar,* November 18, 1988.

109. *Al-Qabas,* September 11 and 13, 1988.

110. *Al-Thawra,* September 11, 1988, and *Al-Khaleej,* September 12, 1988.

111. See Omer Karasapan, "Gulf War Refugees in Turkey," *Middle East Report* 19, no. 1 (January–February 1989): 33–34.

112. *Khaleej Times,* September 9, 1988; *Emirates News,* September 24, 1988; *Al-Khaleej,* September 15, 1988; and *Tercuman,* September 15, 1988.

113. Amnesty International, *Amnesty Action,* September–October 1988, 1. See also Samir al-Khalil, *The Monument: Art, Vulgarity and Responsibility in Iraq* (Berkeley, CA: University of California Press, 1991): 127–128.

114. Amnesty International, *Iraq-Children: Innocent Victims of Political Repression* (New York: Amnesty International USA, n.d.).

115. *Al-Ittihad,* September 30, 1988, and *Middle East Economic Digest,* October 28, 1988, 15.

116. *Al-Qabas,* March 3, 1989.

117. *Gulf News,* April 16, 1989; *Al-Qabas,* June 18, 1989; and *Khaleej Times,* July 22, 1989.

118. *Al-Ittihad,* March 11, 1990.

119. *Gulf News,* September 9 and 11, 1989, and *Al-Thawra,* September 10 and 11, 1989.

120. Judith Miller and Laurie Mylroie, *Saddam Hussein and the Crisis in the Gulf* (New York: Times Books, 1990): 139–140; Elaine Sciolino, *The Outlaw State: Saddam Hussein's Quest for Power and the Gulf Crisis* (New York: Wiley, 1991): 157–160; and Henderson, *Instant Empire,* 180–191.

121. John Simpson, "Along the Streets of Tehran: Life Under Khomeini," *Harper's,* January 1988, 37.

122. Quoted in Miller and Mylroie, *Saddam Hussein,* 143.

123. Ibid., 144, and Sciolino, *The Outlaw State,* 167–168. See also Robert C. Johansen and Michael G. Renner, "Limiting Conflict in the Gulf," *Third World Quarterly* 7, no. 4 (October 1985): 812, and Nader Entessar, "Superpowers and Persian Gulf Security: The Iranian Perspective," *Third World Quarterly* 10, no. 4 (October 1988): 1437.

124. Sciolino, *The Outlaw State,* 158.

125. James A. Bill, "The U.S. Overture to Iran, 1985–1986: An Analysis," in Keddie and Gasiorowski, *Neither East Nor West,* 173.

126. See John Tower, Edmund Muskie, and Brent Scowcroft, *The Tower Commission Report* (New York: Bantam Books, 1987): 112.

127. Ibid., 116.

128. Bill, "The U.S. Overture to Iran," 173–174.

129. Edward W. Said, "Irangate: A Many-Sided Crisis," *Journal of Palestine Studies* 16, no. 4 (Summer 1987): 28.

130. See, for example, Bill, "The U.S. Overture to Iran," 174–175; Beit-Hallahmi, *The Israeli Connection,* 13–16; Jonathan Marshall, Peter Dale Scott, and Jane Hunter, *The Iran-Contra Connection: Secret Teams and Covert Operations in the Reagan Era* (Boston: South End Press, 1987): 167–186; Oliver L. North, *Taking the Stand* (New York: Pocket Books, 1987): 203; Victor Ostrovsky and Claire Hoyt, *By Way of Deception: The Making and Unmaking of a Mossad Officer* (New York: St. Martin's Press, 1990): 326–331, and Tom Segev, *The Iranian Triangle: The Untold Story of Israel's Role in the Iran-Contra Affair* (New York: Free Press, 1988).

131. Quoted in Miller and Mylroie, *Saddam Hussein,* 147–148.

132. Christopher Hitchens, "Realpolitik in the Gulf: A Game Gone Tilt," in Micah L. Sifry and Christopher Cerf, eds., *The Gulf War Reader: History, Documents, Opinions* (New York: Times Books/Random House, 1991): 112–113. For an example of a generally sympathetic scholarly account of Iraq's foreign policy in the 1980s, see Laurie A. Mylroie, "After the Guns Fell Silent: Iraq in the Middle East," *Middle East Journal* 43, no. 1 (Winter 1989): 51–67.

133. Hitchens, "Realpolitik," 113.

134. Stephen C. Pelletiere, Douglas V. Johnson II, and Leif R. Rosenberger, *Iraqi Power and U.S. Security in the Middle East* (Carlisle Barracks, PA: Strategic Studies Institute, U.S. Army War College, 1990): 74–75.

135. Ibid., 56.

136. For a good summary of the events leading to the 1991 Gulf War, see James Ridgeway, ed., *The March to War* (New York: Four Walls Eight Windows, 1991), and Sifry and Cerf, *The Gulf War.*

137. See "America's Stake in the Gulf," *Department of State Dispatch* 1, no. 2 (September 10, 1990): 70.

138. Edward W. Said, "On Linkage, Language, and Identity," in Sifry and Cerf, *The Gulf War,* 439.

139. Sciolino, *The Outlaw State,* 215.

140. *Iran Times,* August 17, 1990.

141. *Iran Times,* August 31, 1990.

142. *New York Times,* January 28, 1991. See also Laizer, *Into Kurdistan,*

112–128.

143. *Manchester Guardian Weekly*, February 24, 1991.

144. *Iran Times*, April 12, 1991.

145. Eric Hooglund, "The Other Face of War," *Middle East Report* 21, no. 4 (July–August 1991): 7 and 10–11.

146. *Christian Science Monitor*, April 18, 1991.

147. Joost Hiltermann, "Eyewitness Iraq," *Middle East Report* 21, no. 4 (July–August 1991): 8–9.

148. "What Sort of New Order?" *The Middle East*, no. 199 (May 1991): 5–8.

149. Lamia Lahoud, "We Never Give Up Hope," *The Middle East*, no. 198 (April 1991): 18.

150. *USA Today*, July 3, 1991.

151. Al-Khalil, *The Monument*, 127–128.

152. *New York Times*, April 25, 1991.

153. Jim Muir, "Why the Kurdish Leaders Went to Baghdad," *Middle East International*, no. 399 (May 3, 1991): 3. See aslo *Christian Science Monitor*, April 30, 1991; *New York Times*, April 26, 1991; and *Al-Hayyat*, April 21, 1991.

154. Quoted in Moti Zaken, "Precarious Kurdish Unity," *Christian Science Monitor*, May 8, 1991, 19.

155. *Christian Science Monitor*, May 6, 1991.

156. *Iran Times*, June 21, 1991.

157. *Manchester Guardian Weekly*, April 28, 1991.

158. *Iran Times*, June 28, 1991.

159. *Iran Times*, July 5, 1991.

160. Jim Muir, "How Can They Trust Saddam?" *Middle East International*, no. 404 (July 12, 1991): 8.

161. *Christian Science Monitor*, July 23, 1991.

162. *Al-Thawra*, July 23, 1991; *Kayhan*, July 24, 1991; and *Iran Times*, July 26, 1991.

163. *Christian Science Monitor*, March 15, 1991, and *New York Times*, April 4, 1991.

164. *Christian Science Monitor*, April 26, 1991.

165. *Milliyet*, April 9, 1991, and *New York Times*, April 12, 1991.

166. "Safe Haven or Living Hell?" *The Middle East*, no. 200 (June 1991): 10.

167. *Christian Science Monitor*, May 21, 1991.

168. Hugh Pope, "Americans in Charge," *Middle East International*, no. 399 (May 3, 1991): 5, and Wendy Kristianasen, "The Other Kurds Have Their Say," *The Middle East*, no. 202 (August 1991): 20. See also *Hurriyet*, March 31, 1991.

169. Hugh Pope, "Operation Poised Hammer," *Middle East International*, no. 404 (July 12, 1991): 8–9, and *Christian Science Monitor*, July 16, 1991.

170. *Washington Post National Weekly Edition*, July 29–August 4, 1991. See also *New York Times*, February 27, 1991.

171. John Simpson, "Saddam's Plan 'B'," *World Monitor* 4, no. 8 (August 1991): 22.

172. *New York Times*, March 27, 1991.

173. *Washington Post National Weekly Edition*, July 29–August 4, 1991.

174. Shibley Telhami, "Stay Out of Iraq's Civil War," *New York Times*, April 5, 1991, A15.

175. Daniel Pipes, "Why America Can't Save the Kurds," *Wall Street Journal*, April 11, 1991, A15.

176. *Manchester Guardian Weekly*, April 14, 1991, and *Christian Science Monitor*, April 10, 1991.

177. *Washington Post*, April 18, 1991, and *New York Times*, April 18,

1991.
    178. *Christian Science Monitor*, May 2, 1991.
    179. Hugh Pope, "What When They Leave?" *Middle East International*, no. 401 (May 31, 1991): 9.
    180. Pope, "Operation Poised Hammer," 9.
    181. Quoted in *Newsweek*, April 15, 1991, 27.
    182. Bill Frelick, "Troubled Waters in the Middle East: 1990–91," in U.S. Committee for Refugees, *World Refugee Survey, 1991*, 93.
    183. Ibid.
    184. "Safe Haven or Living Hell?" 10.
    185. Ibid. See also *New York Times*, April 18, 1991.
    186. *Kayhan Havai*, April 7, 1991, and David McDowall, "Bedrock of Support," *Middle East International*, no. 399 (May 3, 1991): 5–6.
    187. *Iran Times*, April 26, 1991.
    188. *Jomhooriye Islami*, April 20, 1991.
    189. *Iran Times*, May 3 and 10, 1991, and *Kayhan Havai*, May 8, 1991.
    190. *Iran Times*, May 17, 1991.
    191. "Safe Haven or Living Hell?" 10.

CHAPTER SIX

    1. Entessar, "The Kurdish Mosaic," 98.
    2. Young, *The Politics of Cultural Pluralism*, 402–407.
    3. Charles Tilly, "War and State Power," *Middle East Report* 21, no. 4 (July–August 1991): 39.
    4. Ibid.
    5. Entessar, "The Kurdish Mosaic," 98, and Charles G. MacDonald, "The Kurdish Question in the 1980s," in Esman and Rabinovich, *Ethnicity*, 233–234.
    6. Hooshang Amirahmadi, "A Theory of Ethnic Collective Movements and its Application to Iran," *Ethnic and Racial Studies* 10, no. 4 (October 1987): 369.
    7. For further discussion, see Donald L. Horowitz, *Ethnic Groups in Conflict* (Berkeley, CA: University of California Press, 1985): 230–232.
    8. Ibid., 233–239.
    9. Entessar, "Kurdish Identity," 280. See also MacDonald, "The Kurds," 124–132.
    10. Robert G. Wirsing, "Dimensions of Minority Protection," in Robert G. Wirsing, ed., *Protection of Ethnic Minorities: Comparative Perspectives* (New York: Pergamon Press, 1981): 5–7.
    11. Ibid., 6.
    12. Ted Robert Gurr and James R. Scarritt, "Minorities at Risk: A Global Survey," *Human Rights Quarterly* 11, no. 3 (August 1989): 375–405.
    13. Ibid., 398.
    14. Gudmundur Alfredsson, "International Law, International Organizations, and Indigenous Peoples," *Journal of International Affairs* 36, no. 1 (Spring–Summer 1982): 114.
    15. Ibid., 115–116; James Fawcett, *The International Protection of Minorities* (London: Minority Rights Group, 1979): 5; Buchheit, *Secession;* and Patrick Thornberry, *Minorities and Human Rights Law* (London: Minority Rights Group, 1987): 5.

16. Buchheit, *Secession*, 17.

17. Ibid., 28.

18. Ibid., 29.

19. Quoted in ibid., 87. Also, see Fawcett, *The International Protection*, 5–6.

20. Fawcett, *The International Protection*, 6.

21. David Weissbrodt and Teresa O'Toole, "The Development of International Human Rights Law," in Amnesty International, *The Universal Declaration of Human Rights 1948–1988: Human Rights, the United Nations and Amnesty International* (New York: Amnesty International USA, 1988): 19.

22. Stephen Ryan, "Ethnic Conflict and the United Nations," *Ethnic and Racial Studies* 13, no. 1 (January 1990): 36.

23. Rodolfo Stavenhagen, "Ethnic Conflicts: A Human Rights Perspective," *Ethnic Studies Report* 7, no. 2 (July 1989): 2.

24. Amnesty International, *The Universal Declaration of Human Rights*, appendix 1, 111.

25. Weissbrodt and O'Toole, "The Development of International Human Rights Law," 24. For a succinct description of the UN's machinery and efforts in promoting human rights, see David P. Forsythe, *The Internationalization of Human Rights* (Lexington, MA: Lexington Books, 1991): 55–86.

26. Amnesty International, *The Universal Declaration of Human Rights*, appendix 3, 135.

27. Ryan, "Ethnic Conflict," 40.

28. For a brief review of these treaties, see Gerhard von Glahn, *Law Among Nations: An Introduction to Public International Law*, 5th ed. (New York: Macmillan, 1986): 193–194, 303–305, and Thomas Buergenthal and Harold G. Maier, *Public International Law*, 2nd ed. (St. Paul, MN: West Publishing Company, 1990): 124–125. See also ibid., 39–40, and Stavenhagen, "Ethnic Conflicts," 2–3.

29. Von Glahn, *Law Among Nations*, 303.

30. Ibid., 304.

31. Barbara Harff and Ted Robert Gurr, "Toward Empirical Theory of Genocides and Politicides: Identification and Measurement of Cases since 1945," *International Studies Quarterly* 32, no. 3 (September 1988): 364–365, table 1.

32. Ibid., 360.

33. Ibid., 363–365.

34. For a useful treatment of this topic, see Claire Palley, "The Role of Law in Relation to Minority Groups," in Anthony E. Alcock, Brian K. Taylor, and John M. Welton, eds., *The Future of Cultural Minorities* (London: Macmillan, 1979): 120–160.

35. For details, see ibid., 121–126.

36. Thornberry, *Minorities*, 4.

37. Ibid.

38. Horowitz, *Ethnic Groups*, 623.

39. Ahmad Chalabi, "Iraq: The Past as Prologue?" *Foreign Policy*, no. 83 (Summer 1991): 27–28.

40. Ibid., 29.

41. See Horowitz, *Ethnic Groups*, 602–613.

42. Ibid., 628–633.

SELECTED BIBLIOGRAPHY

Abdulghani, Jasim M. *Iraq and Iran: The Years of Crisis.* Baltimore: Johns Hopkins University Press, 1984.

Abrahamian, Ervand. "Communism and Communalism in Iran: The Tudah and the Firqah-i Dimukrat." *International Journal of Middle East Studies* 1, no. 4 (October 1970): 291–316.

———. *Iran Between Two Revolutions.* Princeton, NJ: Princeton University Press, 1982.

———. *The Iranian Mojahedin.* New Haven, CT: Yale University Press, 1989.

Adamson, David. *The Kurdish War.* London: George Allen & Unwin, 1964.

Aghajanian, Akbar. "Ethnic Inequality in Iran: An Overview." *International Journal of Middle East Studies* 15, no. 2 (May 1983): 211–224.

Aguado, Laura Donnadieu. "The Kurds in the Middle East: Struggle for National Liberation." *Ethnic Studies Report* 5, no. 2 (July 1987): 9–17.

Alaolmolki, Nozar. "The New Iranian Left." *Middle East Journal* 41, no. 2 (Spring 1987): 218–233.

Alfredsson, Gudmundur. "International Law, International Organizations, and Indigenous Peoples." *Journal of International Affairs* 36, no. 1 (Spring–Summer 1982): 113–124.

Al-Khalil, Samir.*The Monument: Art, Vulgarity and Responsibility in Iraq.* Berkeley, CA: University of California Press, 1991.

———. *Republic of Fear: The Inside Story of Saddam's Iraq.* New York: Pantheon Books, 1990.

Al-Rubaiy, Abdul A. "The Failure of Political Integration in Iraq: The Education of the Kurdish Minority." *Intellect* 102, no. 2357 (April 1974): 440–444.

Amirahmadi, Hooshang. "A Theory of Ethnic Collective Movements and its Application to Iran." *Ethnic and Racial Studies* 10, no. 4 (October 1987): 363–391.

Amnesty International. *Iraq-Children: Innocent Victims of Political Repression.* New York: Amnesty International USA, n.d.

———. *Torture in the Eighties.* London: Amnesty International, 1984.

———. *Iraqi Kurds: At Risk of Forcible Repatriation From Turkey and Human Rights Violations in Iraq.* New York: Amnesty International USA, June 1990.

Andrews, F. David, ed.. *The Lost Peoples of the Middle East: Documents of the Struggle for Survival and Independence of the Kurds, Assyrians, and Other Minority Races in the Middle East.* Salisbury, NC: Documentary Publications, 1982.

Arfa, Hassan. *The Kurds: An Historical and Political Study.* London: Oxford University Press, 1966.

At-thawra. *Settlement of the Kurdish Problem in Iraq.* Baghdad: At-thawra Publications, n.d.

Axelgard, Frederick W. *A New Iraq?: The Gulf War and Implications for U.S. Policy.* Washington Papers 133. New York: Praeger Publishers, 1988.

Aziz, Tariq. *On Arab-Iranian Relations.* Baghdad: Ministry of Culture and

Information, 1980.

Bakhash, Shaul. *The Reign of the Ayatollahs: Iran and the Islamic Revolution.* New York: Basic Books, 1984.

Bani-Sadr, Abol Hassan. *My Turn to Speak: Iran, the Revolution & Secret Deals with the U.S.* New York: Brassey's (US), 1991.

Baram, Amazia. "The Impact of Khomeini's Revolution on the Radical Shi'i Movement of Iraq," in David Menashri, ed. *The Iranian Revolution and the Muslim World.* Boulder, CO: Westview Press, 1990: 131–151.

"Barnameh va Assasnameh-e Hezb-e Demokrat-e Kurdistan-e Iran" (The Platform and Constitution of the Kurdish Democratic Party of Iran). Third Congress of the KDPI (1973) and Fourth Congress of the KDPI (1980).

Batatu, Hanna. *The Old Social Classes and the Revolutionary Movements of Iraq: A Study of Iraq's Old Landed and Commercial Classes and of its Communists, Ba'thists, and Free Officers.* Princeton, NJ: Princeton University Press, 1978.

Beit-Hallahmi, Benjamin. *The Israeli Connection: Who Israel Arms and Why.* New York: Pantheon Books, 1987.

Bialer, Uri. "The Iranian Connection in Israel's Foreign Policy—1948–1951." *Middle East Journal* 39, no. 2 (Spring 1985): 292–315.

Bill, James A. *The Eagle and the Lion: The Tragedy of American-Iranian Relations.* New Haven, CT: Yale University Press, 1988.

————. "The U.S. Overture to Iran, 1985–1986: An Analysis," in Nikki R. Keddie and Mark J. Gasiorowski, eds. *Neither East Nor West: Iran, the Soviet Union, and the United States.* New Haven, CT: Yale University Press, 1990: 166–179.

Bitlisi, Sharaf-ed-din Khan. *Sharafnameh.* Tehran: Elmi Publications, n.d.

Bois, Thomas. *The Kurds.* Trans. M.W.M. Welland. Beirut: Khayats, 1966.

Bolukbasi, Suha. "Ankara, Damascus, Baghdad, and the Regionalization of Turkey's Kurdish Secessionism." *Journal of South Asian and Middle Eastern Studies* 14, no. 4 (Summer 1991): 15–36.

Borovali, Fuat. "Iran and Turkey: Permanent Revolution or Islamism in One Country?" in Miron Rezun, ed. *Iran at the Crossroads: Global Relations in a Turbulent Decade.* Boulder, CO: Westview Press, 1990: 81–93.

————. "Kurdish Insurgencies, the Gulf War, and Turkey's Changing Role." *Conflict Quarterly* 7, no. 4 (Fall 1987): 29–45.

Brown, David. "Ethnic Revival: Perspectives on State and Society." *Third World Quarterly* 11, no. 4 (October 1989): 1–16.

Buchheit, Lee C. *Secession: The Legitimacy of Self-Determination.* New Haven, CT: Yale University Press, 1978.

Bulloch, John, and Harvey Morris. *The Gulf War: Its Origins, History and Consequences.* London: Methuen, 1989.

Butorac, Franjo. "Iran's Revolution and the Kurds." *Review of International Affairs* (Belgrade) 31 (April 20, 1980): 17–19.

Ceyhun, Fikret. "Development of Capitalism and Class Struggles in Turkey," in Berch Berberoglu, ed. *Power and Stability in the Middle East.* London: Zed Books, 1989: 55–69.

Chalabi, Ahmad. "Iraq: The Past as Prologue?" *Foreign Policy,* no. 83 (Summer 1991): 20–29.

Chaliand, Gerard, "Introduction," in Gerard Chaliand, ed. *People Without a Country: The Kurds and Kurdistan.* Trans. Michael Pallis. London: Zed Press, 1980: 8–18.

————, ed. *Minority Peoples in the Age of Nation-States.* Trans. Tony Berrett. London: Pluto Press, 1989.

Chamran, Mostafa. *Kurdistan* (in Persian). Tehran: Foundation of Martyr
Chamran, 1985.
Cordesman, Anthony H., and Abraham R. Wagner. *The Lessons of Modern War.*
Vol. 2, *The Iran-Iraq War.* Boulder, CO: Westview Press, 1990.
Cottam, Richard W. *Nationalism in Iran.* Updated edition. Pittsburgh: University
of Pittsburgh Press, 1979.
_____. *Iran and the United States: A Cold War Case Study.* Pittsburgh:
University of Pittsburgh Press, 1988.
Chubin, Shahram, and Charles Tripp. *Iran and Iraq at War.* Boulder, CO: Westview
Press, 1988.
Chubin, Shahram and Sepehr Zabih. *The Foreign Relations of Iran: A Developing
State in a Zone of Great Power Conflict.* Berkeley, CA: University of
California Press, 1974.
Dann, Uriel. "The Kurdish National Movement in Iraq." *Jerusalem Quarterly* 9
(Fall 1978): 131–144.
"Dar Bareh-e Fa'aliyat-e Hezb dar Kurdistan: Assnadi az Mabahes-e Darooni-e
Hezb-e Komonist-e Iran" (About the Activities of the Party in Kurdistan:
Documents from Internal Discussions of the Communist Party of Iran)
(August 1990): 77–93.
Eagleton, William, Jr. *The Kurdish Republic of 1946.* London: Oxford University
Press, 1963.
Edmonds, C. J. "Kurdish Nationalism." *Journal of Contemporary History* 6, no. 1
(1971): 87–107.
_____. *Kurds, Turks and Arabs: Politics, Travel, and Research in North-
Eastern Iraq, 1919–1925.* London: Oxford University Press, 1957.
"E'lamiy-e Hoqooq-e Payi-e Mardome-e Zahmatkesh dar Kurdistan"
(Announcement of the Basic Rights of the Toiling People in Kurdistan).
Besooye Socialism 2, no. 5 (March 1990): 63–69.
Entessar, Nader. "Changing Patterns of Iranian-Arab Relations." *Journal of
Social, Political and Economic Studies* 9, no. 3 (Fall 1984): 341–358.
_____. "The Kurds in Post-Revolutionary Iran and Iraq." *Third World
Quarterly* 6, no. 4 (October 1984): 911–933.
_____. "Egypt and the Persian Gulf." *Conflict* 9, no. 2 (1989): 111–126.
_____. "The Kurdish Mosaic of Discord." *Third World Quarterly* 11, no. 4
(October 1989): 83–100.
_____. "Kurdish Identity in the Middle East." *Current World Leaders* 34, no. 2
(April 1991): 270–282.
Esman, Milton J., "Ethnic Pluralism and International Relations." *Canadian
Review of Studies in Nationalism* 17, nos. 1–2 (1990): 83–93.
Esman, Milton J., and Itamar Rabinovich, "The Study of Ethnic Politics in the
Middle East," in Milton J. Esman and Itamar Rabinovich, eds. *Ethnicity,
Pluralism, and the State in the Middle East.* Ithaca, NY: Cornell University
Press, 1988: 3–24.
Fardoost, Hussein. *Zohoor va Soqoot-e Saltanat-e Pahlavi* (The Rise and Fall of
the Pahlavi Dynasty). Vol. 1. Tehran: Ettela'at Publications, 1991.
Farouk-Sluglett, Marion, and Peter Sluglett. *Iraq Since 1958: From Revolution to
Dictatorship.* London: I. B. Tauris, 1990.
Fawcett, James. *The International Protection of Minorities.* London: Minority
Rights Group, 1979.
Feili, Omar Yahya, and Arlene R. Fromchuck. "The Kurdish Struggle for
Independence." *Middle East Review* 9, no. 1 (Fall 1976): 47–59.
Forsythe, David P. *The Internationalization of Human Rights.* Lexington, MA:
Lexington Books, 1991.

Gasiorowski, Mark J. "Security Relations Between the United States and Iran, 1953–1978," in Nikki R. Keddie and Mark J. Gasiorowski, eds. *Neither East Nor West: Iran, the Soviet Union, and the United States.* New Haven, CT: Yale University Press, 1990: 145–165.

————. *U.S. Foreign Policy and the Shah: Building a Client State in Iran.* Ithaca, NY: Cornell University Press, 1991.

Ghareeb, Edmund. *The Kurdish Question in Iraq.* Syracuse, NY: Syracuse University Press, 1981.

Ghassemlou, Abdul Rahman. *Kurdistan and the Kurds.* Prague: Publishing House of the Czechoslovak Academy of Sciences, 1965.

————. "Kurdistan in Iran," in Gerard Chaliand, ed. *People Without a Country: The Kurds and Kurdistan.* Trans. Michael Pallis. London: Zed Press, 1980: 107–134.

Ghods, M. Reza. *Iran in the Twentieth Century: A Political History.* Boulder, CO: Lynne Rienner Publishers, 1989.

Gotlieb, Yosef. *Self-Determination in the Middle East.* New York: Praeger Publishers, 1982.

Graz, Liesl. *The Turbulent Gulf.* London: I. B. Tauris, 1990.

Gunter, Michael M. "The Kurdish Problem in Turkey." *Middle East Journal* 42, no. 3 (Summer 1988): 389–406.

————. *The Kurds in Turkey: A Political Dilemma.* Boulder, CO: Westview Press, 1990.

Gurr, Ted Robert, and James R. Scarritt. "Minorities at Risk: A Global Survey." *Human Rights Quarterly* 11, no. 3 (August 1989): 375–405.

Harff, Barbara, and Ted Robert Gurr. "Toward Empirical Theory of Genocides and Politicides: Identification and Measurement of Cases since 1945." *International Studies Quarterly* 32, no. 3 (September 1988): 359–371.

Harris, George S. "Ethnic Conflict and the Kurds." *The Annals of the American Academy of Political and Social Science* 433 (September 1977): 112–124.

Hazen, William E. "Minorities in Revolt: The Kurds of Iran, Iraq, Syria, and Turkey," in R. D. McLaurin, ed. *The Political Role of Minority Groups in the Middle East.* New York: Praeger Publishers, 1979: 49–75.

Helfgott, Leonard M. "The Structural Foundations of the National Minority Problem in Revolutionary Iran." *Iranian Studies* 13, nos. 1–4 (1980): 195–214.

Helms, Christine Moss. *Iraq: Eastern Flank of the Arab World.* Washington, DC: Brookings Institution, 1984.

Helsinki Watch. *Destroying Ethnic Identity: The Kurds of Turkey.* New York: Human Rights Watch, 1990.

Henderson, Simon. *Instant Empire: Saddam Hussein's Ambition for Iraq.* San Francisco: Mercury House, 1991.

Higgins, Patricia J. "Minority-State Relations in Contemporary Iran," in Ali Banuazizi and Myron Weiner, eds. *The State, Religion and Ethnic Politics: Afghanistan, Iran, and Pakistan.* Syracuse, NY: Syracuse University Press, 1986: 167–197.

Hiltermann, Joost. "Eyewitness Iraq." *Middle East Report* 21, no. 4 (July–August 1991): 8–9 and 13.

Hitchens, Christopher. "Realpolitik in the Gulf: A Game Gone Tilt," in Micah L. Sifry and Christopher Cerf, eds. *The Gulf War Reader: History, Documents, Opinions.* New York: Times Books/Random House, 1991: 107–118.

Honigman, Gerald A. "British Petroleum Politics, Arab Nationalism and the Kurds." *Middle East Review* 15, nos. 1 and 2 (Fall 1982–Winter 1982/83): 33–39.

Hooglund, Eric. "The Other Face of War." *Middle East Report* 21, no. 4 (July–August 1991): 3–7 and 10–12.

Horowitz, Donald L. *Ethnic Groups in Conflict*. Berkeley, CA: University of California Press, 1985.

Hunter, Shireen T. *Iran and the World: Continuity in a Revolutionary Decade*. Bloomington, IN: Indiana University Press, 1990.

Hyman, Anthony. "Elusive Kurdistan: The Struggle for Recognition." *Conflict Studies* 214 (1988): 1–25.

The Initiative for Human Rights in Kurdistan. *A Report on State Terrorism in Turkish Kurdistan*. Bremen, Germany: Initiative for Human Rights in Kurdistan, 1990.

_____. *Silence Is Killing Them: A Report on the Situation of the Kurdish Refugees in Turkey*. Bremen, Germany: Initiative for Human Rights in Kurdistan, 1990.

Ismael, Tareq Y. *Iraq and Iran: Roots of Conflict*. Syracuse, NY: Syracuse University Press, 1982.

Izady, Mehrdad. "A Kurdish Lingua Franca?" *Kurdish Times* 2, no. 2 (Summer 1988): 13–24.

_____. "Persian Carrot and Turkish Stick: Contrasting Policies Targeted at Gaining State Loyalty from Azeris and Kurds." *Kurdish Times* 3, no. 2 (Fall 1990): 31–47.

Jafar, Majeed R. *Under-Underdevelopment: A Regional Case Study of the Kurdish Area in Turkey*. Helsinki, Finland: Social Policy Association, 1976.

Jawad, Sa'ad. *Iraq & the Kurdish Question 1958–1970*. London: Ithaca Press, 1981.

"Jonbesh-e Moqavemat-e Khalq-e Kurd va Komala" (The Resistance Movement of the Kurdish Masses and Komala). Document series no. 2 (1980): 1–9.

Karasapan, Omer. "Gulf War Refugees in Turkey." *Middle East Report* 19, no. 1 (January–February 1989): 33–35.

Karsh, Efraim, and Inari Rautsi. *Saddam Hussein: A Political Biography*. New York: Free Press, 1991.

Keddie, Nikki R. "The Minorities Question in Iran," in Shirin Tahir-Kheli and Shaheen Ayubi, eds. *The Iran-Iraq War: New Weapons, Old Conflicts*. New York: Praeger Publishers, 1983: 85–108.

Khadduri, Majid. *Republican Iraq: A Study in Iraqi Politics Since the Revolution of 1958*. London: Oxford University Press, 1969.

_____. *Socialist Iraq: A Study in Iraqi Politics Since 1968*. Washington, DC: Middle East Institute, 1978.

Kinnane, Derk. *The Kurds and Kurdistan*. London: Oxford University Press, 1964.

The Kurdish Program. "The Destruction of Iraqi Kurdistan." *Kurdish Times* 2, no. 2 (Summer 1988): 1–6.

Kurdistan: Imperialism va Groohaye Vabaste (Kurdistan: Imperialism and the Dependent Groups). Tehran: Political Bureau of the Islamic Revolutionary Guards Corps, 1980.

Kutschera, Chris. *Le Mouvement National Kurde*. Paris: Flammarion, 1979.

Laizer, Sheri. *Into Kurdistan: Frontiers Under Fire*. London: Zed Books, 1991.

MacDonald, Charles. "The Kurdish Challenge and Revolutionary Iran." *Journal of South Asian and Middle Eastern Studies* 13, nos. 1 and 2 (Fall–Winter 1989): 52–68.

_____. "The Kurdish Question in the 1980s," in Milton J. Esman and Itamar Rabinovich, eds. *Ethnicity, Pluralism, and the State in the Middle East*. Ithaca, NY: Cornell University Press, 1988: 233–252.

_____. "The Kurds." *Journal of Political Science* 19 (1991): 121–139.

Magnarella, Paul J. "A Note on Aspects of Social Life Among the Jewish Kurds of Sanandaj." *Jewish Journal of Sociology* 11, no. 1 (June 1969): 51–58.

Malek, Mohammed H. "Kurdistan in the Middle East Conflict." *New Left Review* 175 (May–June 1989): 79–94.

Marcus, Aliza. "Hearts and Minds in Kurdistan." *Middle East Report* 20, no. 2 (March–April 1990): 41–42 and 44.

Margulies, Ronnie, and Ergin Yildizoglu. "Trade Unions and Turkey's Working Class." *MERIP Reports* 14, no. 2 (February 1984): 15–20 and 31.

Marr, Phebe. *The Modern History of Iraq.* Boulder, CO: Westview Press, 1985.

McDowall, David. *The Kurds.* New edition. London: Minority Rights Group, March 1989.

Menashri, David. "Khomeini's Policy Toward Ethnic and Religious Minorities," in Milton J. Esman and Itamar Rabinovich, eds. *Ethnicity, Pluralism, and the State in the Middle East.* Ithaca, NY: Cornell University Press, 1988: 215–229.

Middle East Watch. *Human Rights in Iraq.* New Haven, CT: Yale University Press, 1990.

Miller, Judith, and Laurie Mylroie. *Saddam Hussein and the Crisis in the Gulf.* New York: Times Books, 1990.

Moddaressi, Koorosh. "Kurdistan va Ayandeh-e Mobarezeh-e An" (Kurdistan and the Future of its Struggle). *Besooye Socialism* 2, no. 5 (March 1990): 1–53.

Mohajer, Nasser. "Ensheab dar Hezb-e Demokrat-e Kurdistan-e Iran" (A Division Within the Kurdish Democratic Party of Iran). *Aghazi No* 7 (Summer 1988): 25–29.

Mohseni, Nasser. *Joghrafiya-e Kurdistan* (The Geography of Kurdistan). Boroojerd, Iran: Lavian Publications, 1948.

Mylroie, Laurie A. "After the Guns Fell Silent: Iraq in the Middle East." *Middle East Journal* 43, no. 1 (Winter 1989): 51–67.

Naby, Eden. "The Iranian Frontier Nationalities: The Kurds, the Assyrians, the Baluchis, and the Turkmens," in William O. McCagg, Jr., and Brian D. Silver, eds. *Soviet Asian Ethnic Frontiers.* New York: Pergamon Press, 1979: 83–114.

————. "Rebellion in Kurdistan." *Harvard International Review* 2, no. 3 (November 1979): 1, 5–7, and 29.

Nagel, Joane. "The Conditions of Ethnic Separatism: The Kurds in Turkey, Iran, and Iraq." *Ethnicity* 7, no. 3 (September 1980): 279–297.

[Nezan], Kendal. "Kurdistan in Turkey," in Gerard Chaliand, ed. *People Without a Country: The Kurds and Kurdistan.* Trans. Michael Pallis. London: Zed Press, 1980: 47–106.

Nisan, Mordechai. *Minorities in the Middle East: A History of Struggle and Self-Expression.* Jefferson, NC: McFarland, 1991.

————. *The Gulf War.* London: Brassey's Defence Publishers, 1988.

————. "The Kurdish Factor in the Gulf War." *Military Review* 61, no. 6 (June 1981): 13–20.

O'Ballance, Edgar. *The Kurdish Revolt: 1961–1970.* Hamden, CT: Archon Books, 1973.

Olson, Robert. *The Emergence of Kurdish Nationalism and the Shaikh Said Rebellion, 1880–1925.* Austin, TX: University of Texas Press, 1989.

————. "The International Consequences of the Sheikh Said Rebellion," in Marc Gaborieau, Alexander Popovic, and Thierry Zarcone, eds. *Naqshbandis: Historical Developments and Present Situation of a Muslim Mystical Order.* Paris: Editions Isis, 1990: 379–406.

————. "The Kocgiri Kurdish Rebellion in 1921 and the Draft Law for a

Proposed Autonomy of Kurdistan." *Oriente Moderno* (new series) 8, nos. 1–6 (January–June 1989): 41–56.

Owrang, Morad. *Kurd Shenasi* (Kurdology). Tehran: Rangin Publications, 1967.

Palley, Claire. "The Role of Law in Relation to Minority Groups," in Anthony E. Alcock, Brian K. Taylor, and John M. Welton, eds. *The Future of Cultural Minorities*. London: Macmillan, 1979: 120–160.

Pelletiere, Stephen C. *The Kurds: An Unstable Element in the Gulf*. Boulder, CO: Westview Press, 1984.

Pelletiere, Stephen C., Douglas V. Johnson II, and Leif R. Rosenberger. *Iraqi Power and U.S. Security in the Middle East*. Carlisle Barracks, PA: Strategic Studies Institute, U.S. Army War College, 1990.

Perry, John R. *Karim Khan Zand: A History of Iran, 1747–1779*. Chicago: University of Chicago Press, 1979.

Physicians for Human Rights. *Winds of Death: Iraq's Use of Poison Gas Against its Kurdish Population*. Somerville, MA: Physicians for Human Rights, 1989.

Ramazani, Rouhollah K. "The Autonomous Republic of Azerbaijan and the Kurdish People's Republic: Their Rise and Fall," in Thomas T. Hammond, ed. *The Anatomy of Communist Takeovers*. New Haven, CT: Yale University Press, 1975: 448–474.

_____. *Revolutionary Iran: Challenge and Response in the Middle East*. Baltimore: Johns Hopkins University Press, 1988.

Raviv, Dan, and Yossi Melman. *Every Spy a Prince: The Complete History of Israel's Intelligence Community*. Boston: Houghton Mifflin Company, 1990.

Reppa, Robert B. *Israel and Iran: Bilateral Relationships and Effects on the Indian Ocean Basin*. New York: Praeger Publishers, 1974.

Ridgeway, James, ed. *The March to War*. New York: Four Walls Eight Windows, 1991.

Robins, Philip. *Turkey and the Middle East*. London and New York: The Royal Institute of International Affairs/Council on Foreign Relations Press, 1991.

Roosevelt, Archie, Jr. "The Kurdish Republic of Mahabad," in Gerard Chaliand, ed. *People Without a Country: The Kurds and Kurdistan*. Trans. Michael Pallis. London: Zed Press, 1980: 135–152.

Roosevelt, Kermit. *Countercoup: The Struggle for the Control of Iran*. New York: McGraw-Hill, 1979.

Rothschild, Joseph. *Ethnopolitics: A Conceptual Framework*. New York: Columbia University Press, 1981.

Rustow, Dankwart A. *Turkey: America's Forgotten Ally*. New York: Council on Foreign Relations Press, 1987.

Ryan, Stephen. "Ethnic Conflict and the United Nations." *Ethnic and Racial Studies* 13, no. 1 (January 1990): 25–49.

Saikal, Amin. *The Rise and Fall of the Shah*. Princeton, NJ: Princeton University Press, 1980.

Sciolino, Elaine. *The Outlaw State: Saddam Hussein's Quest for Power and the Gulf Crisis*. New York: Wiley, 1991.

Segev, Tom. *The Iranian Triangle: The Untold Story of Israel's Role in the Iran-Contra Affair*. New York: Free Press, 1988.

Short, Martin, and Anthony McDermott. *The Kurds*. Third edition. London: Minority Rights Group, March 1977.

Sick, Gary. "Trial by Error: Reflections on the Iran-Iraq War," in R. K. Ramazani, ed. *Iran's Revolution: The Search for Consensus*. Bloomington, IN: Indiana University Press, 1990: 104–124.

Sim, Richard. "Kurdistan: The Search for Recognition." *Conflict Studies* 124 (November 1980): 1–21.

Skocpol, Theda. "Bringing the State Back In: Strategies of Analysis in Current Research," in Peter B. Evans, Dietrich Rueschemeyer, and Theda Skocpol, eds. *Bringing the State Back In.* New York: Cambridge University Press, 1985.

Sluglett, Peter. *Britain in Iraq 1914–1932.* London: Ithaca Press, 1976.

————. "The Kurds," in Committee Against Repression and for Democratic Rights in Iraq, ed. *Saddam's Iraq: Revolution or Reaction?* New updated edition. London: Zed Books, 1989: 177–202.

Sobhani, Sohrab. *The Pragmatic Entente: Israeli-Iranian Relations, 1948–1988.* New York: Praeger Publishers, 1989.

Stavenhagen, Rodolfo. "Ethnic Conflicts: A Human Rights Perspective." *Ethnic Studies Report* 7, no. 2 (July 1989): 1–8.

Thornberry, Patrick. *Minorities and Human Rights Law.* London: Minority Rights Group, 1987.

Tilly, Charles. "War and State Power." *Middle East Report* 21, no. 4 (July–August 1991): 38–40.

Tower, John, Edmund Muskie, and Brent Scowcroft. *The Tower Commission Report.* New York: Bantam Books, 1987.

U.S. Committee for Refugees. *World Refugee Survey 1991.* Washington, DC: U.S. Committee for Refugees, 1991.

Van Bruinessen, Martin. *Agha, Shaikh and State: On the Social and Political Organization of Kurdistan.* Utrecht, The Netherlands: Ryksuniversiteit, 1978.

————. "Between Guerrilla War and Political Murder: The Workers' Party of Kurdistan." *Middle East Report* 18, no. 4 (July–August 1988): 40–42 and 44–46.

————. "Kurdish Tribes and the State of Iran: The Case of Simko's Revolt," in Richard Tapper, ed. *The Conflict of Tribe and State in Iran and Afghanistan.* London: Croom Helm, 1983: 364–400.

————. "The Kurds Between Iran and Iraq." *MERIP Middle East Report* 16, no. 4 (July–August 1986): 14–27.

————. "The Kurds in Turkey." *MERIP Reports* 14, no. 2 (February 1984): 6–12 and 14.

Vanly, Ismet Sheriff. "Kurdistan in Iraq," in Gerard Chaliand, ed. *People Without a Country: The Kurds and Kurdistan.* Trans. Michael Pallis. London: Zed Press, 1980: 153–210.

Weinbaum, Marvin G. "Iran and Israel: The Discreet Entente." *Orbis* 18, no. 4 (Winter 1975): 1070–1087.

Weissbrodt, David, and Teresa O'Toole. "The Development of International Human Rights Law," in Amnesty International. *The Universal Declaration of Human Rights 1948–1988: Human Rights, the United Nations and Amnesty International.* New York: Amnesty International USA, 1988.

Westermann, William Linn. "Kurdish Independence and Russian Expansion." *Foreign Affairs* 70, no. 3 (Summer 1991): 50–54.

"What Is Happening in Kurdistan?" *Review of Iranian Political Economy and History* (RIPEH) 3, no. 2 (Fall 1979): 55–59.

Whitley, Andrew. "The Kurds: Pressures and Prospects." *The Round Table* 279 (July 1980): 245–257.

Wirsing, Robert G. "Dimensions of Minority Protection," in Robert G. Wirsing, ed. *Protection of Ethnic Minorities: Comparative Perspectives.* New York: Pergamon Press, 1981: 3–17.

Yalda, Nariman. "Federalism and Self-Rule for Minorities: A Case Study of Iran and Kurdistan." Ph.D. diss., Claremont Graduate School, 1980.

Yassemi, Rashid. *Kurd va Payvastegi-e Nejadi va Tarikhi-e Uo* (The Kurd and His Racial and Historical Bonds). Tehran: Amir Kabir Publications, 1984.

Young, Crawford. *The Politics of Cultural Pluralism.* Madison, WI: University of Wisconsin Press, 1976.

Zabih, Sepehr. *Iran Since the Revolution.* Baltimore: Johns Hopkins University Press, 1982.

————. *The Left in Contemporary Iran.* London and Stanford, CA: Croom Helm/Hoover Institution Press, 1986.

Zangeneh, Mozaffar. *Doodeman-e Aryai: Kurd va Kurdistan* (The Aryan Lineage: Kurd and Kurdistan). Tehran: Chehr Publications, 1968.

Zemzemi, Abdel-Magid. *La Guerre Irak-Iran: Islam et Nationalismes.* Paris: Albatroos, 1985.

Zonis, Marvin. *Majestic Failure: The Fall of the Shah.* Chicago: University of Chicago Press, 1991.

Newspapers, Magazines, and Specialized Kurdish Publications

Al-Ahram
Al-Ittihad
Al-Khaleej
Al-Nahar
Al-Qabas
Al-Thawra
Ayandegan
Christian Science Monitor
Cumhuriyet
Ettela'at
Gulf News
Hurriyet
Information and Liaison Bulletin (Kurdish Institute, Paris)
Iran Times
Kayhan
Khaleej Times
Kurdish Liberation
Kurdish Times
Kurdistan
Manchester Guardian Weekly
The Middle East
Middle East International
Milliyet
New York Times
Pesh Merga
Pishrow
Tercuman
Voice of Kurdistan
Washington Post

INDEX

202

ABOUT THE BOOK
AND THE AUTHOR

Kurdish nationalism has long been a source of instability, intercommunal conflict, and ethnic strife in the Middle East, and demands for Kurdish self-determination have grown increasingly frequent and loud. Nader Entessar explores the nature of Kurdish solidarity, the reasons for its political activation in recent years, and the policies that have been adopted in response to it.

After providing a historical context, Entessar analyzes the political, social, and legal dimensions of Kurdish integration into the mainstream of sociopolitical life in Iran, Iraq, and Turkey. How have these countries handled the phenomenon of Kurdish ethnonationalism? How has this phenomenon affected the nation-state system in the Middle East? Do state policies aimed at, variously, assimilation, pluralism, or segregation succeed in achieving multi-ethnic harmony? The impact of international events since the 1970s—e.g., the Iran-Iraq war—on the plight of the Kurds is also considered. In the final chapter of this balanced and well-grounded study, Entessar looks to the future of Kurdistan.

NADER ENTESSAR is professor of political science and international relations, and chair of the Social Science Division at Spring Hill College.